W9-CMQ-723

A CONCISE HISTORY OF BOSNIA

A Concise History of Bosnia integrates the political, economic and cultural history of this fascinating, beautiful, but much misunderstood country. Drawing on a wide range of primary and secondary literature, this objective and engaging history covers developments in the region up to the present day and offers an accessible interpretation of an often contested and controversial history. Importantly, Cathie Carmichael looks at Bosnia over the long term, moving away from a narrow focus on the 1990s to offer a historical rather than a nationalist perspective on events. Integrated within the narrative account, there is a particular focus on the themes of culture and religion and the effect of geography and regional changes in the landscape on Bosnian history. Engaging and authoritative, the book succinctly explores how Bosnia has changed over many centuries, and focuses on the dynamic and creative aspects of Bosnia's past as well as on the darker elements.

CATHIE CARMICHAEL is Professor of History and Head of the School of History at the University of East Anglia. She is the author and editor of several books including *Slovenia and the Slovenes: A Small State in the New Europe* (with James Gow), *Language and Nationalism in Europe* (co-edited with the late Stephen Barbour), *The Routledge History of Genocide* (co-edited with Richard Maguire), *Ethnic Cleansing in the Balkans: Nationalism and the Destruction of Tradition* and *Genocide before the Holocaust*.

CAMBRIDGE CONCISE HISTORIES

This is a series of illustrated 'concise histories' of selected individual countries, intended both as university and college textbooks and as general historical introductions for general readers, travellers and members of the business community.

A full list of titles in the series can be found at:
www.cambridge.org/concisehistories

A Concise History of Bosnia

CATHIE CARMICHAEL
University of East Anglia

CAMBRIDGE
UNIVERSITY PRESS

CAMBRIDGE
UNIVERSITY PRESS

University Printing House, Cambridge CB2 8BS, United Kingdom

Cambridge University Press is part of the University of Cambridge.

It furthers the University's mission by disseminating knowledge in the pursuit of education, learning and research at the highest international levels of excellence.

www.cambridge.org
Information on this title: www.cambridge.org/9781107016156

© Cambridge University Press 2015

First published 2015

Printed in the United Kingdom by TJ International Ltd. Padstow Cornwall

A catalogue record for this publication is available from the British Library

Library of Congress Cataloguing in Publication data
Carmichael, Cathie.
A concise history of Bosnia / Cathie Carmichael, University of East Anglia.
pages cm. – (Cambridge concise histories)
Includes bibliographical references and index.
ISBN 978-1-107-01615-6 (hbk) – ISBN 978-1-107-60218-2 (pbk)
1. Bosnia and Herzegovina–History. I. Title.
DR1685.C37 2015
949.742–dc23
2015003680

ISBN 978-1-107-01615-6 Hardback
ISBN 978-1-107-60218-2 Paperback

CONTENTS

FIGURES

MAPS

ACKNOWLEDGEMENTS

The academic literature on Bosnia is excellent. So too is the cultural representation of Bosnian life in the arts, film and literature. As I was writing this book, the work of Bojan Baskar, Cornelia Sorabji, Mark Thompson, Edina Bećirević, Ademir Kenović, James Gow, Pjer Žalica, Marko Hoare, Stef Jansen, Richard Mills, Vladimir Dedijer, Ivana Maček, Božidar Jezernik, Vjekoslav Perica, Jasmila Žbanić, Mak Dizdar, Mitja Velikonja, Ivo Goldstein, Tomislav Dulić, Wendy Bracewell, William G. Lockwood, Munevera Hadžišehović, Sabrina P. Ramet, Ivan Čolović, Ivo Žanić, Marko Živković, Bob Donia and Adil Zulfikarpašić significantly influenced the way in which I thought about an issue or problem. I was also lucky enough to talk to or correspond with many of the living among them and would like to extend my profound gratitude to them for their inspirational work.

Students and colleagues have continually challenged me and given me help in innumerable ways. In particular, I would like to thank Chris Jones, Matt Willer, Alistair Dickins, Mark Vincent, Kate Ferguson, Luke Roberts, Elliot Short, Djordje Stefanović, Dejan Djokić, Josip Glaurdić, Bethany Quinn, Matthias Neumann, Sanja Malbaša Thompson, Nicholas Vincent, Aurèlia Mañé-Estrada, Andy Wood, Melanie Watling, Yvonne Tasker, Ollie Carlisle, Caroline Woolsgrove and Jordan Claridge. Matt Willer, Sam Foster, Jessica Sharkey and Richard Mills gave me some of their incredible photographs to illustrate the book for which I am very grateful. Thanks to the Bošnjački institut – Fondacija Adila Zulfikarpašića, Sarajevo for their permission to reproduce the fine painting on the cover.

The editors at Cambridge University Press – Michael Watson, Liz Friend-Smith, Rebecca Taylor and Rosalyn Scott – are simply marvellous and galvanized me to finish the book even when my role as Head of the School of History at the University of East Anglia took me in (many) other directions. Thanks also to Rob Wilkinson at Out of House Publishing.

Most fundamentally, my family gave me enormous support and indulgence. Thank you Mike, Christina, Jacob, Mum, Dad, David, Valeria, David, Mary, Kirsten, Paul, Roz, Pete, Clare and Olivia. Thanks to all the 'Horners' as well, especially Frances Carey for all their love.

PREFACE

Since 1988, I have been to the country formally known as Yugoslavia almost every year. I was lucky enough to receive a British Council Studentship in 1989 that allowed me to study at the University of Ljubljana, which proved a great base not only to read about but to explore the region. At that time, Bosnians lived in every republic of the country taking their culture, food, religious practices and upbeat worldview with them. There was a discernible uneasiness about daily interactions between Yugoslavs by this time and the political system looked shaky. Nationalism seemed to be on the rise and almost everywhere I went people would stop me to talk about the wrongs that had been committed against their nation. The exception to this general pattern of urgency and radicalization seemed to be in Bosnia. Staying with a Croat family in Hercegovina in 1990, I was told about the way in which they respected the religion of their neighbours while we all watched an Orthodox service on the television. This embrace of tolerance, which has sometimes been described as the Bosnian spirit (*bosanski duh*), was not just the forced repetition of the Communist regime's mantra of brotherhood and unity and it came from the heart. If Bosnia came late to nationalism, then it suffered the most for its tardiness and the belief of its citizens that a multi-faith society was possible, even preferable.

As a historian I have always been fascinated by the change that occurs over time as well as the deeper currents that only move very slowly. It is unlikely that many regions have changed as much in those years. In just one generation, Bosnia has generated more history than most of its inhabitants would have wanted. I started to write this book in the summer of 2011 in Sarajevo and travelled through many of the towns mentioned here including Bugojno, Jajce, Livno and Travnik and was at all times struck by the energy, intellectual zest and vision of the Bosnians that I met. But it has always proved impossible to accept every aspect about the current status quo and to even contemplate a return to Mostar, last visited on a hot April day in 1990. The rationale behind this decision is that, although the paramilitaries destroyed the sixteenth-century bridge in 1993, they have not destroyed my memory of it. The eighteenth-century Sarajevan chronicler Mula Mustafa Ševki Bašeskija believed that only those ideas that are committed to paper endure and that which is mere memory will eventually disappear.

In the book, I have used the terms 'Muslim', 'Catholic', 'Jewish' and 'Orthodox' as well as 'Roma', 'Vlach', 'Bosniak', 'Croat' and 'Serb'. I would have preferred simply to use the word 'Bosnian' and do not intend to engage in an essentialist discussion about who has or does not have the right to belong. In my view, essentialism is a long-term symptom of violence and a rejection of the very notion of overlapping identities and shared heritage. One symptom of an attack can be defensiveness and a desire to reify that aspect of the self that is being targeted, but this very defensiveness can also be a form of intellectual capitulation. It would be giving Vjekoslav Luburić or Ratko Mladić too much power if one were to reject all that is positive about Croat or Serb civilization because of their actions. The primary cause of genocide in 1941 was the fascist Ustaša movement. Although it represented a very small minority among the Croats, they were in power long enough to attempt to wipe out the Serb population of the Independent State of Croatia, which included modern-day Bosnia and Hercegovina. Similarly the primary cause of conflict in 1992 was a small group of Serb radicals who galvanized a larger part of the Orthodox population to support a disastrous fratricidal war aimed at driving a large part of the non-Serb population out of those parts of the country that they claimed. In carrying out this strategy, those radicals were prepared to commit genocide. Once conflicts begin, the balance of responsibility for any ensuing violence is clearly more complex, but in cases of genocide, it is important to establish the *intent* to destroy a people in whole or in part.

Hundreds of thousands of Bosnians of all religious affiliations know the real meaning of genocide and now live in places miles away from their hometowns, often fundamentally disconnected to the past at least physically. But in this book, I wanted to tell a story that conveys Bosnia's stunning and positive qualities as well as acknowledging the suffering that came with the modern era and the three wars that have been fought by Bosnians in the past 100 years. This book is primarily intended for readers who currently know little about the history of an incredible and diverse European country. The existing literature on Bosnia is very rich and there are excellent academic books and articles to capture the imagination of the reader. Bosnia has also inspired great novelists, poets, artists, sculptors and filmmakers, whose work almost never feels parochial or small and easily compares in terms of literary depth and quality to the best of the canon of any civilization.

CHRONOLOGY OF EVENTS IN BOSNIAN HISTORY

168 BC	Illyria (including much of modern Bosnia) was taken over by the Romans.
Seventh century	Arrival of Slavs in the Balkans.
Ninth century	Bosnians converted to Christianity.
Tenth century	Constantine VII Porphyrogenitus writes *De administrando imperio* in Greek, which mentions the place name Βόσονα or Bosona for the first time.
1189, 29 August	The Charter of Ban Kulin (*Kulinova povelja*), a trade agreement between Bosnia and the Ragusan Republic (nowadays Dubrovnik) was written.
1291	The Franciscan Order started its ministry in Bosnia.
1377	Stjepan Tvrtko became king of Bosnia, the first in the Kotromanić Dynasty.
1389, 28 June	Battle of Kosovo polje. Bosnian King Stjepan Tvrtko fought under the command of Serbian Prince Lazar.
1463	Ottoman conquest of Bosnia. Execution of the last Christian king Stjepan Tomašević. Conversions to Islam and Orthodoxy commenced and the Franciscan Order retained the right to minister to the Catholic *rayah*.

1526	The Battle of Mohács. Orthodox-born Mehmed-paša Sokolović fought on the side of the Ottomans against a Hungarian Alliance.
1531	Gazi Husrev-beg mosque founded in Sarajevo
1566	An Ottoman bridge, later known as *Stari Most* was built in Mostar over the Neretva river. The bridge was destroyed in 1993 and subsequently rebuilt, reopening in 2004.
1570s	Construction of the Mehmed Paša Sokolović Bridge on the Drina at Višegrad.
1656	Turkish writer Evliya Çelebi described Bosnia in his travel book *Seyâhatnâme*.
1699	Prince Eugen of Savoy attacked and burned Sarajevo.
1783–1786	Plague in Bosnia.
1809	Napoleon Bonaparte annexed the Illyrian Provinces, which were restored to the Habsburgs in 1815.
1831–1833	The Great Bosnian Revolt (1831–1833) led by Husein Gradaščević in protest against the Tanzimat reforms of the Ottoman Empire.
1875–1876	Christian peasants rebelled against the Ottomans.
1878, 13 July	Treaty of Berlin divided South-East Europe. Bosnia came under Habsburg administration.
1881	Pope Leo XIII established new Catholic dioceses in Sarajevo, Banja Luka and Mostar.
1900	At the *Exposition Universelle*, a world fair in Paris, the Bosnian pavilion was decorated by Alphonse Mucha.
1908	Bosnia and Hercegovina were formally annexed by the Habsburg monarchy.
1912–1913	The Balkan Wars lead to the enlargement of the states of Serbia and Montenegro.
1914, 28 June	Habsburg Heir Archduke Franz Ferdinand and his wife Sophie assassinated in Sarajevo by Gavrilo Princip.

1914–1917	Bosnian troops fight on the Eastern Front against Imperial Russia.
1915–1917	Bosnian legions fight on the Isonzo Front against Italy.
1918, 28 April	Gavrilo Princip died in prison of tuberculosis.
1918, 1 December	The Kingdom of Serbs, Croats and Slovenes created under the Serbian Karadjordjević Dynasty.
1919	Lawyer Mehmed Spaho founded the Yugoslav Muslim Organization (*Jugoslovenska Muslimanska Organizacija*).
1920	Strike by Bosnian miners (*Husinska buna*).
1929	Bosnia divided into districts of *banovine* called Drinska, Zetska, Primorska and Vrbaška.
1934	Assassination of King Aleksandar in Marseilles by a gunman financed by the fascist Ustaša.
1939	The *Sporazum* (Mutual Agreement) gave the Croatians some territorial autonomy within Royalist Yugoslavia and included some Bosnian towns that had been in Primorska.
1941	Collapse of Royalist Yugoslavia in April after invasion by the Third Reich under Adolf Hitler. Bosnia incorporated into the fascist Independent State of Croatia led by the Ustaša under Ante Pavelić. Atrocities against Serbs, Jews and Roma perpetrated by the Ustaša.
1941	Catholic nuns from Pale were killed in Goražde by Serbs nationalist guerrillas or Četniks in December and thrown into the River Drina. The so-called 'Drina martyrs' were beatified by the pope in 2011. Atrocities against Muslims perpetrated by the Četniks.

1942	The Second Proletarian Brigade was formed in March by Josip Broz Tito, the head of the Yugoslav Communists and now leader of the left-wing Partisan guerrillas.
1943, 29 November	Tito formed a temporary government in Jajce.
1944, 7 May	German attack on Drvar. Tito escaped by rope from a cave. After his death, the town was renamed Titov Drvar in his honour.
1945	Partisan victory is accompanied by reprisals against fascists and Četniks as well as the expulsion of ethnic Germans from Bosnia. Some Ustaša leaders escaped to Austria and Italy.
1946, 1 January	The victorious Communist Partisans create a new Constitution. Bosnia-Hercegovina was given the status as a Yugoslav Republic.
1948	Yugoslavia expelled from Cominform. Trials of Muslim leaders in Sarajevo, including Alija Izetbegović who was imprisoned.
1950	Peasant uprising (*Cazinska buna*) against the Communist regime in Cazin.
1959	Death of Ante Pavelić in Madrid.
1961	Ivo Andrić won the Nobel Prize for Literature.
1971	Muslims allowed to identify as such in the Yugoslavian census.
1972	The Bugojno group (*Bugojanska skupina*) tried to start an armed uprising against the Communists codenamed Phoenix (*Feniks*).
1980, 4 May	Josip Broz Tito, Communist leader of Yugoslavia since 1945, died.

1981	Apparitions of the Virgin Mary began in Medjugorje.
1983	Alija Izetbegović imprisoned for religious beliefs and released in 1988.
1984	Winter Olympics held in Sarajevo in February.
1984	Vojislav Šešelj imprisoned for nationalism and released in 1986.
1990, 31 July	Bosnia-Hercegovina declared a democratic state of equal citizens, free elections followed in November.
1990	The foundation of new political parties. The Serb Democratic Party (SDS) was founded by Radovan Karadžić, the Croatian Democratic Union of Bosnia and Hercegovina (HDZ BiH) inspired by Franjo Tudjman's party and the Party of Democratic Action (SDA) founded by Alija Izetbegović.
1991, 25 June	Croatia and Slovenia declared independence from Yugoslavia in June. Fall of the Croatian town of Vukovar in November accompanied by war crimes.
1992, 29 February	Bosnia-Hercegovina voted for independence from Yugoslavia but the referendum was boycotted by the Bosnian Serbs.
1992, 6 April	The European Community recognized Bosnia-Hercegovina as an independent state, followed by the USA.
1992	Fighting engulfed Bosnia. War crimes committed and the capital Sarajevo under siege for more than three years.
1992	Extension of United Nations Protection Force mandate to Bosnia in June.
1993	Creation of the United Nations 'safe areas' in Sarajevo, Žepa, Srebrenica, Goražde, Tuzla and Bihać.
1993	Failure of the Vance-Owen Peace Plan.

1993	Break down of Muslim-Croat Alliance. Creation of Herceg-Bosna.
1994	NATO jets shot down four Serb aircraft in February for allegedly violating the UN no-fly zone.
1994	Washington Peace Agreement ended the war between Croats and Bosniaks.
1994, 5 February	Massacre of shoppers at the Markale market in Sarajevo. Another bomb fell on the market on 28 April 1995.
1995	Ratko Mladić took the town of Srebrenica; 8,000 Muslim men and boys killed by Serb soldiers under his command.
1995, 21 November	Dayton Peace Treaty signed by Slobodan Milošević, Franjo Tudjman and Alija Izetbegović. Division of Bosnia into 'Federation' (51 per cent) and 'Serb Republic' (49 per cent). Right of return for refugees established. Brčko District became an International Protectorate. Appointment of a European High Representative.
1997	Bosnian government signed the Ottawa Treaty, which aimed to stop the use of anti-personnel mines in military combat. Landmines remained a particular problem in Bosnia after the 1992–1995 war.
1998	The Neum Agreement allowed Croatian vehicles to pass through Bosnia territory on the Adriatic coast unimpeded.
2003	Death of Alija Izetbegović.
2004	Massacre at Srebrenica in 1995 deemed to be a case of genocide in The Hague.
2008	Radovan Karadžić arrested and sent for trial to The Hague.
2011	Ratko Mladić apprehended and sent for trial to The Hague.

2013   The Bosnian census reported an overall
                decline in population by 585,411 com-
                pared to the previous census of 1991, or
                about 13 per cent of the population.
2014   Austerity protests in Tuzla dubbed the
                'Bosnian Spring'.

I

Introduction

Bosnia and Hercegovina is extraordinary and beautiful, a country of extremes in landscapes, personalities and history. Visually stunning and able to draw in thousands of tourists despite the devastation of civil war in the 1990s, it combines climatic zones and both Eastern and Western styles of living. In Livanjsko polje, an almost completely flat valley where wild horses graze, there is an intriguing disappearing karst river called the Jaruga.[1] At Vrelo Bune, extremely cold and clean water flows out of a small cave from a huge subterranean lake carrying a large variety of fish with it. In Visoko there is a rare symmetrical pyramid, a type of hill that is known to geologists as a flatiron. It looks like an ancient Egyptian temple that has been covered in shrubs and trees and it draws in tourists from around the world. The series of salt lakes in the centre of the city of Tuzla are rare to Europe and are a small remnant of the once vast Pannonian sea. Bosnia's highest peak Maglić, in the Sutjeska National Park, forms part of the border with Montenegro and stands 2,386 metres above the sea. Beneath it lies the virgin forest of Perućica, one of the wildest and least accessible parts of Europe where bears and wolves live almost undisturbed by humans. In the Middle Ages, the remote towns of Vratar and Vratac were only accessible by single file and were a place of refuge during political crises. Bosnia's scenery such as the waterfall at Jajce has been captured by numerous writers and

---

[1] Hoernes, Moritz *Dinarsiche Wanderungen: Cultur- und Landschaftsbilder aus Bosnien und der Hercegovina* (Vienna: C. Graeser, 1894), p. 296.

artists, both native and foreign. Sketches of daily life, the costumes worn by locals and their houses, musical instruments and food have all been carefully recorded for posterity.

Bosnia has a rich natural heritage, but has been subject to almost every major social movement or ideological experiment in the last millennium. This long-term instability has had its inescapable impact on the people and their destiny. Indeed before the referendum in 1992, Bosnia had not been an independent state in any form since the Middle Ages. In this concise history, a discussion of long-term structural trends has been woven into the micro-narratives of towns, cities and villages. Events in Sarajevo, Medjugorje, Jajce and Srebrenica have had lasting significance and put Bosnia on an international map. Several themes run through this discussion are crucial to the evolution of modern Bosnia. The most important of these themes is its boundaries with neighbouring lands and peoples, which are linguistic, ethnic, geographical and political. Modern Bosnia and Hercegovina has a unique national heritage, but it also shares a great deal with its immediate neighbours. For most of its history Bosnia has been ruled from outside the country and the legacy of empires and wars and of rule from Istanbul, Vienna or Belgrade is a constant theme. Bosnia is a country where the past matters and is lived experience for most. Writers from Veselin Čajkanović to Vera Stein Erlich have stressed how the people of the region saw themselves very much as part of a infolding chain of history. This sense of connectedness comes through very strongly in memoirs and autobiographies written by Bosnians. Growing up in Oglavak in the 1920s and 1930s, osteologist Dr Nadžija Gajić-Sikirić knew that it was her great-great-grandfather (*prapradjed*) who had built the *tekija* (Dervish monastery) in Fojnica.[2]

The impact of religion especially Sunni Islam, the Franciscan Order and the Orthodox Church and the disparities in wealth, opportunity and privilege that divisions entailed are also constant themes in the narrative here. Many scholars of Bosnia have focused upon the overlaps and blurred edges between those religious beliefs, of the Bosnian Muslims who stored bottles of alcohol for their Catholic friends, for the Christians who refrained from eating in

---

[2] Gajić-Sikirić, Nadžija *Sjećanja iz Bosne* (Raleigh, NC: Lulu, 2012), p. 8.

public during Ramadan or the Orthodox who believed that hospitality was one of the tenets of Christianity (rather than a pillar of Islam) and that church bells signalled a call to prayer. Although Bosnia produced plenty of religious radicals, it also produced many people who took personal risks to protect their neighbours. Among the prisoners at the prison camp at Omarska in 1992 were 'two Serb women arrested for protesting the behaviour of Serb soldiers and reservists towards their neighbours'.[3] Perhaps most striking of all the themes is the élan, bravery, creativity, but also sometimes destructiveness of many of its people. For the novelist Ivo Andrić there were 'few countries with such firm belief, elevated strength of character, so much tenderness and loving passion, such depth of feeling, of loyalty and unshakeable devotion, or with such a thirst for justice. But in secret depths underneath all this hide burning hatreds, entire hurricanes of tethered and compressed hatreds maturing and awaiting their hour.'[4]

Scientific evidence suggests that the modern population of Bosnia and Hercegovina is largely descended from Palaeolithic and Mesolithic populations. An article by Damir Marjanović and several co-authors that appeared in the *Annals of Human Genetics* in 2005 aimed to demonstrate that 'the three main groups of Bosnia-Hercegovina ... share a large fraction of the same ancient gene pool distinctive for the Balkan area'.[5] In other words, most modern Bosnians are descended from folk that lived in the region before the arrival of the Slavs, before Christianity and before Islam. The population was augmented over the centuries by settlement by speakers of South Slavonic, Vlach, Ladino and Turkish languages. There were also migrations from Central Europe under the Habsburgs and various parts of the former Yugoslavia. All of the population movements were significant in the making of modern

---

[3] Hukanović, Rezak *The Tenth Circle of Hell: A Memoir of Life in the Death Camps of Bosnia* (London: Abacus, 1998), p. 41.

[4] 'Letter from 1920' from Andrić, Ivo *The Damned Yard and Other Stories*, (Dufour: Forest Books, 1993), p. 115.

[5] Marjanović, Damir, Fornarino, S., Montagna, S., Primorac, D., Hadžiselimović, R., Vidović, S., Pojskić, N., Battaglia, V., Achilli, A., Drobnić, K., Andjelinović, S., Torroni, A., Santachiara-Benerecetti, A.S. and Semino, O. 'The Peopling of Modern Bosnia-Herzegovina: Y-chromosome Haplogroups in the Three Main Ethnic Groups', *Annals of Human Genetics* 69, 2005, pp. 757–763.

Bosnia and no one group can claim to be any more 'autochthonous' or genuine than any other.

The peoples of the Dinaric region of mountains are often very tall and certainly the loftiest in Europe in this century.[6] At 2.2 m, the basketball player Bojan Dodik, originally from Sarajevo, is one of the tallest men in the world. In the early twentieth century, racial theorists were convinced that the Dinaric people were part of the distinct 'race' and vestiges of similar beliefs linger in popular culture to this day. Height levels may have been nurtured by historically high protein consumption and a diet of lamb, goat, eggs and cheese. Red meat often forms the staple for a meal. *Ćevapi* or *Ćevapčići* are made with spiced minced meat and onion and usually don't contain pork in Bosnia. Meat is often served a preserved with a winter vegetable (*zimnica*), such as the red pepper relish *ajvar*. Bosnians produce hard crumbling cheeses, and softer varieties were introduced by the Ottomans. *Vlašićki* is a ewe's cheese that resembles feta, whereas *kajmak* is a curd cheese. British archaeologist Arthur Evans, well-known for his work on the Minoan civilization, spent some time studying the antiquities in Bosnia and left us animated and detailed descriptions of everyday life in the region in the 1870s. Staying with the Franciscans in the Guča Gora Monastery just east of Travnik, he remembered, 'we met with most sumptuous entertainment – as we thought it at the time – consisting of some lumps of mutton, good brown bread, eggs poached in cheesy milk, vermicelli, and a sweet melon'.[7]

Both Orthodox believers and Catholics are traditionally obliged to fast and not eat meat on some days and before mass. Muslims fast for Ramadan, which means that no food is consumed during the daylight hours. This habit and practice meshed particularly well with Ottoman cuisine, which is rich in cultivated food with a strong emphasis on vegetables. Casseroles could be prepared in advance for meat free days or for the evenings. *Sarma* is generally

[6] Pineau, Jean-Claude, Delamarche, Paul and Bozinovic, Stipe 'Les Alpes Dinariques: un peuple de sujets de grande taille' *Comptes Rendus Biologies* 328, 2005, pp. 841–846.

[7] Evans, Arthur J. *Through Bosnia and the Herzegóvina on Foot During the Insurrection, August and September 1875* (London: Longmans, Green, 1876), Vol. I, p. 181.

made from beef, onion and rice wrapped in cabbage leaves and served with *pavlaka* (sour cream). A similar dish known as *japrak* in Bosnia is made with vine leaves. When the dish was prepared, some of the leaf parcels only contained rice and vegetables for the fasting days. Local habits could sometimes lead to misunderstandings. British writer George Arbuthnot, who would later become MP for Hereford visited Vidosa (Vidoši) in early 1860 and found that 'the priest was profuse in his apologies for the absence of meat, proffering as an excuse that Roman Catholics do not eat it on Friday, a reason which would scarcely hold good, as I arrived on a Saturday. Of eggs and vegetables, however, there was no lack.'[8]

Bosnia and Hercegovina has had somewhat 'soft' borders with its neighbours in terms of religion, language and family connections, which often confound nationalism. There was continual Dinaric transhumance and then more permanent population movements between Hercegovina, old Montenegro and Serbia. The father of the Dubrovnik Jesuit scientist Rudjer Bošković came from Orahov Do in Hercegovina. As a result, the physicist who had a type of lunar crater (now known as a Boscovich) named after him is variously claimed to be Serb, Croat, Italian or even Montenegrin in origin. In time of crisis, the porosity of the borders suited people well. Bosnians could flee the state and take up residence in neighbouring regions. During the 1875 rebellion, the Adriatic port of Dubrovnik became a refuge for the people from the hinterland as it had been centuries earlier during the Ottoman invasions. In 1992, Bosnians who left their war-torn state most frequently went to other former Yugoslav republics. Modern Bosnia-Hercegovina has borders with three countries: Montenegro, Croatia and Serbia. Bosnia's neighbours all speak the same language with minor variants, which creates a potential problem if language is to be seen as one of the major determinants of nationality. Bosnian Croats and Serbs were particularly influenced by nationalist currents emanating from their neighbours. The break-up of the Ottoman State exposed the potential geopolitical vulnerability of Bosnia just as the collapse of both Yugoslav states was to do in the twentieth century.

---

[8] Arbuthnot, George *Herzegovina: or Omer Pacha and the Christian Rebels* (London: Longman, Green, Longman, Roberts, & Green, 1862), p. 264.

Modern Bosnians are also only a generation away from belonging to a unified state with its neighbours and a devastating war
in which its neighbours were aggressors. Bosnia's borders are also
relatively permeable because they are easy to breach. The Drina can
be swum across, as can the Adriatic at Neum, one can see Croatia
from the banks of the Sava and a shepherd or hiker could wander
into Montenegro without passing a border guard.

Bosnia has contrasting geographical regions that cover different zones of civilization. Heinrich Renner described the transition from the relatively lush Adriatic to the bare rocks of
Hercegovina: 'Greenery ... disappeared altogether and the wildest most magnificent mountain scenery surrounded us. Nothing
but grey, bare mountain peaks all around, on which guard houses
(*Karaulen*) stand everywhere ... the road climbed sharply to traverse the border between the Hercegovina and Dalmatia. In the
depth of individual valleys (*Dolinen*), are lonely farmsteads which
hardly stand out against the grey rock.'[9] Other travellers compared
the craggy Hercegovinian landscape to the moon.[10] The interplay
between these zones is one of the most intriguing motifs in Bosnian
history. The Adriatic region and its small coastal towns are suscep-
tible to earthquakes. Although the mountains separate Bosnia from
some of the worst tectonic instability, nevertheless it remains vulnerable. The terrible earthquake that destroyed the historic centre
of Dubrovnik in 1667 was felt in Trebinje some 15 miles away.

The Dinaric range extends like a spine along the western part of
Bosnia. Blown by a dry wind – the *bura* (or sometimes *bora*) that
comes in from the Adriatic – the rock is limestone, often dry and
difficult to traverse. Arriving in Mostar in 1893, Guillaume Capus
remembered that '[t]he bora blowing furiously, the sky was heavily
overcast ... The tremors were violent enough to crack houses ... and
bring a terrible confusion.'[11] Known as 'karst' from the local word
kras, its study has become a distinctive subject and its contours
have been carefully charted by earth scientists. The area around

[9] Renner, Heinrich *Durch Bosnien und die Hercegovina kreuz und quer* (Berlin:
   D. Reimer, 1896), p. 322.
[10] Evans, *Through Bosnia and the Herzegovina*, p. 355.
[11] Capus, Guillaume *A travers la Bosnie et l'Herzégovine. Études et impressions de
   voyage* (Paris: Librairie Hachette, 1896), p. 200.

Livno is one the largest of the karst fields or *polje* in the world and was submerged under water in the Neolithic era. Local idioms and words were adapted in the nineteenth century when the region was explored by researchers. The standard word for a sinkhole where water collects in the earth sciences is *dolina*, which comes from the word used by local people in the Dinarics and the term *uvala*, also used by geologists, means a coalescence of sinkholes. Describing the landscape, Émile de Laveleye found '[t]he surface of the ground is covered with large blocks of white limestone, which seems to be thrown down by chance, like the ruins of Cyclopean monuments. Water is almost everywhere very scarce; there are no springs, and the rivers issue ready made from grottos, giving rise in winter to lakes in the closed-up valleys; then they disappear again under the ground.'[12] In places, settlements have been hewn into the rock such as the medieval fort at Blagaj known as Stjepan grad.

Historically, many Bosnians lived in stone farmsteads with their extended families in what were known as *zadruge*.[13] Living with a larger group gave people a strong sense of their identity and mutual obligations. The concept of *moba* (mutual aid in times of need such as harvest) reinforced the obligations of traditional life. Fields full of stones, lack of water and the fact that it is hard for a pastoralist to become rich or to substantially change their life may have also contributed to the often noted fatalism of the Dinaric peoples.[14] The Bosnian word for destiny is *sudbina*, but sometimes the Turkish word *ksmet* has also been used, according to the geographer Jovan Cvijić.[15] Soil rarely settles for long enough for serious cultivation to take place so that fields are sparse and far better suited to ruminant animals than agriculture in Hercegovina. British writer Gerald Brenan, later known for his vivid descriptions of daily life in Andalucía, visited Hercegovina in his youth. 'Wherever I went

---

[12] de Laveleye, Émile *The Balkan Peninsula* (New York: G. P. Putnams, 1887), pp. 119–120.

[13] This could be translated as 'commune' and was close in concept to the Russian *obshchina*.

[14] Stein Erlich, Vera *Family in Transition: A Study of 300 Yugoslav Villages* (Princeton, NJ: Princeton University Press, 1966), p. 78.

[15] Cvijić, Jovan *La péninsule balkanique: Geographie humaine* (Paris: A. Colin, 1918), p. 297.

Map 1. Relief map of Bosnia

there was the same emptiness – the land too poor or too rocky to cultivate, the settlements rare, the farms few, and the ground either greyish white or ribbed and streaked with snow. The blank denuded look of the country is what I best remember – bare stony plains scattered with thin clumps of oak or fir tree, bare stony valleys without streams or rivers, hills that when not covered were ribs of whitish limestone rock.'[16] In some places, traditional lifestyles have survived to the present day. Muslims still live a pastoralist life in the nomadic village of Lukomir, which is inaccessible for months every year due to harsh local weather. The elderly inhabitants live in antique stone houses with cherrywood roof shingles, a vestige of

[16] Brenan, Gerald *A Life of One's Own: Childhood and Youth* (Cambridge University Press, 1979), p. 163.

a different age. They still spin and wear the clothes they produce including a type of heavy waistcoat known as a *zobun* and small caps called the *krmez*. Knitting is an important part of the preparations for marriage and men traditionally wore heavy long socks made for them by their female relatives. In 2010, a Dutch documentary crew made the film *Winterslaap in Lukomir*, which captured the desolation of the village during its 'hibernation', the drifts of snow and the sound of the wind.

Alongside the harsh landscapes of the mountains, there is also the Bosnia of rivers and small towns where fruit, tobacco and cereal crops can be grown. Fruit trees flourish, cows graze in lush meadows and the ground is kept moist by innumerable streams. Traditional houses (*Bosanske kuće*), often plastered and painted white, tended to have balconies and to be narrower at ground level. Their interiors were sometimes panelled with wood and then decorated with carpets. Passing from the mountains into the fertile valleys, Brenan discovered the other Bosnia: 'as I travelled south and east, the landscape began to alter. I came on mountain ranges that were dark with forest, valleys with clear rivers flowing in them, small towns and villages that in place of churches had minarets and mosques.'[17] In 1909 Maude Holbach visited the former Bosnian capital of Travnik, '[a] garden city with its mosques and minarets lying under the protecting walls of its ancient fortress', where she found herself 'wandering in the narrow streets of the old quarter, where the quaint Turkish houses have projecting upper stories, shaded by broad eaves and harem windows of muscharabiah work in the whitewashed walls'.[18] The novel *Travnička hronika* (1945), written about the town where author Ivo Andrić went to school but set more than a century earlier, evokes the imaginary smell of tallow, sounds and attitudes of an Ottoman-era city.

Historically Bosnia has had a small coast on the Adriatic since 1718 when it was taken over by the Ottomans. The sea and the recollection of visiting it for the first time became an important *lieu de mémoire* for Bosnians.[19] Although they often went to Dubrovnik

---

[17] Brenan, *A Life of One's Own*, p. 163.
[18] Holbach, Maude *Bosnia and Herzegovina, Some Wayside Wanderings* (New York: J. Lane, 1910), pp. 83–84.
[19] Gajić-Sikirić, *Sjećanja iz Bosne*, p. 22.

(Ragusa) rather that Neum, most of Bosnia is culturally very far from the sea. When Heinrich Renner visited in the 1890s, he described this small area of Bosnian coast as a 'Turkish wedge between Ragusa and Venice', which was still referred to by Dalmatian peasants as 'Turkey'.[20] The town of Neum and its environs including the islands of Veliki i Mali Školj remain very similar in economy to the rest of the littoral. Like neighbouring towns, it is also overwhelmingly Catholic. Neum has a stunning small church, Sveta Ana, and the folk costumes worn by local people are Dalmatian in style but clearly influenced by Ottoman traditions. The belt (*tkanica*) was made from woven material and not dissimilar to Turkish weaving in both styles and colour. Men wore the small cap or *bareta* and women covered their heads with white kerchiefs. Leather shoes with toes that turned up at the end (*opanci*) were worn across the Balkans and crossed the Dinaric Dalmatian divide. Other local traditions have preserved the *lindjo* folk dances accompanied by a lyre (*lijerica*). A cappella singing known as *klapa*, which involved the (usually male) tenor, baritone and base singers forming a semicircle also links Neum to the rest of the Dalmatian littoral. The long-term relationship between the Adriatic world and the hinterland is a constant historical theme in this region. Merchants from Dubrovnik traded in the old Ottoman towns such as Srebrenica. With them they bought knowledge of a wider Mediterranean culture of fish, wine and olive oil as well as the literacy of the Catholic world.

Much of the history of Bosnia and Hercegovina before the modern era is carved in stone. In 1976, Palaeolithic era carvings were found in the Badanj caves near Stolac. The image discovered probably represents the figure of a horse and as such is not unusual for Mediterranean region art from this era. Pottery has been found from the Neolithic era in Butmir and Obre with incised geometric patterns such as spirals and rhytons (drinking vessels). Until the early twentieth century, rural women tattooed themselves with vegetable dyes in similar patterns to those found on tombstones and even Neolithic figurines. For historians the written sources for the period between the fall of the Roman Empire and the medieval Bosnian kingdom are relatively sparce. In 168 BC, Illyria (which

[20] Renner, *Durch Bosnien und die Hercegovina*, p. 328.

included modern Bosnia) was taken over by the Romans. Several Bosnian towns have an Illyrian heritage, including Daelminium (which is now called Tomislavgrad and was previously known as Duvno) and Vranduk, which may be the ancient town of Arduba. Scholars have debated whether the city of Bistue Nova was Vitez, Zenica or close by to modern Bugojno[21] or even Rogatica. Illyria was ruled from Constantinople rather than Rome after 395 BC. In subsequent centuries, Bosnia continued to remain on a crucial fault line between Byzantium and Rome.

Christianity had reached Bosnia in the seventh and eighth centuries, thanks to the missionary work of Cyril and Methodius, two brothers born in Thessaloniki who reached Balkan peoples through the medium of their Slavonic dialect. Most Bosnians became nominal Christians and remained so until the sixteenth century and mass conversions to Islam. The Bosnian state and the forerunner of Hercegovina known as Hum (or sometimes Zahumlje) nestled between the authority of Rome and Constantinople and had overlapping borders with the modern states of Montenegro, Croatia and Serbia, which changed frequently with dynastic fortunes. Bosnia (or what is referred to as Βόσονα or Bosona) is mentioned for the first time as a geographically distinct entity in a tenth-century Greek treatise by the Byzantine Emperor Constantine VII Porphyrogenitus 'Πρὸς τὸν ἴδιον υἱὸν Ρωμανόν' ('For my Son, Romanos').[22] He also named the region of Travunia (Τερβουνια), which corresponds to the area around the city of Trebinje. The Neretva Delta region was populated by a tribe who were unbaptized and referred to as Pagani. The treatise is generally known now by its Latin title, *De administrando imperio*. Mihajlo Višević was recorded as being ruler in Hercegovina (which included the coast in the early tenth century). Porphyrogenitus believed that Mihajlo was a Slav whose forebears had migrated from the Vistula river region. Mihajlo is also described by a near contemporary Venetian chronicler known as John the Deacon in *Chronicon Sagornini*.

[21] Šašel Kos, Marjeta 'Bistue Nova', *Enzyklopädie der Antike* 2, 1997, p. 696.

[22] Goldstein, Ivo 'Zemljica 'Bosna – to horion Bosona u "De administrando imperio" Konstantina VII Porfirogeneta', in Marko Karamatić (ed.) *Zbornik o Pavlu Andjeliću* (Sarajevo: Franjevačka Teologija, 2008), pp. 97–110.

The banate of Bosnia, initially a vassal state of Hungary created in the twelfth century, emerged as a distinct polity by the fourteenth. After the Battle of Zemun in 1167, the defeated Hungarians lost much of their control in the region and sued for peace, thus recognizing Byzantine control over Bosnia. Bosnia's ruler, Ban Kulin – whose title can be translated as 'Lord' – was a vassal to the Byzantine Emperor Manuel I Komnenos and came to power in 1180. The Charter of Ban Kulin (*Kulinova povelja*), a trade agreement between Bosnia and the Ragusan Republic (nowadays Dubrovnik) written on 29 August 1189, effectively regulated Ragusan trade rights in Bosnia. Kulin is widely seen as one of the most important medieval rulers and established authority over a banate, which his son Stjepan Kulinić took over in 1204. Stjepan Kulinić was deposed by Matej Ninoslav, who as Ban continued to maintain strong relations with Dubrovnik. In 1250, the Catholic Kotromanić Dynasty took control of the banate and ruled Bosnia until they were destroyed by the Ottomans. Kotromanić power still rested on their status as Hungarian vassals and, in the fourteenth century, a number of rulers tried to create an independent Bosnian state. By 1329 Stjepan Kotromanić had gained much of Hum in a war with the Serbian King Stefan Dečanski. Stjepan Tvrtko managed to gain independence from Hungary, establishing rule over a country with similar borders to modern Bosnia in 1353. With its capital in Jajce, in 1377 Bosnia then became a kingdom under Tvrtko, who also claimed to be a Nemanjić successor to the Serbian crown through his grandmother Elizabeta. His important reign is celebrated with a statue in contemporary Tuzla. It is believed that his coronation actually took place in the Orthodox monastery of Mileševa, which is in contemporary Serbia. Tvrtko fought with the Serbian Prince Lazar at Battle of Kosovo polje in 1389 and survived the battle (unlike Lazar, who was captured and beheaded). Facing the army of the Ottoman Sultan Murad I many miles south, the battle brought Christian rulers together despite their differences and counter-claims. Like Lazar, Murad was also killed at the battle and possibly assassinated by a Serbian knight, Miloš Obilić, and was succeeded by his son Bayezid. In his 1998 novel *Elegy for Kosovo* (*Tri këngë zie për Kosovën*), the Albanian novelist Ismail Kadare saw this as a catastrophic turning point and an ominous sign for all the Balkan Christian rulers. 'Everyone ran. Unknown men, short sword in hand, glared with wild eyes ... Through all the mayhem shreds of violence news were heard.... King Tvrtko, having by now lost his crown, was hurrying back to Bosnia.'[23]

Although the Bosnian kingdom existed for several more decades, it was eventually overrun by the army of Sultan Bayezid. Tvrtko's successor, Stjepan Dabiša, who died in 1395, was unable to defend Bosnia against either the Turks or Hungarians. He was succeeded by his wife Jelena Gruba, the only female head of state in medieval Bosnia, who ruled for three years. It is not clear how she acquired the name 'Gruba' (coarse or ugly) and she may have been Orthodox rather than Catholic. She was ousted as queen in 1398 but remained at court as the late king's widow. The leader who had deposed her, Stjepan Ostoja, was temporarily ousted himself after he tried to ally himself with the Hungarians to the north, only managing to triumph over his rival Stjepan Tvrtko II in 1408. The last medieval king of Bosnia, Stjepan Tomašević, who had killed his own father Stjepan Ostoja, was defeated and subsequently beheaded by Sultan Mahommed II in 1463. Medieval Bosnia was noted for its complexity and individuality and a high degree of secularism as Ivan Lovrenović notes.[24] The hilltop town of Visoki, which overlooks modern Visoko, had a university and was the seat of several medieval kings.

It was during the Middle Ages that tombstones unique to this region, the *stećak* (plural *stećci*) were constructed. In popular Bosnian, these stones are sometimes referred to as *mramorovi* (marble stones). Some *stećci* are marked with a unique script, *bosančica*, which is similar to old Cyrillic, while others have scenes of dancing and symbols that may link them to a more ancient past. The fleur-de-lis, a symbol of Bosnia statehood, is sometimes found on these early tombstones. They often contain pithy inscriptions about the person buried there. Sometimes there is simply 'here lies...' (*a se leži*). 'Here lies Ljuben Dragota, on his noble land ... Pass by peacefully and do not overturn my tombstone, for I do not have anyone

---

[23] Kadare, Ismail *Elegy for Kosovo: A Novel* (London: Vintage Classics, 2010), pp. 39–40.

[24] Lovrenović, Ivan *Bosnia: A Cultural History* (London: Saqi, 2007), pp. 45–80.

Fig. 1 Medieval tombstones known as *stećci* (by Sam Foster)

there to right it'. From 1268, there was 'here lies Kulduk Krilić ...
I followed the way of reason, not of the heart. And now I regret
it.'[25] Visually, *stećci* are often very large and striking and are the
same greyish white of the surrounding limestone. Although they are
found beyond the Bosnian border in Montenegro and Croatia, they
are primarily constructed as part of the Bosnian cultural heritage
and often used to promote tourism. Much of the scholarly research
on the *stećci* was undertaken by the American art historian Marian
Wenzel, who was known affectionately as 'Marija Stećkova'.[26] The
poet Mak Dizdar famously described the tombstones as 'stone, but
also the word, earth but also the sky, solid but also spirit, death but
also life, the past, but also the future'.[27] He believed that the mysteries

[25] 'A se leži Ljuben Dragota na svojini na plemenitoj...Ne krejti u moj kam jer ja
    nikgoh nejmam da ga obaljenog vrejti (1405. po Gospodu godne)'. 'A se leži
    Kulduk Krilić ... Sljedih put razuma ne srdca. I sad mi je togda žal' in Tanović,
    Nenad *Stećci ili Oblici Bosanskih Duša* (Sarajevo: Bosanska riječ, 1994), p. 9.
[26] Wenzel, Marian *Ukrasni motivi na stećcima* (Sarajevo: Masleša, 1965).
[27] 'Jest kamen, ali jeste i riječ, jest zemlja, ali jeste i nebo, jeste materija, ali jeste i
    duh, jest krik, ali jeste i pjesma, jest smrt, ali jeste i život, jest prošlost, ali jeste

of the region were inscribed there waiting to be revealed. The art of the *stećak* was dominated by Christian symbolism, which drew upon the necessary aesthetics of limestone. Artist Maude Holbach described 'a curious rock-hewn tomb in what appeared from the other side merely a huge boulder that had become detached from the mountainside'.[28] In some respects the Islamic era gravestones or *türbe* continued this tradition by utilizing the whiteness of the stone to great aesthetic effect.

The nature of the Bosnian Church in the early Middle Ages is one of the most controversial subjects in the early history of the region and has become intertwined with questions of national identity in the modern era. Medieval Christendom was beset with heresy and schisms, perhaps linked to extant local traditions, the impact of illiteracy, poor nutrition and ergot-induced hallucinations. Members of the medieval Bosnian Church referred to themselves as *krstjani* (Christians) and were led by religious houses (*hiže*) similar to Catholic monasteries. The apparent radicalism of the Church led the Croat Catholic priest Franjo Rački to deduce that they were Manicheans (and thus similar to the Cathars of Western Europe). Manicheans believed that the universe was created by the devil rather than God and rejected the material world and the worship of a wooden cross as idolatrous. In his book *Bogomili i paterini*, written in 1869, Rački argued that Dualism (or the belief in a struggle between forces of good and evil) was an existential threat to the Catholic Church and its tenets of faith in many parts of Europe.[29] However many historians since Rački have disputed whether the Bosnian Church was heretical at all. Lovrenović reminds us that, in the cultural material of medieval Bosnia, there are no Bogomil elements, nor those of any other recorded heresy. The key texts – from the *Bilino Polje Abjuration* of 1203[30] down to the 1466 *Will of Gost Radin*[31] – quite explicitly operate within Orthodox Christian

---

i budućnost' in Isaković, Alija (ed.) *Biserje: izbor iz muslimanske književnosti* (Zagreb: Globus, 1972), p. 35.

[28] Holbach, *Bosnia and Herzegovina*, p. 148.

[29] Paterini is the name for Manicheans used on the Dalmatian coast.

[30] A *confessio* signed by seven *krstjani* for the legate John de Casamaris who was sent by Pope Innocent to investigate the church in Bosnia under Ban Kulin.

[31] The merchant Radin Butović has often been seen as an adherent of the Bosnian Church. See, for example, Truhelka, Ćiro 'Testament gosta

formulae and terminology.[32] In the early thirteenth century, Bosnia narrowly avoided the fate that befell Languedoc, which had been subject to a violent campaign to wipe out heresy from 1209 to 1229, known euphemistically as the Albigensian Crusade. In 1233, Vladimir, bishop of the Bosnian Diocese, was forced to step down by Pope Gregory IX for failing to crack down on heresy. The new bishop, Johannes von Wildeshausen, was not from the region, but was a German scholar known for his precision and piety. Another point of controversy was the notion that medieval adherents of the Bosnian Church, perhaps already heretically inclined and outside the Catholic fold, converted en masse to Islam after the arrival of the Ottomans. According to this hypothesis, Manicheanism was closer to Islam than Christianity, which made the process of changing faith less complicated. Conversion to Islam ensured the continuity of landownership and gave the Muslims legitimacy as the 'authentic' inheritor of Bosnian particularity. As Bojan Baskar has noted, 'slightly modified variants of this argument still dominate the accounts of conversion in Bosniak textbooks'.[33]

Linguistically, Bosnia is one of the most unified regions in the Balkans, with the vast majority of people speaking or understanding the variant of Bosnian (*bosanski*) called *neoštokavian ijekavski*, which can be written in Cyrillic or Latin (and is also referred to as *srpski*, *bošnjački*, *hrvatski* or *srpsko-hrvatski* depending on the preference of the speaker). In the fifth century, South Slavonic speakers from Eastern Europe began to arrive in the area and their language and culture spread quickly even to the remote mountains. At some stage between the late medieval and early modern age, the majority of the population began to speak the Slavonic Bosnian language.[34] Medieval scholar Florin Curta has suggested

Radina – Prinos paterenskom pitanju', *Glasnik Zemaljskog muzeja*, 24, 1911, pp. 355–376.

[32] Lovrenović, *Bosnia: A Cultural History*, p. 53.

[33] Baskar, Bojan 'Komišluk and Taking Care of the Neighbor's Shrine in Bosnia-Herzegovina' in Dionigi Albera and Maria Couroucl (eds.) *Sharing Sacred Spaces in the Mediterranean: Christians, Muslims, and Jews at Shrines and Sanctuaries* (Bloomington, IN: Indiana University Press, 2012), p. 59.

[34] The language spoken in Bosnia has variously been called Bosnian, Serbian, Serbo-Croat, Croatian or Bosniak. Native speakers sometimes call it simply '*naški*', i.e., our language.

Map 2. Bosnia in the Middle Ages

that a proto-Slavonic language spread as much by trade, migration and agriculture as by conquest. Prior to the seventeenth century, the Vlachs living in more remote areas of Bosnia spoke a language closely related to modern Romanian, a vestige from the Roman Empire. Some Vlach words survive in the region. The word for a mountain dog, *Tornjak*, is probably Vlach in origin. *Zarica* is a dry sour cheese from north-western Bosnia, which can be served grated and is etymologically of Vlach origin.[35] Roma peoples speaking a language distantly related to Sanskrit arrived in the region between the twelfth and fourteenth centuries and most in Bosnia converted

---

[35] Malcolm, Noel *Bosnia: A Short History* (London: Macmillan, 1994), p. 74.

to Islam. Turkish, Hungarian and German (the languages of the imperial metropoles) never fully replaced *bosanski.*

In the seventeenth century, the lexicographer and Jesuit Giacomo Micaglia wrote that there were many forms and variations of the 'Illyrian' tongue, but that the Bosnian language was the 'most beautiful'.[36] The process of Slavization in which Slavonic variants gradually replaced older idioms such as Vlach was largely completed by the time that Micaglia was writing. Nevertheless, in Bosnia, scholarship by Muslim scholars remained in Turkish or Arabic until the mid-nineteenth century at a time when much of the literature about the region was also being written down in German or Italian by Habsburg citizens and other Central Europeans. There are also a lot of words from Turkish (or, even more distantly, Arabic) in contemporary Bosnian including the words for cotton (*pamuk*), button (*dugme*) and socks (*čarape*). According to Srdjan Vucetić, there is also a genre of jokes that ridicule use of putative Turkish words in Bosnian, intended to illustrate their provincialism: 'a police officer is said to be called *pendrek-efendija* (baton mister) and *maksuz pendrek-efendija* (for special police: big time baton mister). An army tank is called *belaj-bager* (trouble-plower) and a female figure skater is called *zvrk-hanuma* (twist-woman).'[37] Fran Markowitz has suggested that 'the Turkish and Arabic words and expressions that dot Bosnian … can serve as an ominous reminder to Bosnian Serbs and Bosnian Croats that their ancestors once toiled under the Ottoman yoke, and that they might once again fall prey to the dominion of the Muslims'.[38] When compiling his influential dictionary, *Srpski rječnik istolkovan njemačkim i latinskim rječima*, which was first published in Vienna in 1818, Vuk Karadžić specifically did want to take out Turkish loanwords from the Serbian language.[39]

Both first and surnames are intimate to the rich history of the region. Goran means 'man from the mountain' suitable enough for

---

[36] Olivier, Louis Pierre Frédéric *La Bosnie et l'Herzégovine* (Paris: A. Colin, 1890), p. 94.

[37] Vucetić, Srdjan 'Identity is a Joking Matter: Intergroup Humor in Bosnia', *Spaces of Identity* 4(1), 2004.

[38] Markowitz, Fran *Sarajevo: A Bosnian Kaleidoscope* (Urbana, IL: University of Illinois Press, 2010), pp. 164–165.

[39] Peco, Asim *Turcizmi u Vukovim Rječnicima* (Belgrade: Vuk Karadžić, 1987).

the terrain and Davor is an old Slavonic name equivalent to the god Mars. Vlahović would suggest Vlach ancestry and many names are of Arabic or Turkish origin such as Begović, Damir, Adil or Esma. Ljubomir and Branimir (lover of and defender of peace, respectively) are Slavonic in origin. Christian saints are well represented, with names like Filipović (son of Philip) and Pavlović (son of Paul). The variations of Vuk (i.e., Vukić, Vuković, Vucić, Vujić) have embedded combat with the wolf (*vuk*). Perhaps inspired by the double dose in his given name and patronymic, legend has it that a heroic knight, Vuk Vukoslavić, saved Ban Stjepan Kotromanić in battle in the fourteenth century. First names often have male and female variants: Zoran/Zora (dawn), Zlata/Zlatan (gold) and Vjera/Vjeran (faith). It is often possible to guess the religion of a Bosnian by their name, but equally some names are shared by all faith groups. The Bosnian language is exceptionally rich in metaphors and archaisms, which are frequently lost when translated into English. A language with inflections where the nouns have genders and adjectives agree with them, it adapts well in verse. For example in first two sentences of Musa Ćazim Ćatić's 1902 poem 'Islamu',[40] 'O Islamu, vjero moja sveta, Spasu duše griješničke moje' (Islam, the faith of my world, that saves my sins), all the words end in vowel sounds. This poem has been memorized for its beauty by Muslims across the world.

[40] Terzić, Smail F. *Musa Ćazim Ćatić* (Sarajevo: Bosanska riječ, 1996), p. 24.

2

Bosnia, Hercegovina and the Ottoman Empire (1463–1912)

Over several centuries, Bosnia found itself at the centre of struggles between great powers and civilizations, which all left their imprint on the land and people as the hilltop towns with their churches and castles were taken one by one. Ottoman forces advanced slowly through the Balkans in the late medieval period and their arrival was anticipated. Fleeing the conquerors, Orthodox Serbs had started to pour into Bosnia from the 1430s onwards. By 1451 the Ottomans had taken Sarajevo, much of the rest of Bosnia fell in 1463 and Hercegovina by 1481. Jajce remained under the Hungarians until 1527 after the Turks lost possession of the town. Bihać was the last Bosnian city to fall and by the sixteenth century the Ottomans were in control not only of modern-day Bosnia and Hercegovina, but also Lika and parts of Slavonia known as the Bosnian Eyalet from 1580. What defeat by the Turks actually meant to ordinary Bosnians we can surmise from the surviving fragments of evidence, but it is likely to have been traumatic for many. Dalmatia served a safe haven for those escaping from Ottoman rule and many of its cities had fortifications erected to protect them against Turkish incursions. The family of the Renaissance humanist who experimented with the design of the parachute, Faust Vrančić (known also by his Venetian name Fausto Veranzio), is believed to have fled from Bosnia in the sixteenth century and settled in Šibenik. Some Bosnians were sold into slavery in the empire. Some seized the moment to change religion. Stjepan Hercegović, brother of the last Christian ruler of Hercegovina Vladislav, changed his name to Ahmed in 1473 and served the sultan as grand vizier in Constantinople. A *tekija* or Sufi monastery was built in the second decade of the sixteenth century on the Buna river near Blagaj and became well-known for Dervish religious devotion.

Bosnia had been a largely Catholic land with autonomous traditions and Hum largely Orthodox, but conquest completely changed the religious demographic patterns. Conversion from Catholicism to Orthodoxy and to Islam largely took place in the early decades of the sixteenth century. Most religious houses and monasteries in Bosnia and Hercegovina were converted into mosques or deserted. John Fine believes that by the fifteenth century, many areas of Bosnia had no Christian clergy at all.[1] Catholic priests had to find new ways to reach their scattered flock. There is an underground chapel in Jajce, which is similar to the catacombs that hid the early Christians in Rome.[2] According to the eighteenth-century friar Bono Benić, the monks of the Kraljeva Sutjeska monastery travelled disguised as shepherds in the nearby hills, sleeping rough or in caves and giving communion to or hearing the confession of the Catholic population.[3] Bosnia is already divided by its high peaks and fertile valleys. Conversion to Islam reinforced a difference between hills and towns, which persists to this day. Those unwilling to adopt the new religion may have converted to Orthodoxy rather than wait for the ministrations of the Franciscans, who were the only Catholics allowed to remain in the Ottoman lands. The number of Orthodox people in the West of Bosnia in the modern era (at least before the 1990s) indicates a distinct change from medieval religious population distribution.[4] Catholicism and Orthodoxy shared many of the basic tenets, although they differ on the question of sin and whether it can ever be 'erased' from the soul.

Defterler or Turkish cadasters indicate that this was a gradual process of conversion. Sons have Muslim names, but their fathers

[1] Fine, John V.A. 'The Medieval and Ottoman Roots of Modern Bosnian Society' in Mark Pinson (ed.) *The Muslims of Bosnia-Herzegovina. Their Historic Development from the Middle Ages to the Dissolution of Yugoslavia* (Cambridge, MA: Harvard University Press, 1996), p. 13.
[2] Lovrenović, *Bosnia: A Cultural History*, pp. 63–64.
[3] Holbach, *Bosnia and Herzegovina*, p. 238.
[4] Malcolm, *Bosnia*, p. 71.

still carry the names they were given in baptism. In the absence of strong and well-organized alternatives, Islam must have offered a great deal of structure and consolation for believers. Mosques and medresas became places of beauty, learning and contemplation. Islam must also have looked dynamic and new as its tenets were spread by articulate mullahs. The new adherents of Islam were spared from many taxes and became in effect a new ruling class (although many Muslims also remained poor). The millet system that categorized Ottoman subjects by the conversions of the early years of conquest reinforced divisions between Muslim landowners (*begovi*), the army (*spahija*) and civil servants and the peasantry, referred to as *rayah* from the Arabic word for flock. In the cities, merchants were classified as *muâf-nâme*.[5] This basic division in Bosnia was difficult to overcome. In contemporary slang the word *rayah* is still used to mean 'the common people'. In the Ottoman Empire a kind of religious separation was maintained through the millet system. Bosnian Muslims became an economically as well as culturally distinctive group. Because they also had links with wider communities outside the boundaries of their respective states, they often had transnational identities as well.

Some Ottoman practices that were introduced at the time of the conquest were radically different from Christian rule and often deeply resented by the *rayah*. According to the Janissary system or *devşirme*, bright promising Christian boys were taken from both the Balkans and Anatolia to Constantinople to work in the service of the state. There they converted to Islam and were expected to be loyal to the empire.

Thousands were taken in the last decade of the sixteenth century from Bosnia. The number of Janissaries grew to more than 100,000 in the next two centuries and many lost their connection to military or state service. The Janissary system (which comes from the Turkish work *yeniçeri*) was not abolished until 1826–1827 and it bound Christians to Muslims with ties of family. Some boys who had been spirited away did not forget their homeland. The grand

---

[5] Koller, Markus 'Introduction: An Approach to Bosnian History' in Markus Koller and Kemal H. Karpat (eds.) *Ottoman Bosnia: A History in Peril* (Madison, WI: University of Wisconsin Press, 2004), pp. 21–22.

Fig. 2 Mehmed Paša Sokolović Bridge at Višegrad (by
Richard Mills)

vizier Mehmed Paša Sokolović was born in a small village in eastern
Bosnia in the first decade of the sixteenth century. It is likely that his
family were Orthodox shepherds. Like many of his contemporaries,
he was taken as a slave to serve the sultan but soon rose through
the ranks because of his flair for languages and his incisive, pragmatic leadership style. He fought at the Battle of Mohács and the
1529 Siege of Vienna. During a long, illustrious career he took on
many important political offices including admiral and governor of
Rumelia (the Turkish term for the Southern Balkans), loyally serving three sultans. He commissioned many architectural structures,
including the eponymous bridge in Višegrad.

In the mid-seventeenth century, Bosnia was described in some
detail by the celebrated Ottoman traveller Evliya Çelebi. His trav-
elogue or *Seyâhatnâme* tells us that Ottoman culture was already
well-established by this date and had become a habit of the heart in
the region. Çelebi visited what he described as the 'peerless' stone
bridge in Mostar, which had been first commissioned during the

Map 3. Bosnia under the Ottomans

reign of Suleiman the Magnificent and its chief architect was Mimar Hayruddin. Stonemasons were brought in from the Dalmatian coast to build the bridge, which almost resembled a Muslim crescent. The architect Hayruddin was an apprentice of perhaps the most famous Ottoman architect, Mimar Sinan, who designed the Mehmed Paša Sokolović Bridge, which stretches across the Drina in Višegrad, in the 1570s. Sinan and his pupils defined an elegant characteristically Ottoman style found across the empire from Hercegovina to Anatolia. They used local materials but retained the elements of light coloured stone and ambitiously proportioned curving arches. The sixteenth century was an Ottoman Renaissance and a great era of bridge and mosque building. It was also an era in which beautiful Orthodox churches were constructed or decorated. Vicko, son of the famous Lovro Dobričević from Kotor, travelled to

Fig. 3 The old bridge at Mostar and Karst Mountains (by Matt Willer)

the monastery at Tvrdoš near Trebinje to paint murals in the early sixteenth century. The white monastery at Žitomislić was probably finished by the first decade of the seventeenth century, having been commissioned by pious local Serbs. For perhaps as long as the bridge in Mostar had stood, there has been a local tradition of jumping in the Neretva river from the top of the bridge, a custom also described by Çelebi: 'some brave boys stand ready at the bridge and cry *Ya Allah* (dear God!) and leap into the river, flying like birds … somersaulting or plunging upside down or sitting cross legged; on they go in twos or three, embracing each other and leaping into the water. God keeps them unharmed and they immediately clamber onto the shore.'[6]

Sarajevo, Jajce and Travnik all served as capitals before the 1870s. As a city, Sarajevo has many layers of identity. Prior to the Ottoman conquest, it was known as Vrhbosna and has been the sight of

[6] Dankoff, Robert and Kim, Sooyong (eds.) *An Ottoman Traveller: Selections from the Book of Travels of Evliya Çelebi*, 2nd edn (London: Eland Publishing, 2011), p. 215.

settlement since the Neolithic period. Its modern-day name is a fusion of the word for the walled seclusion of women (*seraglio* or *serraglio*), combined with a Slavonic word ending. Its late nineteenth-century buildings are similar to dozens of towns in Central Europe, but its small centre represents a unique synthesis between the local and the Ottoman. Gazi Husrev-Beg (1480–1541), who is buried in the city, did much to augment the small settlements in the area. Like many of his contemporaries, Husrev-Beg distinguished himself in the service of Suleiman the Magnificent at the 1526 Battle of Mohács, which allowed the Ottomans to take the city of Buda. This victory probably represented the highpoint of Ottoman power and the confidence and élan of its leaders is reflected in the plans for the cities in their empire. It was during his time as ruler of Bosnia that the city began to develop in terms of political importance. The first mention of the city and its new name comes in the work of the Venetian traveller Caterino Zeno, who discussed the journey from Spalato (Split) to Serraglio (Sarajevo) in 1550. In many ways, Sarajevo became the perfect village city, nestling in a beautiful golden valley with parks and gardens. But it was never an easy city to defend and was vulnerable to attack from the surrounding mountains. Sarajevo grew as an important Ottoman trading centre with important links to the Adriatic and the rest of the empire. Egyptian merchants developed their skills in calligraphy. In its *bedestan* or covered market, silk fabrics were found from all over the Middle East. For more than 300 years, from 1621 onwards, the *Fondaco dei Turchi* on the Grand Canal in Venice was used to house all Muslims merchants including Bosnians. The Venetian building was adapted to include a space for prayer and Turkish baths. It is likely that several hundred merchants a year visited the city and were thus separated from other visitors according to the wishes of the Venetian authorities.[7] They traded in wool, lead, dyes and leather. The blue dye so valued by artists in Dubrovnik was a by-product of the production of silver extraction from Bosnia.[8]

[7] Faroqhi, Suraiya *Travel and Artisans in the Ottoman Empire: Employment and Mobility in the Early Modern Era* (London: I.B. Tauris: 2014), p. 76.

[8] Belamarić, Joško 'Cloth and Geography. Townplanning and Architectural Aspects of the First Industry in Dubrovnik in the Fifteenth Century' in Alina Payne (ed.) *Dalmatia and the Mediterranean: Portable Archaeology and the Poetics of Influence* (Leiden: Brill, 2013), p. 285.

The Ottomans lost most of the territory in modern-day Croatia at the Treaty of Karlowitz in 1699, a date that is generally regarded as the high point of Ottoman power in Europe. Areas of present-day Croatia originally taken by the Turks were re-Christianized. In 1693, the Venetians captured Gabela, which had been under the Ottomans. The so-called 'sultan's mosque' was turned into the church, Sveti Stjepan. Near to Zadar, a port that was subject to constant attacks by the Ottomans, are two villages that used to be a single settlement with the Turkish name of *Saddislam* (wall of Islam). Islam Grčki (Orthodox) and Islam Latinski (Catholic) have since become separate villages with populations of different religions (but with no remaining Muslims). Habsburg campaigns in the Balkans led by Prince Eugen of Savoy led to the sacking and torching of Sarajevo in 1697. He recorded in his diary: 'On the 24th [October] I stayed near Sarajevo. We completely burnt down the town and all its surroundings. Our troops, which pursued the enemy, brought back booty and many women and children, after killing many Turks.'[9] Fires also devastated the city in 1879, hence the local prevalence of *dirne* or thick fire doors.

A century after Çelebi, the scholar and former Janissary Mula Mustafa Ševki Bašeskija recorded a chronicle (*Ljetopis*) about life in Bosnia's largest city from 1746 until 1804, describing the different districts (*mahalle*) of the city, some of which were named after the flowers that grew there. Of these mahalle, two were Jewish, 12 were Christian and 90 were Muslim. Bašeskija wrote the text in the dialect of Turkish used in Sarajevo, but spoke Bosnian in his everyday life. Pilgrimages to Mecca by his contemporaries were recorded in spirited detail. Going to the holy city would mean that pilgrims and their ancestors could add 'Hadži' to the beginning of their patronymic (creating distinctive Bosniak surnames such as Hadžišehović). Christian pilgrims to Jerusalem could also add 'Hadži', which has meant that some non-Muslims also have had surnames that link them to an Ottoman past. In particular Bašeskija

---

[9] Džaja, Srećko 'Bosnian Historical Reality and its reflection in myth' in Pål Kolstø (ed.) *Myths and Boundaries in South-Eastern Europe* (London: Hurst, 2005), pp. 106–129.

recorded the devastation of the plague that raged for three years after 1783 and killed thousands across Bosnia.

One of the best extant sources on Ottoman-era Bosnia is the travel account by Croat Matija Mažuranić. His 1839 journey published as *Pogled u Bosnu* (*A View of Bosnia*) gave Habsburg readers a sense of another more Oriental world just to the south and east. He was in his early twenties when he made the short journey across the Sava into Bosnia. The book gives an insight into a country that was effectively a foreign country for those living on the nearby Dalmatian coast and Mažuranić dwells on the more obvious differences in dress, the stratification of society and language. He depicted the Bosniaks as a caste who despised the *rayah* and asserted their privileges in manifold petty ways. The Bosniaks who did not see themselves as Ottoman but rather as local, insisted that the words they used that were different from the Illyrian idioms of coastal Croatian were native and not borrowed from the Turks. Nevertheless Mažuranić took playful delight in trying to capture the difference in their language by using their Turkish words such as *valaha* and *murafet*.[10]

In the early nineteenth century, the Serbian writer Vuk Stefanović Karadžić, whose ancestors came from the Hercegovina clan of Drobnjaci, recorded some the popular poems and songs from Bosnian people. Karadžić, who had spent many years studying with the linguist and imperial librarian Jernej Kopitar in Vienna, was one of the scholars responsible for codifying and thus elevating the scattered ballads of the guslars into a national literary canon.[11] One of his main informants was a blind gusle player, Filip Višnjić, from north-east Bosnia. Daily and epic struggles against the Ottoman Turks were a central theme of these poems, which also indicate that, at least by the early nineteenth century, the border between Serbia and Ottoman Bosnia was quite porous. Reading the memoirs by Matija Nenadović of the first uprising against the Dahije rulers in 1804, it is clear that the Drina river was regarded as a fairly easy border to traverse and the border between Bosnia

---

[10] Mažuranić, Matija *Pogled u Bosnu ili kratak put u onu krajinu, učinjen 1839–40* (Zagreb: Ljudevita Gaja, 1842), p. 25.
[11] Malcolm, *Bosnia*, pp. 79–80.

and Serbia was becoming less distinct by the early nineteenth century. Ivan Mažuranić, brother of Matija, who came from northern coastal Croatia, at that time under the Habsburgs, was one writer who significantly helped to form our contemporary views of Slavonic Muslims. His poem *Smrt Smail-age Čengića* (*The Death of Smail-aga Čengić*), published in 1846 consciously drew upon the epic Dinaric style of guslari and bards and concerns a feud between clans. Čengić had been a general in the Ottoman army and was well-known to his contemporaries. Born in Bosnia in the late 1780s, the poem recreates the circumstances of his death at about the age of 50 at the hand of the Montenegrin *hajduk*[12] Novica Cerović. Like its near contemporary work, *Gorski Vijenac* (*The Mountain Wreath*) (1847) by Petar II Petrović-Njegoš, the main theme of *Smrt Smail-age Čengića* is the long term poor state of relations between the Muslims and the Orthodox.

In the following decade, another Croatian writer Luka Botić, originally from Split, wrote sympathetically about the Bosnian Muslims in poems such as *Dilber Hasan* (*Hasan the Suitor*). Central to Botić's evocation of Bosnian culture is the role of the *sevdalinka*.[13] The romanticism of some Croatian writers is very different from the antipathy in Serbian/Montenegrin literature, which tended towards a clearer repudiation of all aspects of the Islamic heritage. It would be too much to state that the lines of division between Croat and Serb views of Bosnia were drawn in the mid-nineteenth century, but a general accommodation of Islam was more closely reflected in the Habsburg monarchy than in the Ottoman successor states to the south. *Sevdalinke* are traditional love songs mostly performed by Bosnian Muslim women, although men can sing them as well. The old Turkish word *sevdah* could be roughly translated as 'the melancholy of being in love' with a Slavonic diminutive. The *sevdalinka* can be seen as a unique and authentically Balkan genre, which often mixes Turkish and

---

[12] A word that means a rebel or bandit in Serbian, Croatian or Bosnias, *hajduci* were often seen as folk heroes.

[13] Solić, Mirna 'Women in Ottoman Bosnia as Seen Through the Eyes of Luka Botić, a Christian poet' in A. Buturović and I. Ç. Schlick (eds.) *Women in the Ottoman Balkans: Gender, Culture, and History* (London: I.B. Tauris, 2007), p. 328.

Slavonic words. The songs *Moj dilbere* (*My Lover*) and *Simbil cveće* (*Hyacinth Flowers*) jumble words of different etymological origins and are both popular in the repertoire today. A poet from Mostar, Aleksa Šantić, consciously imitated this style when he wrote *Emina* in 1902 about the joy and pain of his unrequited desire for a young girl, while evoking the flowing water and the Oriental scents of jasmine, roses and hyacinths in her garden. Šantić was a Serb and his neighbour, Emina Sefić, a Muslim and the daughter of an imam. Many years earlier, the Venetian traveller Alberto Fortis had journeyed along the Dalmatian coast and recorded the melancholy song of the wife of Hasan-Aga known as *Hasanaginica*, a tragedy about a man who divorces his wife by ordering her out of the house after a misunderstanding. Forced to marry another man and leave her children, she dies of a broken heart. The song was first recorded in Imotski, close to the contemporary Croatian-Bosnian border, and was translated by numerous writers including Walter Scott and Alexander Pushkin.

Away from the Dalmatian coast, Bosnian music was influenced by traditions of transhumance and proximity to the cultural world of the Ottoman Empire. *Gajde* or bagpipes were played by shepherds and made from the hides of goats or sheep. Polyphonic choirs were often accompanied by long-necked lutes known as *tamburice* or *šargije* (similar to the modern Greek bouzouki). Elaborated and lengthy poems was sung or recited by singers known as *guslari* who played a simple single stringed *gusle*. The poems typically mixed the contemporary with the historic collective in a style that came to shape later Serbian discourses. There was some role for artistic elaboration by *guslari* such as Filip Višnjić who could adapt the core poem according to the audience and occasion. Perhaps one of the reasons why American-style rap has been so readily adopted in contemporary Bosnia by performers such as Edo Maajka, originally from Brčko, is that local audiences are receptive to yarns spun in rather long and idiosyncratic ways.

Government by the Turks had a profound impact on all the peoples in the region, whatever their original religious conviction. Large numbers of Slavonic-speaking people appear to have converted voluntarily to Islam and, by the end of the Ottoman period, represented more than a third of the population of Bosnia and Hercegovina.

Their version of Islam had many local characteristics, giving us some crucial insight into the way in which Muslim beliefs spread. Although the henna tattoos of Muslim and Catholic women look like a Middle Eastern habit (linked to fertility, the anti-fungal properties of henna and ritual ablutions) the patterns used predate Islam. The Ottoman legacy is not the sole preserve of the descendants of Muslim converts. A wave of refugees arrived from Spain in the late fifteenth and early sixteenth centuries. In the nineteenth century it was reported that their language was 'the same as that spoken in Spain at the time of their expulsion, and is very nearly that in which "Don Quixote" is written'.[14] The descendants of the Jews that settled in Sarajevo still speak their Ladino Spanish to the present day, but the number of Jews that survived the Holocaust in the city was very few. A Jewish courtyard (*cortijo*) known as the Mahalla Judia was constructed in the late sixteenth century near to the market that housed artisans and craftsmen. Although the converts to Islam were perhaps the most profoundly affected by Turkish hegemony, it permeated the folk beliefs and language of the region. Bosnians will say *mashallah* if they are presently surprised, but also *inshallah* (or *ako Bog da*) to cover other eventualities. *Merhaba* as a greeting tends to be used by Muslims. In the late nineteenth century, Maude Holbach, a painter, visited Jajce and observed the extent of acculturation of Christians to Islamic practices. In the Catholic Church she spied men with shaven heads, save a small pigtail, kneeling on prayer rugs with their arms outstretched in the Muslim fashion: 'It is curious to see how Moslem customs have had their influence on the Christians of these countries; witness that of prostrating the body in the act of worship so that the forehead touches the ground, and raising the hands, palms upwards, at the blessing.'[15] Red turbans were worn by Serbs in the Trebinje region in the nineteenth century, although the Muslims did tend to wear gaudier colours (Christians were forbidden to wear green). Many sources stress both significant acculturation and mutual respect between the religious groups. In the 1870s, Franciscans wore the fez, which made

[14] Muir Sebright Mackenzie, Georgina Mary and Irby, Adelina Paulina *The Turks, Greeks and Slavons: Travels in the Slavonic Provinces of Turkey-in Europe*, (London: Bell and Daldy 1877), p. 18.

[15] Holbach, Bosnia and Herzegovina, p. 63.

them difficult to distinguish from the other Bosnians.[16] In Azići in 1930s Alija Izetbegović remembered that his elderly Serb neighbour Risto Berjan would turn his head away in respect when he greeted women in their gardens in order to respect Muslim customs.[17] Serbs tended to respect the Muslim prohibition of pork and did not eat in public during Ramadan.

Links with the Ottoman world meant that Bosnia became a colourful theatre set for many Europeans who went there during the nineteenth and early twentieth century. A young Anglo-Irish traveller, Evelyn Wrench, bought from Mustapha, a tailor in Sarajevo, 'a fez, a Zouave jacket and trousers of pale blue, a bodice of striped material, a red sash and red shoes ... As usual the population was half Christian and half Mahommedan; it seems extraordinary how both sects live in peace with each other ... One could see that one had left ordinary Europe behind, as all the people were in costume that reminded me very much of the East.'[18] Many travellers commented on the baggy trousers (*dimije*) in orange and red that Christians and Muslim women both wore. Despite high levels of acculturation, some differences persisted. Rose petal jam seems only to have been eaten by Muslims, who also ate carrots and other vegetables raw rather that cooking them. Honey was also drunk diluted by Muslims who added it to their food as well.[19] Lard was never used in the Muslim kitchen, which meant that, although Christians could be guests of Muslims, invitations could never be returned as the 'purity' of the kitchen and other domestic habits would not be acceptable. In 1936, Slovene-American writer Louis Adamič observed that 'hospitality in a Sarajevo Moslem home ... is not the spontaneous almost orgiastic business that it is in Christian homes in Yugoslavia, but extremely formal and restrained'.[20] All Bosnians shared the culture of drinking coffee on settees,[21] although the Bosnian language has

---

[16] Blau, Otto and Kiepert, Heinrich *Reisen in Bosnien und der Hertzegowina* (Berlin: D. Reimer, 1877), p. 38.

[17] Izetbegović, Alija *Sjećanja: autobiografski zapis* (Sarajevo: OKO 2005), p. 31.

[18] Wrench, Evelyn British Library Add. Manuscript 59566, vol. XVI, 1901.

[19] Hangi, Antun *Die Moslim's in Bosnien-Hercegovina* (Sarajevo: D.A. Kajon, 1907), p. 103.

[20] Adamič, Louis 'Sarajevo – Mustafa's Home Town', *The Rotarian*, 1936, p. 72.

[21] On the culture of coffee in the Balkans as well as a detailed discussion of the Ottoman legacy, see Jezernik, Božidar *Wild Europe: The Balkans in the Gaze of Western Travellers* (London: Saqi, 2004).

different words for the little cup that they used (*fildžan* for Muslims and *šoljica* for Christians). Travelling in Hercegovina in the 1870s, Arthur Evans remembered that 'the only refreshment we could obtain in this terrible waste was the never-failing coffee'.[22] All wore slippers instead of shoes indoors in the Middle Eastern fashion. In the domestic sphere, Muslim houses tended to have more walls and higher fences and never had pigsties. Differences remained and survived into the twentieth century. Cornelia Sorabji's 1980s fieldwork in Sarajevo contained an important observation that Muslims mocked the Christian habit of crying and wailing at funerals; they preferred silence and ritual prayers at their ceremonies. Muslims also neglected their gravestones. 'Falling down like a Turkish graveyard' means falling into disrepair in the Croatian and Serbian languages. Muslim cemeteries became one of the most distinctive sights on the Bosnian landscape. George Arbuthnot remarked in Mostar in 1860s: 'As usual in a Turkish town, dogs and gravestones were to be found in abundance, the latter with their turbaned heads looking spectral and grim in the cold moonlight.'[23]

Although Bosnians had earlier converted to Christianity, vestiges of a far older traditional culture have survived into the modern era. These beliefs connect Bosnians of all religious groups to the land and landscape around them. In order to evoke rain, pebbles are thrown into the river and a *dova* or prayer is uttered. The ceremony sometimes takes place on the first day of spring, with Sufi mystics leading the prayers. One vestige of an older culture is the practice of going on picnics, considered to be a Bogomil legacy by Adil Zulfikarpašić. In many parts of Bosnia, a belief in a thunder god, Perun, survived. Alindjun or Ilindan is celebrated by Serbs and Muslims together as St Ilias Day. The ethnographer Miroslav Niškanović studied the festivities (known as *dernek*) in Gerzovo in 1978 concluding that the Muslim and Serb celebrations were syncretic and parallel to one another rather than stemming from the same ceremony.[24] In Foča, the stone of Ivko of Jogatica (*Ivkov kamen*) was revered by Muslims and Christians, who believed that

---

[22] Evans, *Through Bosnia and the Herzegóvina*, p. 356.
[23] Arbuthnot, *Herzegovina*, p. 30.
[24] Niškanović, Miroslav 'Ilindanski dernek kod turbeta Djerzelez Alije u Gerzovu', *Novopazarski zbornik* 2, 1978, pp. 163–186; Baskar, 'Komišluk and Taking Care of the Neighbor's Shrine', p. 54.

Fig. 4 Muslim headstones in a Sarajevo graveyard
(by Matt Willer)

if they drank the water that fell in the cavity of the fallen hero's
gravestone, that they would be cured of illness.[25]
The ritual of *pobratimstvo* (ritual blood brotherhood) is found
among and between Serbs and Muslims in Hercegovina.[26] Blood
brothers usually shared blood by cutting their arms and mixing
the two together. The ritual could also involve women and in that
case was called *posestrimstvo*. The wives of sworn brothers would
become sisters and through rituals they were bound to help each
other in times of crisis as an extended and deeper version of *moba*
or mutual obligation. The notion of 'family' was also extended by
the institution of *kumstvo* (similar to the idea of godparenthood)
in which *kumovi* (godparents) would promise to protect children of
close friends. This practice could also unite Christians and Muslims
in deep friendship and pacts of obligation. Christian couples seeking a marriage or divorce might turn to a Muslim *kadi*. In 1935, in

---

[25] Renner, *Durch Bosnien und die Hercegovina*, p. 120.
[26] Grandits, Hannes *Herrschaft und Loyalität in der spätosmanischen Gesellschaft.
Das Beispiel der multikonfessionellen Herzegowina* (Vienna: Böhlau 2008).

Gacko, the Homer scholar Milman Parry noted the blood brotherhood between Serb Stojan Janković and Muslim Ramo Katurnica while he was collecting epic poems.[27] Professor Parry and his young assistant, Albert Bates Lord, arrived in Bosnia in 1934 to record the lived tradition of poetry that they heard in the *kafana* or coffee bar on aluminium discs. Lord's own 1960 work *The Singer of Tales* also drew extensively on this fieldwork and is considered to be one of the most influential texts on the subject.

At some crucial levels, Islamic norms also failed to permeate Bosnian society. The colourful profanities of the Bosnian language are used by all people (especially men), although strictly speaking Muslims should not swear. In the 1860s, Arbuthnot noted that 'the use of foul and indelicate language is almost universal, men, women, and children employing it in common conversation'.[28] Monogamy remained standard and it remained rare for Bosnian men to take more than one wife.[29] Some women did not wear the veil, although most women wore headscarves until the 1920s. Alcohol, traditionally wine and raki(ja) brandy were enjoyed by all religions. Arthur Evans remembered that, in Doboj in 1875, '[o]ur Mahometan, with the greatest *sang froid*, ordered a bottle of thick red Slavonian wine, and proceeded to consume it before our eyes; but the wine-bar in the upper town had already familiarized us with the laxity of true believers'.[30]

The Ottoman Empire had offered Bosnians a new structure after the dynastic fighting of the Middle Ages. It had given them new words and ways of life. In the 1880s, Salih Sidki Hadžihuseinović produced a *Tarih-i-Bosna* (*History of Bosnia*) written in Turkish and drawing on many of the primary sources that were lost during the fire in the Vijećnica during the siege of Sarajevo. It looks back with nostalgia at the entire period from the Ottoman conquest to annexation by the Habsburgs in 1878. Nevertheless,

[27] Vidan, Aida *Embroidered with Gold, Strung with Pearls: The Traditional Ballads of Bosnian Women* (Cambridge, MA: Harvard University Press 2003), p. 168.
[28] Arbuthnot, *Herzegovina*, p. 46.
[29] Unusually President Alija Izetbegović married four times, in accordance with Islamic practice elsewhere. For his views on 'married love' see Izetbegović, Alija *Islam between East and West* (Selangor: Islamic Book Trust 1993), p. 234.
[30] Evans, *Through Bosnia and the Herzegóvina*, p. 107.

Fig. 5 Interior of Mehmed Koski pašina džamija (mosque), Mostar (by Sam Foster)

this civilization began to crumble in the early nineteenth century just as it had started to make widespread changes. Attempting to reverse hundreds of years of legal discrimination, Sultan Mahmut II (1808–1839) had said 'one is a Christian when in church and a Muslim in a mosque, but all are equally my subjects'.[31] But this sentiment came too late for Bosnia, which was beset by rebellions as both Muslims, angry at the loss of privilege, and Christians, inspired by the Serbs and the Greeks, began to lose faith in the Ottoman Empire. The Great Bosnian Revolt (1831–1833) was led by the general Husein Gradaščević, the so-called 'dragon (*zmaj*) from Bosnia' who opposed some of the Tanzimat reforms that were beginning to change Ottoman rule. Before he led an anti-Ottoman force in Bosnia he had been the local ruler in Gradačac. While in

[31] Karpat, Kemal H. 'The Migration of the Bosnian Muslims to the Ottoman State 1878–1914. An Account based on Turkish Sources' in Markus Koller and Kemal H. Karpat (eds.) *Ottoman Bosnia: A History in Peril* (Madison, WI: University of Wisconsin Press, 2004), p. 126.

power he had commissioned some of the local landmarks, including the tower at the castle in 1824 and an exquisite white mosque (*Džamija Husejnija*) with a tall and elegant minaret some two years later. For several years, Gradaščević took over Bosnia and tried to roll back the impact of the changes, but was defeated militarily by another Bosnian Muslim who had initially supported the uprising, Ali-paša Rizvanbegović. Until his execution by the sultan in 1851, Rizvanbegović ruled Bosnia as vizier. Harsh treatment of Christians in the final years of the empire, led to a reaction, particularly in Hercegovina. The Orthodox formed themselves into armed bands, drawing on the *hayduk* or bandit traditions in the Dinarics. Their defiance of the Muslim *begovi* was to become important in the mythology of self-defence in the region. Despite the political instability of the mid-nineteenth century, in many respects Bosnia and Hercegovina remained mired in tradition and local practices. Tradition was to weigh heavily on all the political leaders who tried to change Bosnia in subsequent years. Coming from a country where axles had been made with iron for centuries, in 1860 George Arbuthnot noted the 'long strings of carts drawn by eight bullocks were employed in carrying wood to the villages in the plain of Duvno. These carts are roughly built enough, but answer the purpose for which they are intended, viz. slow traffic in the plains. The axle-trees and linch-pins are made of wood, and indeed no iron at all is used in their construction.'[32] Twenty years earlier Matija Mažuranić had thought that the Bosnians he met valued their watermill as if it were as precious as a steam engine (*parna makina*).[33]

---

[32] Arbuthnot, *Herzegovina*, p. 233. Mary Edith Durham made the same observation about Montenegro in her *Diary from 1900*, Royal Anthropological Institute (RAI MS), 42(1).

[33] Mažuranić, *Pogled u Bosnu*, p. 25.

3

Rebellion, war and the Habsburgs (1875–1918)

HABSBURG RULE

In the nineteenth century, as Ottoman imperial power collapsed in the Balkans, national groups and states vied to replace its domination. The Bosnian lands were caught in a greater regional struggle for power that involved the British Empire, Imperial Russia and the Central European powers, as well as all the Balkan states. This struggle became known as the Eastern Question and preoccupied the European diplomatic communities until the establishment of the modern Balkan states from 1912 to 1918 and Turkey in 1923. Horror at atrocities committed during the long break of Turkey-in-Europe often dominated news coverage. In 1875, the Ottomans began to lose control after a rebellion in Hercegovina, which was linked to the spread of nationalist aspirations in neighbouring Montenegro and Serbia. The small village of Nevesinje lit the spark that spread across the region. After a bad harvest, the villagers were unable to pay their tithes. In order to avoid Ottoman retribution, they fled to Montenegro. The remaining *rayah*, too old to flee, were slaughtered in their homes by Muslims. In revenge, the inhabitants of Nevesinje committed atrocities against Muslims once they had returned and forced many of their neighbours to join the rebellion. Rebel Bosnians were killed after attempting to overthrow the Ottomans, but soon began to turn the tide against the authorities as Catholics from Hercegovina also joined the uprising. A vivid account of the events was set down by the archaeologist

Arthur J. Evans who sent his reports to the *Manchester Guardian* and later wrote his experiences up in a book. He was sympathetic to the rebels who he saw as oppressed by centuries of Ottoman rule. Nevertheless, Evans also recorded crimes committed by them and the use of coercion: 'If a village refused to throw in its lot with the rebels, they first burnt one house or one maize-plot, and then another, till the unhappy villagers, forced to choose between ruin and rebellion, consented to join their ranks. As to the way in which the insurgents were conducting the war, it was almost too horrible to be repeated ... they would often shut up whole families of Moslems in their houses, to which they then set fire.'[1]

After several years of uncertainty, the Bosnian vilayet and the Sandžak of Novi Pazar was effectively wrested from Ottoman control, at least in name. In 1878 the Treaty of Berlin allowed the Habsburg monarchy ruled by Emperor Franz Joseph to administer Bosnia, which created an enormous opportunity for the Viennese power to expand their territory. It also meant that most Slavonic Muslims were under Habsburg and not Ottoman or Serbian control. Franz Joseph had been emperor for 30 years in 1878 and the biggest challenge he had faced was from growing nationalism. The loss of the wealthiest parts of northern Italy in the 1860s, including the cities of Milan and Venice, had dealt an economic blow to the monarchy. The retention of the Adriatic port of Trieste had meant that many Italians saw the predominantly Italian-speaking city as theirs by right and wanted to 'redeem' this territory for their new state. Many Bosnians would later fight on the Isonzo Front against Italy from 1915 to 1918. The conservative alternative that Franz Joseph offered was *Kaisertreue* or loyalty to his dynasty, which in many respects was ideal for the South Slavs who had been divided by religious confession for centuries. In 1867, after significant unrest and the growth of Hungarian Magyar nationalist sentiment, Franz Joseph had divided the monarchy into two regions, but he remained emperor in both. Cisleithania came under direct Austrian rule, whereas Transleithania was governed by the Hungarians. Bosnia was jointly administered by both halves of the empire, Dalmatia was under Austrian control and Croatia was governed

[1] Evans, *Through Bosnia and the Herzegóvina*, pp. 327–328.

from Budapest. The inclusion of Bosnia united the Dalmatian coast with its Balkan hinterland in a single state for the first time in centuries and addressed the security concerns of the Viennese state. For centuries, the Habsburgs had had a difficult frontier with the Ottomans and over the years many Serbs had settled on the Habsburg side of the border in Krajina, Slavonia and Vojvodina. This change in power and status created a potential nationalist tinderbox as the Serb population of the monarchy mushroomed in size. The decision of the diplomats who settled on this new solution in Otto von Bismarck's Germany was initially treated with suspicion on the ground. A local imam Salih Vilajetović, known as Hadži Lojo, preached fervently against the new regime in the streets of Sarajevo. In a rapid and effective military operation consisting of more than a quarter of a million troops, Bosnia was quelled.[2] The Austrian army surrounded the hills around Sarajevo, but armed resistance was organized in the city by a local Muslim, Muhamed Hadžijamaković. He bravely fought his captors and managed to injure some of his guards, but was eventually hanged from an oak tree along with seven other defiant Muslim leaders. Both Serbs and Muslims had resisted the annexation, in other words, 80 per cent of the total population of Bosnia and Hercegovina. Eventually the Muslims were pacified by the authorities, but the Serbs remained implacably opposed to rule from either Vienna or Budapest (as authority was shared between the two capitals of the empire after the official annexation of the province in 1908). The mufti of Sarajevo, Mustafa Hilmi Hadžiomerović, encouraged cooperation with the new authorities and discouraged migration to Istanbul, even though he maintained strong personal connections to the Ottoman Empire. This did not stop some pious Bosnians leaving, although not all made it all the way to Anatolia. Some went to Skopje in Macedonia or Edirne in Thrace. The Albanian villages of Koxhas and Borake near Shijak were established by Muslim settlers who left in 1878.[3]

[2] Donia, Robert and Fine, John *Bosnia and Hercegovina: A Tradition Betrayed* (London: Hurst, 1994), p. 94.
[3] Beci, Bahri 'Les minorités ethniques en Albanie' in Denise Eeckaute-Bardery (ed.) *Les oubliés des Balkans* (Paris: Publications Langues'O, 1998), p. 24.

In the 36 years that Bosnia was under the Habsburgs, it underwent a dramatic but very partial modernization. In 1881, a military law was passed obliging Bosnians to serve in the Kaiser's army. Their uniform included a red fez and one of the most popular Habsburg military marches was *Die Bosniaken kommen* (*The Bosnians are Coming*), composed by Eduard Wagnes in 1895. In a hotel in Mostar in 1893, the architect Thomas Graham Jackson recalled that 'the place was full of Austrian officers and their families, and instead of plunging as we had expected into semi-barbarism we found ourselves in a whirl of gay society that recalled Trieste or Vienna itself.'[4] The new authorities took on the task of modernization with enthusiasm, building railways, bridges and roads and introducing educational reforms to a previously largely illiterate population. Agricultural products were highly valued. Bosnia was an excellent place to grow apples, chestnuts, plums and grapes[5] and modern kilns were introduced to dry plums and plum brandy was exported.[6] Education was a vital part of the Habsburg strategy as Robin Okey has argued in his study of the 'civilizing mission' that the Viennese undertook. The Habsburg strategy neglected industrial development so the roots of modernization were weak.[7] The lofty peaks of Bosnia (*Bosna ponosna*) that had been difficult to traverse had new roads and railways by 1914. Railways were constructed by *corvée* (i.e., unpaid) labour, which meant that the peasants worked on the construction projects in lieu of paying some taxes. A tram network was opened in Sarajevo that still operates today. The country was open to modern tourism and travel in a way that had been impossible just a few years earlier and every part of the country was touched by the change. Émile de Lavelaye was told by Count Gustav Kálnoky, 'we do dream of conquests, but of such as in your character of political economist you will approve. It is

[4] Jackson, Thomas Graham *Memories of Travel* (Cambridge: Cambridge University Press, 1923), p. 110.
[5] Hoernes, *Dinarsiche Wanderungen*, p. 71.
[6] Sugar, Peter F. *Industrialization of Bosnia-Hercegovina, 1878–1918* (Seattle: University of Washington Press, 1963), p. 164.
[7] Pinson, Mark 'The Muslims of Bosnia-Herzegovina under Austrian Rule 1878–1918' in Mark Pinson (ed.) *The Muslims of Bosnia-Herzegovina: Their Historic Development from the Middle Ages to the Dissolution of Yugoslavia* (Cambridge, MA: Harvard University Press, 1996), p. 118.

Map 4. Bosnia under the Habsburgs

those to be made by our manufactures, our commerce, our civilization. But to realize them we must have railways in Servia, Bulgaria, Bosnia, Macedonia.'[8]

The Muslim population was eventually reconciled to Habsburg rule, but the Orthodox resented both Austrian and Hungarian

[8] de Laveleye, *Balkan Peninsula*, p. 5.

influence and looked to Serbia and Montenegro to protect their interests. For centuries, the primary political, cultural and religious divide in the Western Balkans was between the towns and the mountains. In nineteenth-century Montenegro and Serbia, the towns were violently 'de-Ottomanized', but Bosnian towns had remained largely Islamic. Valuing their Muslim subjects and encouraging aspects of tradition, the Habsburgs cultivated the townspeople of Bosnia, but did little to address the growing poverty of the Orthodox peasants and pastoralists who represented about half the population. Often they continued to live in dire poverty in less accessible areas. Whereas Serbian and Montenegrin independence in the nineteenth century had involved expulsion and 'cleansings' of Muslims, the Habsburg protection and subsequent annexation of Bosnia in all likelihood prevented this process being repeated in the nineteenth century. Furthermore, it increased Catholic influence in the region, especially in Sarajevo. Bosnia cost the Habsburgs more than they were able to extract from the region, even if its incorporation did give them a hinterland for the Dalmatian coast they had acquired in 1815. In the long run, the political unification of the Hercegovina Karst was to bring those Catholics so long ministered solely by Franciscans closer to a Croat or at least Dalmatian world. However, the appointment of non-Franciscans led to antagonisms in local politics in the region.

From 1882 until his death in 1903, Benjamin von Kállay was imperial minister of finance and chief secretary for Bosnia. Although a Hungarian by birth, he knew the region very well, having written a history of the Serbs published as *Geschichte der Serben* in Budapest in 1878. Through his mother, who was of Serbian descent, he also spoke Bosnian. Impeccably *Kaisertreue*, he governed Bosnia with careful attention while it was still nominally under Habsburg administration. He believed that all Bosnians of all the religious affiliations constituted a single Bosnian nation, which was a radical departure from the millet divisions of the Ottoman period. His concept of *bošnajštvo* (Bosnian identity) was also an active challenge to Serbian and Croatian national ambitions. During his time as chief secretary, he encouraged research and cultural developments that stressed the diverse nature of the region as part of its essential character. Writing in 1909–1910, Maude Holbach felt that 'from the

Fig. 6 The Vijećnica, showing signs of wartime damage (by
Richard Mills)

point of view of the mere sojourner and passer-by, the administration inaugurated by the late Minister von Kally [sic] seems to have
brought peace and prosperity to a land which little more than a
generation ago was given up to bloodshed and sedition through the
inability of the Turkish Government of that day to repress robbery
and clear the country of agitators who incited the people to crime'.[9]

Sarajevo was the focus for much of the administrative 'improve-
ment' and was settled by Catholics (and a small number of Ashkenazi
Jews) from outside the region. The city's population rose from just
over 20,000 in 1885 to 50,000 by 1900. Many Catholic citizens emi-
grated to the Bosnian capital after the late 1870s. Among them was
the architect Karel Pařík. Like Antoni Gaudí in Barcelona, Pařík's
vision for *fin de siècle* Sarajevo was to give the city much of its
architectural personality. Wanting to preserve the old Islamic quar-
ters, he designed many of the art nouveau buildings in the rest of the

---

[9] Holbach, *Bosnia and Herzegovina*, p. 21.

city. In 1902, a new synagogue was designed for the recently arrived Ashkenazi Jews from the Habsburg lands. He continued to work on important Bosnian buildings into the Karadjordjević era and in the 1930s helped to renovate the Franciscan monastery of Sveti Luka, which stands beside the river in Jajce. On Pařík's gravestone is the warm remembrance 'Czech by birth, but elective Sarajevan'. His vision for the City Hall, the Vijećnica that later became the National Library, linked the world of Central European modernism with an Islamic neo-Moorish aesthetic. Although the project was taken on by other architects, including Alexander Wittek, this romantic association was Pařík's great achievement. When Franz Ferdinand arrived at the Vijećnica after the first assassination attempt against him he was greeted by the assembled and mostly Muslim elders of the city. A house had previously stood on the spot where the Vijećnica was constructed and the displaced owner built a new version brick by brick called 'Inat kuća' on the opposite bank of the Miljacka 'from spite'. During the siege of Sarajevo, the library was targeted with incendiary devices that damaged most of the interior, destroying millions of books and monuments.

In other respects the art nouveau or *Jugendstil* of the Viennese lent itself to the embrace of Bosnian tradition. Czech architect František Blažek designed hotels for visitors taking in the waters in the spa town of Ilidža, which was linked to Sarajevo by tram. In 1900, at the Exposition Universelle, a huge world fair that also hosted the Olympic Games in Paris, each country financed a pavilion to showcase local art. The Bosnian pavilion was decorated by one of the best-known artists of the period, the Czech Alphonse Mucha. The white building had a small tower and windows with wooden Islamic-style fretwork and balconies. The interior walls were decorated by Mucha's paintings and there were cabinets displaying local art. The latest technology was used, including a diorama theatre scene of Sarajevo market life at the Baščaršija. Visitors were guided by people in Bosnian costumes which Mucha has designed after a research visit to Bosnia in 1899. Aiming to represent the folklore and traditions of all the Bosnian people, the artist attended to every detail, including the menu, which featured an alluring woman offering a tray with a Turkish-style coffee pot and cups (*fildžan*), an image that is stylized but not outside the European imaginary.

Through Mucha, Bosnian Muslim traditions were tamed and made appealing to tourists. Ironically the Serb nationalist journal *Srpkinja* published in Sarajevo in 1913 drew on the same art nouveau aesthetic. Indeed Serb anti-Habsburg sentiments were stoked in Vienna and in the high schools that the Austrian administration had built.

For centuries Croatians had thought themselves to be the 'bulwark of Christianity' against the Ottomans (*antemurale Christianitatis*). With Bosnia's inclusion into the monarchy, Croat intellectuals renewed their interest in their neighbours, although this engagement often came at the expense of the Orthodox Bosnians. The founder of the Croatian Party of Rights, Ante Starčević, reinforced this trend by defining the Bosnian Muslims as Croats.[10] The Croatian archaeologist Ćiro Truhelka also immersed himself in the study of Bosnia and when the National Museum (*Zemaljski Muzej Bosne i Hercegovine*) was founded in Sarajevo in 1888, he became one of its first 'kustos' or curators. A number of his archaeological finds connected Bosnia to its long-forgotten Catholic past, including the discovery of the alleged remains of the fifteenth century King Stjepan Tomašević, who was beheaded by the Ottomans. In 1907, Truhelka published an anonymous pamphlet *Hrvatska Bosna (Mi i 'Oni tamo')*[11] in which he discussed the racial characteristics of the people of the region. He concluded that Muslims and Croats had broader chests, a higher incidence of blue eyes and fairer hair than the Orthodox Serbs who represented a 'swarthy, physically weaker developed type'.[12] Starčević had also written about putative Serb inferiority calling them an 'unclean race' bound together by their servile nature'.[13] Sadly the pseudoscientific racial politics of Central Europe had arrived in the Balkans and stoked the mistrust that had been long since kindled by the millet system and rural poverty.

The period between Habsburg annexation and the First World War still saw significant interest in the Muslim heritage of towns

---

[10] Spalatin, Mario S. 'The Croatian Nationalism of Ante Starčević, 1845–1871', *Journal of Croatian Studies* 16, 1975, pp. 94–100.

[11] 'Croatian Bosnia (us and "them over there")'.

[12] Bartulin, Nevenko *The Racial Idea in the Independent State of Croatia: Origins and Theory* (Leiden: Brill, 2014), pp. 52–54.

[13] Banac, Ivo *The National Question in Yugoslavia: Origins, History, Politics* (Ithaca: Cornell University Press, 1984), p. 87.

in the interior, perhaps encouraged as part of official government policy. Austrian academic writers recorded much of the local colour. Friedrich Salomon Krauss' 1885 collection *Sitte und Brauch der Südslaven* captured some of the folktales of the Bosnians. One of the founding fathers of psychiatry as a discipline, the Viennese doctor Sigmund Freud went to Hercegovina in 1898 as part of an Austrian medical delegation. In Trebinje, a town with a mixed Muslim and Christian population, he began to think about his first essay on the mechanics of the unconscious, which he wrote shortly after this visit.[14] This was the time during which Freud developed his idea of notion of *Signorelli parapraxis* (often referred to as the 'Freudian slip').[15] Freud probably began to see sexual drive differently at this time and this change in attitude was reflected in his own sexual habits and practices. As he dwelt on the brevity of life and the imminence of death, he made a personal decision that one should always seize the moment ('carpe diem').[16] He spoke to many Muslim patients and noticed their fatalism and the importance that they attached to maintaining their sexual drive. According to the notes that Freud made during his trip, one patient had told his local doctor, 'when that no longer works, life has no worth'. Freud concluded that 'These Turks value the sexual drive above all else and if their drive fails, they fall into a despondency'.[17] Freud was clearly working towards his celebrated theory concerning the drive for creativity (*Eros*) or oblivion (*Thanatos/Mortido*). He was fascinated by what he saw as the fatalism of the Bosnian Muslims, recounting that the carers of a mortally sick person would answer: 'Sir, what is there to be said? I know that if he could have been saved, then you would have done so'.[18] The impact of the visit to Hercegovina remained with Freud, changing some of his basic views on human

---

[14] Bjelić, Dušan I. *Normalizing the Balkans: Geopolitics of Psychoanalysis and Psychiatry* (Exeter: Ashgate, 2011).

[15] Swales, Peter 'Freud, Death and Sexual Pleasures: On the Psychical Mechanism of Dr. Sigm. Freud', *Arc de Cercle* 1, 2003, pp. 4–74.

[16] Freud, Sigmund *Die Traumdeutung* (Leipzig/Wien: Franz Deuticke, 1914), pp. 156–157.

[17] Freud, Sigmund *Zur Psychopathologie des Alltagslebens (Über Vergessen, Versprechen, Vergreifen, Aberglaube und Irrtum)* (Berlin: Verlag von S. Karger, 1904), pp. 5–6.

[18] Ibid., p. 5.

nature. It was not until many years later that Freud used the term
'der Narzissmus der kleinen Differenzen' (the narcissism of minor
differences) when comparing the 'relatively harmless appeasement
of an inclination towards aggression' between neighbours such as
Portugal and Spain who might 'feud' or 'ridicule' each other.[19] This
phrase was used frequently by commentators during the Bosnian
War without acknowledgement to Freud or indeed the context in
which he was writing. Given the Habsburg emphasis on cultural
differences within their new acquisition (and the postcards that
Austrians sent home that all depict colourful native Bosnians in
fezzes or with baggy trousers), it is likely that Freud thought of this
notion much earlier in the late nineteenth century.

Habsburg citizens quickly adopted the new part of their monarchy and guidebooks and ethnographies were published. In 1893,
an opera was performed in Vienna at the Hoftheater called *Eine
Hochzeit in Bosnien* (*A Marriage in Bosnia*) featuring a 'picaresque
staging of minarets, church towers and a throng of assorted Bosnians
in colourful costumes, dancing native dances before Austrian tourists until the latter taught them a waltz'.[20] Writing in the 1890s,
Heinrich Renner was pleased that beer was being brewed in Bosnia
and that there were already three breweries in Sarajevo.[21] For travellers from Dubrovnik, a day trip to Trebinje was recommended by
the Baedeker guidebooks. This excursion was also seen as relatively
safe for women travellers. The Adriatic coast with its strong regional
traditions was frequently contrasted with the Turkish-style interior,
despite the fact that Dubrovnik had had very close trading links
with the Ottomans for centuries. Mary Edith Durham recorded in
her diary in 1900 as they approached the city from the Adriatic coast
that they were 'getting nearer and nearer to the East'.[22] Sometimes,
travel to the interior became part of a 'moral journey', with praise
frequently lavished on the new Habsburg administration. Maude
Holbach wrote that 'even Turkish Trebinje has gained in cleanliness

---

[19] Freud, Sigmund *Das Unbehagen in der Kultur* (Wien: Internationaler Psycho-
    analytischer Verlag, 1930), p. 85.
[20] Okey, Robin *Taming Balkan Nationalism: The Habsburg 'Civilizing Mission' in
    Bosnia, 1878–1914* (Oxford: Oxford University Press, 2007), pp. 71–72.
[21] Renner, *Durch Bosnien und die Hercegovina*, p. 83.
[22] Durham, *Diary from 1900*.

by coming into touch with European standards, but its picturesqueness remains. Our visit was on a Friday, and as we sauntered down the main street all the male population were engaged in ablutions preparatory to visiting the mosques. The feet-washing was a wonderfully simple performance.'[23]

The stability of the Habsburg monarchy depended very much on the dynasty itself. Franz Joseph's son Rudolf committed suicide in 1889 and after the death of the emperor's brother, Karl Ludwig, the succession passed to his nephew Franz Ferdinand. Relations between the emperor and his heir were notoriously unstable, which weakened the state in its final years. In October 1908, Franz Joseph announced the annexation of Bosnia and Hercegovina together with a formal Habsburg withdrawal from the Sandžak of Novi Pazar (which was subsequently taken from the Ottomans by Serbia and Montenegro during the Balkans Wars of 1912–1913). This triggered a flashpoint in international relations, which has become known as the Bosnian Crisis, and exposed the fragility of the peaceful order in Europe. In part, Franz Joseph was prompted by a fear that the Ottoman Empire might revive under new leadership and try to take Bosnia back. His foreign minister, Alois Aerenthal, had come to a secret agreement with his Russian counterpart, Isvolsky, the previous month that basically ignored Serbia's claims to Bosnia. Habsburg relations with the Serbs continued to deteriorate. When Franz Joseph visited Bosnia in 1910, he compounded the problem further. He did not visit an Orthodox church, but did take time to visit Catholic churches and mosques. Some Austrian citizens remained sceptical about their new addition. The Viennese satirical paper *Kikiriki* mocked the annexation in its 15 October 1908 edition. It was expensive to run Bosnia and increased the number of Serbs in the Habsburg Monarchy.

Habsburg hegemony was also challenged by the growth of pro-Yugoslav ideologies. The idea of a political union of South Slav peoples speaking similar languages has its intellectual origins well

---

[23] Holbach, Maude *Dalmatia The Land where East meets West* (London: J. Lane, 1910), p. 162. Given that ritual feet-washing took place in Trebinje long before the arrival of the Habsburgs, the sentiments expressed here seem rather clichéd.

before 1908 and the creation of a Yugoslav state in 1918. The memory of medieval states remained in literary circles and peasants in Hercegovina continued to sing about Kosovo polje into the nineteenth century. In the late sixteenth century, the linguist and historian Pavao Ritter Vitezović had seen Bosnians as part of what he called 'Illyria' (from the Latin term for South-East Europe). Between 1809 and 1813, Napoleon Bonaparte had challenged the Habsburg monarchy, albeit temporarily, by creating the 'Illyrian Provinces', which stretched from Slovenia to Dalmatia. By the time the Habsburgs had regained control of its Slovenian and Croatian regions and added Dalmatia to its possessions in 1815, pro-Illyrian ideas had started to grow and were fuelled by poets and journalists. In early nineteenth-century Bosnia, the Franciscan bishop and educationalist Marijan Šunjić maintained contacts with Croatian literary scholars. By 1850, the languages of the region had been codified into a standard that was quite close to the Bosnian spoken by most people. Until the 1870s, Bosnia was still a *de facto* part of the Ottoman Empire (and remained so *de jure* until 1908). Its thinkers and writers were largely steeped in Islamic learning, but nevertheless were aware of the currents in neighbouring lands. The annexation of Bosnia by the Habsburgs in 1908 as well as the decline of the Ottoman Empire and the growth of Serbia and Montenegro fuelled pro-Slavonic sentiment across the Monarchy and intensified the profound rivalry between the states.

The 1911 law on landownership meant that peasants were obliged to pay for land they had worked for centuries (like the serfs in Russia after the emancipation of 1861), which threw many into crippling levels of debt. These legal reforms hit the Orthodox much harder than the Muslims. By 1914, a considerable number of Bosnia's Serbs looked south for political leadership rather than to Vienna. Serb radicalization led to the carefully planned assassination of the heir to the Habsburg monarchy, Archduke Franz Ferdinand, in 1914 in Sarajevo by Gavrilo Princip, a youth from Obljaj. Princip has come to represent a Serb terrorist striking an ancient dynasty in an era when other European royal houses were the target of bomb-throwers. In the month prior to the assassination, when he and his friends plotted the deed, he decided to use his life to become a Serb hero. In his celebrated account of the events, Communist historian Vladimir Dedijer called Princip and his comrades 'primitive rebels ... unable to adapt themselves to the modern ideologies of mass movements against systems of oppression'.[24] Inspired by the Russian Narodniks and by the canon of Serbian literature, he and the other assassins that lined the Appelquai along the banks of the Miljacka river in Sarajevo had all memorized *Gorski Vijenac*, a blood-curdling Montenegrin epic of genuine poetic value, which could be read as a call to violent action for the Orthodox across the region. They were also inspired by more recent events, namely the attempted assassination of the Bosnian governor Marijan Varešanin in 1910, by a student, Bogdan Žerajić.[25] Although Žerajić failed to kill his target and managed to fatally shoot himself, his example inspired his friend Vladimir Gaćinović, one of the founders of Mlada Bosna or 'young Bosnia', a revolutionary movement that had imbibed Serb or even Yugoslav patriotism at school. Another prominent member of Mlada Bosna was the writer Petar Kočić. Originally from a small village near Banja Luka, he wrote for a patriotic but anti-Habsburg journal *Otadžbina*, which was published for the first time on 28 June 1907, exactly seven years before the assassination of Franz Ferdinand. One of his plays *Jazavac pred sudom* (*The Badger on Trial*) is a satire on the political situation in Bosnia. A farmer, David Štrbac, tries to incriminate a badger (meant to represent the *Švabe* or Austrians) for eating his crops. First distributed in 1903, this satirical tale inspired a generation to oppose rule from Vienna. Bosnian Serb poets Jovan Dučić and Aleksa Šantić also inspired the young with ideas of liberation from the oppressor.

Princip and his friends became involved in a secret Black Hand (*Crna Ruka*) society that had made previous assassination attempts on the Habsburg royal family. Their emblem was the skull and crossbones, later used by Serb nationalists in the Second World War. Princip had travelled to Serbia earlier in the year and under the patient supervision of the rogue Colonel Dragutin Dimitrijević

[24] Dedijer, Vladimir *The Road to Sarajevo*, (London: MacGibbon and Kee, 1967), p. 446.
[25] Ivan Čolović, 'Sarajevski atentat i kosovski mit', http://fenomeni.me/ sarajevski-atentat-kosovski-mit/ (accessed 30 June 2014).

(also known as 'Apis') became a crack shot. He practised repeatedly in a Belgrade park until he was the most accomplished marksman in his circle. The murder weapon was a Browning, issued by Apis. Security on the day of Franz Ferdinand's visit was rather light with the local police rather than the army in view on Sarajevo's central streets. The route had been published in a local paper, although not primarily as an assassin's *vade mecum*. The streets were thinly lined with welcoming crowds and Franz Ferdinand abandoned Habsburg protocol by taking his wife in the royal car with him.[26] The assassins would not have stood out and it is likely that the regime wished to demonstrate that it ruled by consent rather than coercion. Franz Ferdinand had chosen to visit Sarajevo on 28 June, which was Vidovdan (St Vitus' Day). This was a central event in Orthodox mythopoeia when South Slavs would reflect on the heavenly kingdom gained in 1389 at the Battle of Kosovo polje. This timing seems to have been a particularly obtuse decision on Franz Ferdinand's part. Radical Serbs had already made the conflation between Ottoman oppression and the Austrian occupation. For them, rule by one set of foreigners had replaced another and they wanted to liberate their compatriots in what they considered a Serb land. The Habsburg heir travelled in an open-top car with his wife, who may have been pregnant, protected chiefly by his necklace of talismans and a putatively bulletproof vest.

Not all the Sarajevo conspirators were Orthodox. Muhamed Mehmedbašić was a relatively mature Muslim carpenter from Stolac who had tried unsuccessfully to kill the Bosnian governor Oskar Potiorek on a previous occasion. Potiorek, who was travelling with the royal couple in their car on 28 June 1914, was unhurt again. Although Mehmedbašić was the first assassin to see the royal car, he hesitated because a policeman was allegedly standing behind him. He managed to slip out of Bosnia to neighbouring Montenegro and was arrested and held in Nikšić. He broke out of custody there and lived as a free and pardoned man between the wars. The Ustaša

---

[26] Although an aristocrat herself, Sophie was not considered high enough in status by birth to be the wife of the future Habsburg emperor. Franz Joseph had only agreed to the marriage on the condition that it was morganatic (i.e., that their children would not be heirs to the monarchy). Normally she did not accompany her husband on official public duties.

effectively rescinded his pardon and finally executed him in Sarajevo in 1943. He was the only Muslim conspirator, but his involvement shows that national identities were still fluid at this time and some still resisted Habsburg rule.

One of the conspirators, Nedeljko Čabrinović, also terminally ill with tuberculosis, threw a bomb at the royal car. Its nimble chauffeur Franz Urban saw the bomb in the air and accelerated. It then exploded in the path of the car behind, injuring several of the passengers including Eric von Merizzi and Count Boos-Waldeck. Čabrinović swallowed his dud cyanide capsule, which failed to kill him, and jumped in the shallow Miljacka River, but was easily apprehended by the Habsburg authorities. Franz Ferdinand's car sped on to the National Library (Vijećnica), an elegant hybrid monument to Habsburg-Muslim mutual understanding and an obvious place to meet local dignitaries. Still raw with anger, he barked at the city authorities, reprimanding them for their poor welcome. Franz Ferdinand then decided to visit the wounded in hospital. Like Tsar Alexander II, who was killed by a bomb after he stepped out of his carriage to console a wounded guard, it was the archduke's act of compassion or sense of duty that was to lead to his death. Gavrilo Princip had heard Čabrinović's bomb explode, but knew that the assassination attempt had failed. He had gone to Schiller's patisserie near the riverfront and had just come back onto the street when the archduke's car stalled in front of him. Able to see his targets at this short range of a few feet, he aimed at Franz Ferdinand's carotid artery and dealt him a slow, but fatal blow.[27] Sophie slumped forward, also fatally wounded in the stomach (and it is this shooting of a pregnant women that some loyal Sarajevans remembered with particular indignation). The Imperial Graf und Stift car was driven away quickly but it was too late to save the royal couple, who were given the last rites by a Jesuit, Anton Puntigam. Princip had intended to kill the hated Potiorek and not Sophie. Before he could complete his act by committing suicide, Princip was swiftly arrested by bystanders, which almost certainly saved him from lynching by the angry crowd. Count Franz von Harrach had stood on the car's fender in order to protect the couple and he recounted

[27] Dedijer, *The Road to Sarajevo*, p. 12.

Fig. 7 Miljacka River in Sarajevo close to where Nedeljko
Čabrinović threw himself in the water (by Matt Willer)

how the archduke died slowly from his wounds. For many years,
the heir to the Habsburg monarchy was an avid, almost compulsive
hunter. He shot thousands of animals in his peculiar, obsessive way
and his castle was a morgue for many of the wild species of Central
Europe. He ended his life as the hunted beast, the target of Bosnia's
enraged youth. Princip's act was an important landmark in the history of political violence. His violent nationalism provoked a significantly more violent response and initiated the biggest diplomatic
and military crisis in Europe to that date. It was in effect the trigger
that created the conditions for a rapid deterioration into interstate
violence and was thus the direct spark that lead to the First World
War between Imperial Germany, the Habsburg monarchy, Bulgaria
and the Ottoman Empire on one side and Imperial Russia, Great
Britain, France, Serbia, Montenegro, Italy and the United States on
the other.

Initially on 28 June it was just Princip and Čabrinović who were
caught. Both refused to speak or to betray their co-conspirators.
The other youths involved were only arrested after Danilo Ilić confessed his involvement when the authorities had traced Princip's

movements back to his accommodation. Trifko Grabež, the son of an Orthodox priest from Pale, died of tuberculosis in captivity. Danilo Ilić, Veljko Čubrilović from Gradiška and Miško Jovanović from Tuzla, who were over 20 years old at the time of the assassination, were hanged in 1915. The death sentences given to these very young accomplices aroused anger across Europe, but particularly in Slavonic-speaking countries. The remaining captured conspirators were given lighter sentences and were released at the end of the war when the Habsburg monarchy collapsed. Cvijetko Popović became a custodian in the Ethnographic Department of the Sarajevo Museum. Vaso Čubrilović, whose older brother was hanged, lived until 1990 and became an eminent historian. His Serb nationalism often guided him in later life. Under Austrian law, Čabrinović could not be executed. He and Princip were both spared and sentenced to 20 years' imprisonment, both dying of tuberculosis during the war. Čabrinović succumbed quickly, but Princip did not actually die until the early months of 1918, enduring years of pain and the amputation of an infected limb. From his prison cell in 1914, he would have been able to hear the guns from the Battle of Cer as the Serbian army fought in the Drina region and may have expected to be rescued according to the vivid and fanciful account of the Sarajevo assassination by Rebecca West in her 1937 travel journal *Black Lamb and Grey Falcon*.[28] Princip would also have heard the gunfire dying down, an ominous sign of Serbia's military rout as the frontline receded.

In many ways, Princip should also be seen as a representative of a generation of young, desperate and angry poor whose economic suffering was enflamed by Serb nationalism. Already terminally ill with tuberculosis at the age of 19 and one of three surviving children of impoverished peasants, he did not simply want to waste his life by dying young of this fatal scourge. Tuberculosis was the curse of a generation and imparted an air of fatalism and immediacy into social and cultural interactions. Captain Gojkomir Glogovac received the Military Order of Maria Teresa, the highest recognition for bravery that the Habsburg monarchy bestowed in

---

[28] West, Rebecca *Black Lamb and Grey Falcon: A Journey through Yugoslavia* (Edinburgh: Cannongate, 1993), p. 375.

the First World War in 1917. He died of tuberculosis just five years later, in 1922. The writer Musa Ćazim Ćatić, who died at the age of 37, described his decline while lying in 'his small room' but still inhabiting 'his big world' of the imagination in the poem *Pred Smrt (Before Death)*.[29]

BOSNIA AND THE FIRST WORLD WAR

The Austrian state blamed the authorities in Belgrade, although they had no direct link with the Mlada Bosna assassins, and used the events of the summer to launch war upon its smaller neighbour. There had been a number of disputes including a customs war and the crisis over annexation in 1908 between the two states in the previous decades and many Austrians were determined to teach their smaller neighbour a lesson. Popular anger was unleashed against Serbs, and throughout Bosnia the local Orthodox population were subjected to massacres and atrocities. The Sarajevo newspaper *Narodna Obrana* compared the destruction in the city after anti-Serbian demonstrations to the Russian pogroms. In Sarajevo, posters were put up that called for the eradication of subversive elements by the Catholic bishop Josip Štadler and his assistant Ivan Šarić. The Hotel Evropa, which was owned by a Serb, Gligorije Jevtanović, and was the largest in the city, was demolished by an angry mob at nine o'clock at night on 28 June.[30] Within a month of the assassination, several thousand Serbs had been jailed. Individuals considered to be pro-Serb were also threatened. As the war continued, the Habsburgs continued to destroy the basic traces of Orthodox civilization in the region. Jevto Dedijer had collected ethnographic data on Bosnia for many years before the war, but his personal archive was destroyed by the Habsburg military and all the material was lost. His son Vladimir wrote one of the best-known books on this period, published in English as *The Road to Sarajevo*.

The Habsburg Dynasty, perhaps one of the most tolerable regimes in the history of empires, became excessively cruel in its final years.

---

[29] Ćatić, Musa Ćazim *Pjesme: (izbor)*, edited by Medhija Mušović (Sarajevo: Veselin Masleša, 1991).

[30] Mitrović, Andrej *Serbia's Great War 1914–1918* (London: Hurst, 2007), p. 18.

Austrian military commanders began to attack Orthodox people living within the territory that they had annexed and beyond the state boundaries. In neighbouring Serbia and Montenegro, systematic atrocities were also carried out, villagers and other non-combatants as well as captured soldiers were executed. The atrocities solidified a sense among the Orthodox people of the region that they would be safer in a single state. The Habsburg authorities also deported thousands of Serbs from their territories, thus removing potentially disloyal individuals from sensitive areas near the border. Both Serbia and its neighbour Montenegro, which had gained part of Hercegovina in 1878, had wanted to prevent the incursion of the Habsburgs into Bosnia. The Serbs considered the Orthodox people of Bosnia to be 'unredeemed' Serbs and part of their national territory. Although Bosnia was not a significant theatre of war from 1914 to 1918, the Serbians were quickly pushed back from the Drina. For their population this was a terrible demographic and cultural disaster and their suffering began to evoke sympathy among the Habsburg public who slowly turned against the state themselves. Habsburg troops fought in the south, effectively taking Serbia and Montenegro by the summer of 1916. Civilians were deliberately killed on the orders of the Croat Catholic General Sarkotić von Lovćen in an attempt to rid them from the crown territories. This was a radical disjuncture from policy for a Habsburg general and terminated Emperor Franz Joseph's vision of a land of many peoples, including South Slavs who were united by his dynasty.

Bosnians fought the Italians in the Izonso River region and the Russians in Galicia. On the Eastern Front, there was a high desertion rate from Habsburg troops whose level of demoralization was notorious, especially among the Bosnian Serbs. Like many of the Russian 'peasants in uniform', the South Slavs showed little enthusiasm for war, which made the Balkan Front a really weak link in the empire's war effort. Habsburg General Oskar Potiorek, who had narrowly escaped assassination in Sarajevo in June 1914, was particularly concerned about the loyalty of the Serbs from the Drina valley on the border with Serbia. On the other hand, as the war against Italy continued, the number of Bosnians fighting on the front continued. Forty-two per cent of Habsburg forces who served in this campaign were South Slavs. On the Izonzo front, in steep valleys and on Karst mountains that must have reminded Bosnians of home, and branding studded maces, they went into battle crying '*Živila Austrija!*' (Long live Austria!).[31] The Italians soon came to fear the Bosnian regiments, who were especially skilful at night combat and would favour close attacks with bayonets and knives. The Second Bosnian Regiment became the most decorated on the Isonzo Front, with 42 combat gold medals for bravery.[32] The Czech sculptor Ladislav Jan Kofránek designed a statue of two Bosnian soldiers from the Second Regiment, one of whom was wearing the Habsburg fez, in Lod pod Mangartom in present-day Slovenia. It stands in a graveyard where more than 800 soldiers who died trying to defend Mount Lombon are buried. Rather than being marked with crosses, the graves of the Muslims can be distinguished by their black headstones.

The Habsburg monarchy had begun to implode in the second half of the war. The end of the war saw not only the defeat of the Central European power, but also the disintegration of their state. Some Croat and Bosnian soldiers had crossed over from the Habsburg side to fight against them. In Tuzla in 1915, lawyer Ivo Pilar warned the Catholic South Slavs living under the Habsburg rule that their best hope for national autonomy lay with the preservation of the monarchy. His book *Svjetski rat i hrvati* was published in Zagreb. A second book, *Die suedslawische Frage und der Weltkrieg*, published in Vienna in 1918, was highly critical of Serb expansionist politics. He was one of the first intellectuals to shape an anti-Serbian script and was tried for his views in a political court in 1921. Pilar died in 1933 and it is possible that he was murdered for his political views. Serbian politicians had already begun to conceive of a united South Slav state. When they joined with Habsburg politicians on the Greek island of Corfu, they issue a declaration in July 1917 of their intention to create such a state when the war ended. The authors of the actual text were the Serbian prime minister Nikola Pašić and the Croat Ante Trumbić, the former major

---

[31] Thompson, Mark *The White War: Life and Death on the Italian Front, 1915–1919* (London: Faber, 2008), pp. 80, 93.

[32] Schindler, John R. *Isonzo: The Forgotten Sacrifice of the Great War* (Westport, CO: Greenwood, 2001), p. 247.

of the Dalmatian city Split and president of the London-based Yugoslav Committee. The Bosnian representatives of the Yugoslav Committee at Corfu were Nikola Stojanović and Dušan Vasiljević; both were Serbs.

A South Slav successor state based in Belgrade was constructed after the war and recognized by the United States in February 1919, three months after its formation, and by Great Britain and France in June 1919. For the first time, the majority of South Slavs were in a single state with a unified language and the single political authority of the Karadjordjević Dynasty. Bosnia, although regarded as unredeemed territories by the new Karadjordjević Dynasty, was essentially on the defeated side in the war. Serbia has suffered such huge demographic losses especially among men, that Bosnian Serbs, many of whom had served in the Habsburg emperor's army, were now a far larger proportion of the overall Serb population. Catholic and Muslim men as well as Serbs from Vojvodina, now in their prime, had been Habsburg soldiers just prior to the formation of the new state. It proved hard for some of them to forget their old affiliations and indeed the entire civilization that had been lost in 1918. This proved a difficult legacy to overcome, and Bosnians who had served with the Habsburg armies were not always successfully integrated into the new South Slav state. For Catholics this was to prove harder than for Muslims, whose loyalty to the Habsburgs was relatively recent. For 50 years before 1918, Catholic hegemony in Bosnia had been slowly growing. The combination of angry defeat and lost hegemony were two of the factors that helped to feed the growth of Ustaša ideology after 1929 and many leading Ustašas were Bosnian Croats. The crisis that led to the First World War and its consequences had meant that Bosnia had become more influential in the politics of the entire region, an importance that was to be amplified further during the Second World War.

4

Royalist Yugoslavia, the Independent State of Croatia and the Second World War (1918–1945)

In 1918, the Allies accepted the right of the enemies of the Habsburgs, the Serbian Karadjordjević Dynasty, to create a new state. Many South Slav intellectuals had wanted a union of the peoples who spoke the shared language of the region, but as a union of equals. The creation of a Royalist Yugoslavia that included all of Bosnia and Hercegovina was a radical departure, but for the 23 years of its existence it was weighed down by the past. Initially named the Kingdom of Serbs, Croats and Slovenes, it was known unofficially as Yugoslavia from the outset (and officially by 1929). That the Karadjordjević Dynasty was Serbian and Orthodox mattered to the Muslim and Catholic peoples in Bosnia. For decades they had effectively been ruled from Vienna, and the Austrian regime had retained the privileges of property holders. If the spark that lit the First World War had been fuelled by the poverty of Bosnia's Orthodox community, then the establishment of a Serbian king in power was a kind of nemesis for the remnants of an Ottoman ruling class that had been propped up by the Habsburgs. Land in Bosnia was radically redistributed, leaving many Muslim families facing poverty after 1919. This created a crisis of self-esteem and purpose as well as financial difficulties among Muslims, used for centuries to owning the land.

Being part of Yugoslavia brought some clear benefits, but also disadvantages to Bosnia. Aleksandar Karadjordjević was a brave man who had led the Serbian army into battle during the war, but he had distinctly authoritarian personality traits. He was a personal friend of the Croatian Peasant Party (*Hrvatska seljačka stranka*, HSS) leader Stjepan Radić and sincerely tried to represent the cultures and traditions of all the peoples. However, he had been the head of state of their official enemy when Bosnians had fought in the Austrian army against their southerly neighbours, and divisions of that magnitude were not easily erased by state policy. In 1919, the lawyer Mehmed Spaho founded the Yugoslav Muslim Organization (*Jugoslovenska Muslimanska Organizacija*, JMO) in Sarajevo, which lasted as long as the ban on political parties in 1929, after which time it was tacitly tolerated. Although Spaho had worked hard for recognition of the sacrifices that Bosnians had made for the Habsburgs during the war, he pragmatically recognized the change in power and worked to protect the interests of Yugoslavia's Slavonic Muslims until his death in 1939. A new constitution, which came into effect on 28 June 1921, melded the state together but preserved regional internal boundaries. The JMO had insisted on the insertion of Article 135 of the so-called Vidovdan Constitution – or what the press dubbed the 'Turkish paragraph' – that affirmed the existence of a Bosnian polity since the Middle Ages. Although the constitution was generally accepted by the Muslims, it was opposed by the HSS. At the same time, another pro-Yugoslav but anti-Karadjordjević intelligentsia was developing and genuine fraternization between Yugoslavs was taking place at an informal and interpersonal level. The 1920s was a period of some optimism despite regime constraints.

Muslims in the new Yugoslavia had to deal with the weight of historical anti-Islamic sentiments. Some writers did not believe that the Muslims were much different from other South Slavs. In 1849, Vuk Karadžić had argued in an influential article '*Srbi svi i svuda*' ('Serbs all and everywhere') that there were five million people who spoke the same language, but they remained divided by religious confession.[1] In colloquial Serbian, Bosnian Muslims were often referred

---

[1] Karadžić, Vuk '*Srbi svi i svuda*', in Mirko Grmek, Marc Gjidara and Neven Simac (eds.) *Etničko Čišćenje. Povijesni dokumenti o jednoj srpskoj ideologiji* (Zagreb: Nakladni zavod Globus, 1993), p. 29.

to as *Turci* (Turks) or even more demeaning terms like *balije* (a word for Bosnian Muslim of unclear etymology) rather than the more neutral *Muslimani*. For Karadžić, the Muslims were not actually Turkish because they did not know the Turkish language, but others were less sure that historical differences could be overcome. Vladimir Dvorniković, a Croat who had completed a doctorate in psychology in Vienna, published *Karakterologija Jugoslovena* (*The Study of Character of the Yugoslavs*) in Belgrade in 1939. His assessment of the legacy of the Ottoman period was that it was a 'black historical mire' of 'trouble, lament, tears and shame', which had left its mark on the Yugoslavs.[2] Serb writer Čedomil Mitrinović published *Naši muslimani* (*Our Muslims*) in Belgrade in 1926. While this book attributes virtues to Orthodox Christianity, the author saw the influence of Islam as negative: 'vanity, wastefulness, lasciviousness, sensuality, rooted mysticism, and fatalism'.[3]

During the First World War, a young writer from Travnik, Ivo Andrić, had been detained in an Austrian prison for his anti-war and pro-Yugoslav views. He became the best-known of Bosnia's novelists both inside and outside the country and won the Nobel Prize for Literature in 1961. He completed a doctoral dissertation in Graz in 1924 entitled 'Die Entwicklung des geistigen Leben in Bosnien unter der Entwicklung der türkischen Herrschaft', which examined spiritual life in Bosnia under Turkish rule and in which he developed negative views of the Islamic legacy. Andrić was bought up as a Catholic and the influence of the Church in his early education, particularly the Jesuits, is evident in his writing. In his doctoral thesis he discussed the idea of the Ottoman yoke that still hung upon 'dark' Bosnia, which included indolence and arbitrary cruelty. He also prolonged prejudice through his fiction, although his work was often very subtle. The execution passage from the 1945 novel *Na Drini ćuprija* (*Bridge on the Drina*) describes the Turkish punishment of impalement in detail and remains one of the best known in Balkan literature.

---

[2] Dvorniković, Vladimir *Karakterologija Jugoslovena* (Belgrade: Kosmos, 1939), p. 117.

[3] Aleksov, Bojan. 'Adamant and Treacherous: Serbian Historians on Religious Conversions' in Pal Kolsto (ed.) *Myths and Boundaries in South-Eastern Europe* (London: Hurst, 2005), p. 175.

Former Mlada Bosna activist Vaso Čubrilović penned a notorious memorandum in 1937 to the cabinet in Belgrade, which was given as a lecture at the Srpski kulturni klub. Entitled simply 'The Emigration of the Albanians', it advised the Belgrade government that they needed to break up Albanian influence in the south of the country by force and thus provoke a wave of widespread emigration to Turkey and Albania. Drawing on his own familiarity with Bosnian Muslims, he suggested that to get people to leave it was necessary to create a psychosis. He argued that Muslims were superstitious and fanatical and he advocated targeting religious personnel who could be used to make migration to Turkey seem more attractive.[4] Not content with ridding the state of Albanian Muslims, Čubrilović also advised Tito's government to expel ethnic Germans after the Second World War. He was a professor of history at Belgrade University for most of his career. By the time of his death in Belgrade in 1990, he had come to terms with the regime's policies and distanced himself from the revived nationalism of this era. In his youth he had been one of the assassins in Sarajevo in 1914 and his older brother had been executed by the Habsburgs for his part in the murder of Franz Ferdinand.

In a context where Greece and Turkey had 'resolved' war and conflict through population exchanges in 1923, albeit with much suffering, dislocation and violence, many Bosnians actually chose to move to Turkey, where there are still distinct communities. It is possible to trace the decline of Muslim population to the first decline in Ottoman power. In 1870 the Muslim population of Bosnia and Hercegovina (excluding Sandžak) has been estimated as 694,000. By 1879 it had dropped to 449,000.[5] It appears that the decline of population was particularly acute in Hercegovina. In the process of Muslims moving away from Yugoslavia in 1920s and 1930s, it

---

[4] Čubrilović, Vaso. 'Iseljavanje Arnauta', in Miroslav Brandt, Bože Čović, Radovan Pavić, Zdravko Tomac, Mirko Valentić and Stanko Zuljić (eds.) *Izvori velikosrpske agresije: Rasprave, dokumenti, kartografski prikazi* (Zagreb: August Cesarec, Školska knjiga, 1991), pp. 106–124.

[5] McCarthy, Justin. 'Archival Sources Concerning Serb Rebellions in Bosnia 1875–76' in Markus Koller and Kemal H. Karpat (eds.) *Ottoman Bosnia: A History in Peril* (Madison, WI: University of Wisconsin Press, 2004), p. 144.

was often the most pious who chose to leave rather than compromise their religious practices. The process of migration is part of a general weakening of the Ottoman legacy or what historian Safet Bandžović has called 'de-Ottomanization'. Muslims continued to leave Bosnia in the 1950s.

POVERTY, THE WEIGHT OF THE PAST AND THE 'DINARIC PERSONALITY'

One of the greatest problems that Bosnia faced in the years between 1870s and the Second World War was endemic levels of poverty and the illnesses related to dearth. Some migrated to the Americas 'with their stomachs for bread' ('*s trebuhom za kruhom*'). In the mines of Illinois or the construction sites of Nevada, Bosnians tended to lose their ethnic identity very quickly and many never returned or even kept in contact with the extended families they had left behind. At the beginning of the twentieth century, rural illiteracy rates in Bosnia could be as high as 95 per cent and were especially high among women. The state of the nation's health was a grave concern to many especially the high levels of poverty in the Dinaric region. By the 1950s, after several decades of modernization, which included the provision of hospitals and schools by both the Royalist and Communist regimes, the illiteracy figure was virtually reversed and the scourges of rural life such as tuberculosis and venereal disease were being tackled. In the late 1930s, Yugoslavia was the worse place in Europe in terms of the incidence of tuberculosis, a problem tackled incrementally with great success. Largely due to penicillin inoculations, syphilis was almost eliminated by the early 1950s, thanks to the work of the pioneering physician Ernest Grin who set up rural clinics.[6]

The economist and Croatian Peasant Party supporter Rudolf Bićanić walked across Croatia and Bosnia *apostolski* (like an apostle) in the mid-1930s producing a vivid memoir, *Kako živi narod: Život u pasivnim krajevima (How the People Live: Life in the Passive Regions)*. He has been released from prison for subversive

---

[6] Arslanagić, Naima, Bokonjić, M. and Macanović, K. 'Eradication of Endemic Syphillis in Bosnia', *Genitourin Med* 65(1), 1989, pp. 4–7.

intellectual activity in the mid-1930s and he decided to travel in the Dinarics. He found that the people trapped by such a harsh existence could barely afford to eat, their lives dominated by the tyranny of customs and pride. He noticed that many people would live on cornmeal and little else, although they would carefully preserve their appearance by dressing smartly.[7] Nikola Šop, born in Jajce and rooted in local Catholic traditions, also captured the agony of the needy in his 1926 *Pjesme siromašnog sina sv. Frane (The Poems of a Poor Son of St Francis)*. In 'Prosjaku koji nosi moji šešir', he blesses the beggar who is wearing his stolen hat and adds 'let your poverty have it'.[8] The doctor and former Mlada Bosna activist Mladen Stojanović treated poor patients for nothing at his surgery in Prijedor and paid their hospital fees. His brother Sretan, also a philanthropist was one of the most well-known sculptors from Bosnia. His larger-than-life creations grace many cities in the region including the vast Monument to Liberty or *Sloboda spomenik* in Fruška gora. After his brother was awarded the posthumous honour of people's hero, Streten was commissioned to create a sculpture of him. Many of the intellectuals of the interwar period had the will to create a better country, a desire cut short but not exterminated by the Second World War.

The Dinaric Mountain range covered much of Hercegovina and when Bićanić travelled there in the 1930s, he was already carrying the weight of contemporary ideas about the region with him. Politically liminal and isolated from the Muslim urban culture of Bosnia and Dalmatia's cities, the limestone Karst had produced its own ways of life. By the mid-nineteenth century, a juxtaposition between the Turk and the Christian bandit or *hajduk* was established in literature. The rebellions in Hercegovina in the 1870s had been depicted in journalistic terms as a battle between wild mountaineers and Turks. Prior to this, the writing of Abbé Albero Fortis about the Morlacchi (Vlachs or Orthodox Serbs of the Dalmatian hinterland) had also created the myth of distinctiveness. The way in which mountain peoples from Bosnia were described continued to

7 Bićanić, Rudolf *Kako živi narod: Život u pasivnim krajevima* (Zagreb: Tisak Tipografija, 1936), pp. 102–105.
8 Šop, Nikola *Božanski pastir* (Zagreb: Mozaik knjiga, 1997), p. 93.

be very particular. Louis Adamič made the following observation in Sarajevo's marketplace, the *baščaršija*, in the mid-1930s: 'one notices the enormous Bosnian mountaineer-peasants from the vicinity of Sarajevo who come to sell their products and make their simple purchases. Six-feet-six, thin and raw-boned, with colossal fleshless hands and faces, they walk with the peculiar strides of mountain men. Nearly all of them, Christians and Moslems, wear homespun clothes, crude boat-like sandals and fezzes or turbans. Their breeches have enormous baggy seats which reach below their knees.'[9]

In his 1918 book *La péninsule balkanique*, geographer Jovan Cvijić argued that the men from the Dinaric region were vigorous, courageous and had not forgotten the struggles of the past. Cvijić had travelled widely in the region and collected a vast amount of ethnographic data that he used to build his theories about character. By linking their own daily struggles to a kind of collective historical 'memory' of the medieval Battle of Kosovo polje as a turning point and defeat, he argues that Dinaric men had a sense of revenge on oppressors and a concept of the significance of independence and freedom: 'Dinaric has an ardent desire to avenge Kosovo ... and to resuscitate the Serbian Empire ... even in circumstances where the less courageous or a man of pure reason would have despaired. Betrayed by circumstances and events, abandoned by all, he has never renounced his national and social ideal.'[10] Cvijić also detected the prevalence of bloody-mindedness as well as fatalism.[11] The term '*inat*', which has come into Bosnian from Turkish is often used to describe the kind of bloody-mindedness or spitefulness. Lack of fear or even contempt for death was a traditional sign of bravery in many Mediterranean societies and was found among the ancient Greeks. Ideas about character traits were also prevalent in the writing of the Croatian-American Dinko Tomašić, who published *Personality and Culture in East European Politics* in New York in 1948. Like Bićanić, he had been active in the Croatian Peasant Party in 1930s and was genuinely concerned about the region. Tomašić attributed

[9] Adamič, 'Sarajevo', p. 72.
[10] Cvijić, *La péninsule balkanique*, p. 282.
[11] Ibid., pp. 281–379.

some negative personality features to people in the region, including restlessness, craftiness, deceit, self-aggrandizement and violence, and saw some of the traits in the Orthodox from Hercegovina in particular as negative. He also suggested that the Dinaric region nurtured authoritarian personality types inclined towards political extremes.[12]

Debates about national character remain a popular form of self-deprecation, but can also sometimes constitute a kind of pride in the Dinaric region. Evocation of tradition that still occurs in popular culture is sometimes a way that Croatians distinguish themselves from people from Hercegovina and a way that Sarajevans differentiate themselves from mountain people. Marko Živković has argued that once the stereotypes about Dinaric people were made the topic of scholarly writing they 'percolated back to the popular level, if not directly through Cvijić's writings, then from his numerous popularizers and became firmly entrenched as a genre of folk ethnopsychology'.[13] *Kenjac (The Donkey/Ass)*, directed by Antonio Nuić, is a 2009 film about a small family in Drinovci in Hercegovina, very close to the border with Croatia. Set in the summer of 1995 and against the backdrop of Croatian victory, the film explores the impact of the war on two brothers who have returned home to their village after years apart. Few of the locals are able to express their feelings directly and resort to violence and alcohol abuse. The women also conform to the Dinaric archetypes and are timid and cowed into submission by male behaviour. The film, which won widespread critical acclaim, is also, implicitly, a discourse on the 'Dinaric personality' and this would be understood by its target audience. The drama centres on Lake Krenica, which comes to symbolize suicide, drowning and despair. In the director's statement to the European Film Awards, Nuić, whose own father came from the region, explained: 'Each character in the film, ... swam in the lake on several occasions regardless of its actual danger. With this I want to render a deeply irrational, dark side of the people from

---

[12] Tomašić, Dinko *Personality and Culture in East European Politics* (New York: G.W. Stewart, 1948), pp. 41, 56, 114.

[13] Živković, Marko *Serbian Dreambook: National Imaginary in the Time of Milošević* (Bloomington, IN: Indiana University Press, 2011), p. 79.

Hercegovina, otherwise extremely religious and cautious people.'[14] Anthropologist Stef Jansen has detected what he calls an 'Zagreb urban-centric discourse'. People from Hercegovina – or *Hercegovci*, as they are known – are seen to have a particular style and are thus implicitly different from other Croats. 'Yes, they drove large Mercedes, wore expensive clothes and frequented fancy restaurants. But his Armani suit was put into context by the white socks, and her black leather Prada handbag was put in the shade by just that little bit too much make-up. *Hercegovci*, it was argued, ate in expensive restaurants but gave away their identity by ordering ... pig on a spit.'[15]

THE TIDE OF CROATIAN NATIONALISM AND THE USTAŠA STATE

After the assassination of Stjepan Radić in 1928, King Aleksandar dispensed with parliament believing that democracy and open debate had led to political instability. He effectively tore up the Vidovdan Constitution and ruled as a dictator. The old boundaries were replaced in 1929 by new internal boundaries broadly based on rivers. At this time, Bosnia was divided between Drinska, Zetska, Primorska and Vrbaska. These radical new divisions, known as *banovine*, had they lasted, would have broken up the old Muslim urban civilization and signalled the end of a recognizable Bosnian entity. The significance of rivers in the Western Balkans was thus dramatically enhanced. The Drinska *banovina* stretched from what is now Serbia into Bosnia including the towns of Požega, Obrenovac, Sarajevo and Konjic. Vladimir Dedijer believed that Radić was so saintly that he would have forgiven his assassin Puniša Račić,[16] but many Croat politicians could not forgive the Montenegrin gunman who had opened fire on the HSS leader in parliament. The assassination marked a serious deterioration in Serb–Croat relations that put the future of the infant Yugoslav state in jeopardy. At the public

---

[14] http://europeanfilmawards.eu/en_en/film/160.
[15] Jansen, Stef *Anti-nationalism: Post-Yugoslav Resistance and Narratives of Self and Society*, doctoral dissertation, University of Hull, 2000, p. 141.
[16] Dedijer, Vladimir *The Beloved Land*, (London: MacGibbon and Kee, 1961), p. 128.

funeral procession of Radić in Zagreb, there was open Croat defiance of the regime.

In October 1934 – when Aleksandar Karadjordjević was himself assassinated in Marseilles by a lone gunman, Macedonian Vlado Chernozemski, funded by the Croatian extremist Ustaša group – there was a brief respite to the interethnic rivalries that had beset the country. Prayers were said in mosques, Orthodox churches became places of respect to the late monarch and his body was taken slowly through the country by train so that his subjects could pay their respects. Aleksandar had been travelling in an open-top car from the harbour where his ship had landed and was greeted by cheering crowds. Rushing forward towards the car, which was

Map 5. Bosnia in Yugoslavia, 1929–1939

moving very slowly through the streets, Chernozemski shot both
Aleksandar and the French foreign minister Louis Barthou by standing on the fender and firing at point blank range. The angry crowd
lynched the Macedonian assassin, but the king died almost immediately of his wounds. Many of the culprits linked to the plot, including the Ustaša leader Ante Pavelić, were tried and found guilty and
sentenced to death *in absentia* in Aix en Provence. Pavelić was in
prison in Italy at the time. It was clear that Yugoslavia had been
badly destabilized by the king's death and Adolf Hitler regarded the
state as weak and vulnerable from that point onwards. Prince Pavle
took over as regent when his cousin was killed, as Aleksandar's son
Petar was only 11 years old at the time. The signing of the so-called
Sporazum (mutual agreement) between the prime minister Dragiša
Cvetković and the leader of the Croatian Peasant Party Vladko
Maček created a new Croatian *banovina* and some of the precondi-
tions for Croatian autonomy in 1939. The *banovina* of Primorska
(which included Mostar and Bugojno) was united with Sava, which
included Brčko. By swallowing up coastal Primorska into a distinct section of the monarchy, Croat ambitions in the wider region
were encouraged. What remained of the old Bosnia, surrounded on
two sides by this Croatian entity, was still divided between Vrbaska,
Drinska and Zetska. With the signing of the *Sporazum*, Serb politicians hoped that a Serb *banovina* might also be created in time,
while many Muslim politicians were alarmed at the disappearance
of the old Bosnia.

The regent Prince Pavle had supported the signing of the
Sporazum, but when he signed a non-aggression treaty with Hitler
in March 1941, he was overthrown in an army coup in favour of
his 17-year-old nephew old Petar. Yugoslavia had remained neutral
at the outbreak of the Second World War in 1939, but significant
numbers in the army opposed any deals with the Axis powers on
principle. Still harbouring an Austrian dislike for Serbs as a remnant from the First World War, Hitler decided to destroy Yugoslavia
in April 1941 with a decisive invasion that involved aerial bombing of Belgrade and the capitulation of the monarchy. The young
King Petar and his government fled to exile in London. Unlike his
father, Petar would never lead a Yugoslav army into battle. It was
the Communist Josip Broz Tito and the Partisans who took on that

role, which gave them legitimacy not only in the wider world but among their own people. It would be four years until their final victory against Nazi quislings and local combatants and most of the contest was decided in Bosnia. After the Karadjordjević monarchy collapsed, what had been Bosnia was swallowed up into a new enlarged Croatian state under the fascist Ustaša. The end of the Yugoslavian monarchy, which collapsed in a matter of days after the Nazi assault, exposed the fragility of the region caught between an expansionist Italy and an aggressive Germany.

The Ustaša were a small paramilitary force that was formed primarily in exile after 1929. Numbering just a few hundred men, they hatched plans to destroy Yugoslavia in Italy and Hungary. The Axis decided to install Ante Pavelić in power and he arrived in Zagreb on 13 April 1941 wearing a black shirt and flanked by Italian tanks. There he proclaimed himself *poglavnik* (equivalent to Führer or Duce). Bosnia was incorporated into the new Independent State of Croatia, which returned it to the 1908 borders and was intended to be a definitive break with Serbia and Serbian influence. The bold geographical experimentation carried out by the Ustaša in 1941 may have been encouraged by the sweeping manner in which the Karadjordjević regime changed the map in 1929 and again in 1931 and 1939. The Ustaša attempted to overcome the primary problem the Habsburgs had faced in Bosnia, namely a lack of legitimacy among the Orthodox population of Bosnia, by force. Rory Yeomans has pointed out that 'as early as 14 April 1941 the movement's official daily newspaper warned that the "resurrection" of the Croatian state after eight and half centuries could only be achieved through "bloodily confronting our eternal enemies, our native Serbs"'.[17] While this aim of confrontation could seem more like revenge for Habsburg defeat in 1918, the notion of hundreds of years of antipathy towards the Serbs, although historically poorly grounded, was crucial to the Ustaša. For them, the Serbs had no place in Bosnia or Croatia. Their core aim was the creation of a state to include all the people they considered to be 'Croats', which included Bosnian

---

[17] Yeomans, Rory *Visions of Annihilation: The Ustasha Regime and the Cultural Politics of Fascism, 1941–45* (Pittsburgh: University of Pittsburgh Press 2013), p. 17.

Muslims and Catholics. On 24 July 1941, Eugen Dido Kvaternik, chief of the Ustaša's internal security, said to Branko Pešelj of the Croatian Peasant Party: 'I know that you believe and expect the English to win the war. I agree with you; I too believe that the English will win the war in the end, but there will be no Serbs left in Croatia then. In other words, whoever wins the war will have to accept the situation as he finds it.'[18]

Gaining the support of the Catholic Church was a crucial part of the Ustaša's genocidal strategy. Mass was regularly held at the Jasenovac death camp and some priests wore state uniforms. Former Peasant Party leader Vladko Maček, who was incarcerated rapidly by Pavelić, observed the piety of the guard Ljubo Miloš in Jasenovac, who would pray after committing atrocities and was prepared to 'go to hell' for Croatia.[19] The Catholic bishop of Banja, Luka Josip Garić, witnessed the demolition of the Orthodox cathedral, which was then promptly replaced by a Pavelić Square. Garić had trained as a Franciscan priest in Fojnica. The Ustaša also worked to gain the support of Bosnia's Muslims. The Croatian Peasant Party leader Radić had abandoned that idea that Muslims were Croats before the First World War after travelling in the region, which meant that this belief remained fairly distinctive to the Ustaša. Many leading Ustaša adherents, including the *poglavnik* Pavelić were born as Habsburg citizens in Bosnia or Hercegovina. Growing up near Jajce and attending a *makteb* primary school had given Pavelić some empathy with Islam and he wore a fez on occasion. During his time as *poglavnik*, a mosque was set up in Zagreb. Like the founder of modern Croatian nationalism, Ante Starčević, he defined Catholic and Muslim Bosnians as part of the Croatian nation. The Ustaša movement is unique in that it was the only fascist group from that era to have a significant Muslim component and military uniforms that included the fez. Including the Bosnian Muslims within the Croatian *Volksgemeinschaft* effectively ignored the religious conversions of the sixteenth century and returned Bosnia to its former

[18] Dulić, Tomislav *Utopias of Nation: Local Mass Killing in Bosnia and Herzegovina, 1941–42* (Uppsala: Acta Universitatis Upsaliensis, 2005), p. 100.
[19] Maček, Vladko *In the Struggle for Freedom* (Philadelphia: Pennsylvania State University Press, 1968), p. 245.

status as a Catholic nation. It also meant that the Croatian nation could be rebuilt with its 'purest' (*'najčišći'*) component as they saw it. Pavelić's deputy prime minister Dr Džafer-beg Kulenović, who had become the leader of the JMO after Spaho's death, was a close political ally.

In the law concerning the Eastern Frontier of the Independent State of Croatia (*Nezavisna Država Hrvatska*, NDH) from 4 June 1941, Clause 3 states 'the boundary of the NDH shall run by land to the East from the Drina along the old boundary line between Bosnia and Serbia as it was before 1908'.[20] The Drina is one of the longest Karst rivers in the Western Balkans. It varies from quite shallow in parts to less easily traversable. There are many old and prosperous towns on it banks, including Goražde, Zvornik and Višegrad. Historically the Drina basin had a mixed Orthodox and Muslim population. The towns tended to be more Islamic, the countryside more Orthodox. The numbers of Catholics living in the region was quite small compared to other parts of Bosnia, although there were some descendants of merchants from Dubrovnik in some Drina towns. For the Serb rebels against the Ottomans in the early nineteenth century, the Drina was a fluid but nonetheless tangible boundary between themselves and Bosnia. After the collapse of Ottoman power in Bosnia, the river marked the political border between Austria-Hungary and Serbia until 1918. During the first weeks of the First World War, the river was the military frontline. Two years earlier citizens of Austria-Hungary had even swam across the Drina to join the Serbian irregulars during the Balkan Wars. For decades before 1941, Croatian nationalists had imagined the Drina as the boundary between themselves and the Serbs and, in doing so, drew on a number of articles by classical authors as well as more contemporary sources.[21] Ivo Goldstein emphasizes the role of the writer Milan Šufflay, who used his 1921 trial to publicize his views. Šufflay called the Drina a 'spiritual and cultural

[20] Lemkin, Raphaël *Axis Rule in Occupied Europe. Laws of Occupation, Analysis of Government. Proposals for Redress* (Clark, NJ: The Lawbook Exchange 2005), p. 607.

[21] Goldstein, Ivo 'The Boundary on the Drina: The Meaning and Development of the Mythologem' in Pål Kolstø (ed.) *Myths and Boundaries in South Eastern Europe* (London: Hurst, 2005), pp. 77–105.

boundary', a phrase often repeated in Ustaša propaganda.[22] Other nationalists, far less extreme than the fascists, also wanted border reforms. In 1936, Croatian Peasant Party leader Vlado Maček even called for a plebiscite with the intention of splitting Yugoslavia into two parts (cisDrina and transDrina). He felt that this decidedly Habsburg-style solution to Yugoslavia's national questions would mean that 'Vojvodina, Bosnia and Hercegovina, Montenegro, Macedonia and even Dalmatia could opt the way they want to or according to the vote of the delegates'.[23]

The NDH experienced problems from the outset. It was economically unviable and subject to Axis exploitation and almost immediately beset by food shortages and inflation, which led to a black market. However, the new regime spent a lot of energy in creating an image of its new border to reinforce their sense of legitimacy. This included propaganda and ceremonial events that accompanied the campaign of atrocities that they unleashed within weeks of coming to power. The 1942 film *Wacht an der Drina (Straža na Drini)*, directed by Branko Marjanović and produced by Hrvatski Slikopis, was aimed not only at NDH citizens but their German-speaking allies. They also produced another propaganda film to create a legitimizing link to the past about Ante Starčević entitled *Otac Domovine (Father of the Nation)*.[24] The German narrative is interspersed with long passages of classical music, although there is also a choral version of *Pozdrav domovini* (a Croatian anthem). The content of the film was very far from the reality of wartime conflict, lack of authority and confusion in the region. More accurately it was an attempt to create a Croatian *Volksgemeinschaft* (i.e., an ethnic community in the fascist sense) through propaganda for German viewers, including Wehrmacht troops.

The film opens with the statement that the Drina marks the old boundary between 'Eastern' and 'Western' Europe, which had become a central tenet of Ustaša ideology. The narrator then continues by explaining that nowhere is more pure Croatian spoken

---

[22] Ibid., p. 82.
[23] Krestić, Vasilije *La grande Croatie: le génocide comme projet politique* (Paris: L'Age d'Homme Editions, 2000), p. 111.
[24] Yeomans, *Visions of Annihilation*, p. 212.

Map 6. Bosnia under occupation in the Independent State of Croatia

than in the Bosnian mountains, which again bound the Bosnians more closely to their Catholic neighbours. The fall of medieval Bosnia under the 'Croatian ruler' Stjepan Tomašević (who was the last Kotromanić monarch and a Catholic) is then addressed and the narrator explains that a 'segment' of the Bosnian people converted to Islam and lived together with Christians. The historical commentary in the film is brief and at no point mentions any Serbian state or indeed separate Bosnian statehood in the Middle Ages. The omission of Serbs from the film is not accidental and gives us an insight into an important aspect of Ustaša ideology. The audience is later informed that the Muslims are of 'pure Croatian blood' (echoing beliefs held by Starčević) and that their 'spiritual leaders have led prayers for a beautiful future for the Croatian people', implicitly binding Islam and Catholicism together. Towards the end, the film envisages a rustic NDH in which the Croatian and Muslim peasants are protected by the Ustaša. The narrator talks about the opponents of the NDH without naming the Serbs directly. Only when the film discusses the 'sign under which they fight' do we see Cyrillic letters (and thus the implicit conflation between Serbs and Russians). Against a background of blazing farmsteads, the film announces that 'Bandits began to burn, destroy, murder and to plunder'. At this stage in the film, fascist black legion soldiers appear (as Wagner's 'Ritt der Walküren' from the *Ring Cycle* is played in the background), joined by tanks from the Croatian army. At times in the film, the NDH soldiers appear wearing the fez. The 'bandits' are then named as Partisans, 'the left flank of the Soviet Army'. The 'bandits' are never named as Četniks at any point and nor are violent anti-Muslim actions in the Drina region by the Serb nationalists alluded to. Indeed apart from the rounding up of bandits, one could imagine from the content of the film that the Ustaša were firmly in charge in the border areas of the NDH. The military reality was that the Ustaša regime found itself desperately overstretched in the Drina region. The film narrator promises that the *poglavnik* Ante Pavelić will never desert his people and that no trace of the enemy will remain. Shots of captured Partisans who strongly resemble Serb peasants are accompanied by the announcement that 'at present, the Black Legion is cleansing the eastern border of Croatia'. Both Pavelić and his close associate Vjekoslav Luburić appear frequently in the film.

In 1943, when Italy collapsed, the NDH reached its apogee and the Dalmatian coast, including Kotor and Zadar, was given to an enlarged Croatian state. For many Croat nationalists, the ephemeral 1943 borders were the culmination of their boldest aspirations

Fig. 8 Ante Pavelić 12 kuna stamp from 1944, Independent State of Croatia

Fig. 9 Guarding the River Drina in eastern Bosnia: 19 kuna stamp from 1944, Independent State of Croatia

because they included Bosnia as well as Dalmatia. As far as the Ustaša were concerned, the primary obstacle in the way of Bosnia becoming part of Croatia remained the Orthodox population, many of whom were not generally considered to be 'redeemable', although there were some forced conversions. Hundreds of thousands were murdered on the grounds of race or religion by the Ustaša especially between the summer of 1941 and 1942. The fascist regime launched a campaign of extermination of the Orthodox peoples of the region and, as allies of the Nazis, allowed the deportation of Sarajevo's Ladino-speaking Jewish population to the death camps.

Muslim leaders were initially quite sceptical about the Ustaša until the intervention of the grand mufti of Jerusalem, Haj Amin el-Husseini, who persuaded many of them to support the Third Reich. Adolf Hitler was enthusiastic about keeping alive links between the Nazis and Islam and was persuaded by Heinrich Himmler that the Bosnian Muslims would make a suitable division of the Schutzstaffel or SS. Some of the older Bosnians had fought for the Habsburgs just over 20 years earlier, including Husejin Biščević. Muhamed Hadžiefendić, who had served in both the Habsburg and Yugoslavian armies, organized a Muslim militia in the Tuzla region before joining the 13th SS Handschar Division in 1943, which 12,000 men volunteered to join. He and his men were surrounded by the Communist Partisans in Tuzla in the autumn of 1943 and died in the struggle. The name that the SS battalion adopted referred to the dagger that was their collective symbol. Some attempts were made to mark their Muslim heritage and their rations excluded alcohol and pork. As in the First World War, their dead were honoured as *šehidi* (Muslim martyrs). As part of their uniform, the Handschar wore a fez with two further symbols: the SS skull and an eagle astride a swastika. Bosnian Handschar soldiers were among the defenders of Berlin in 1945 when it fell to the Soviets.

Ustaša troops carried out the genocide so rapidly in the early summer of 1941, that some confused Serbs reported their actions to the authorities, largely because they could not believe that these actions could be sanctioned by a legitimate government and must be the work of terrorists. Tomislav Dulić has calculated that approximately 75 per cent of Jewish and Roma communities of the NDH and up to 17 per cent of Serbs died as 'victims of fascism'. Six per cent of Croats died, many killed in 1945 by Communists and 9 per cent of Muslims also died, many killed by Četniks.[25] The Ustaša used the term 'Vlach' to refer to Serbs, as if they were aliens in the

---

[25] Dulić, Tomislav 'Mass Killing in the Independent State of Croatia, 1941–1945: A Case for Comparative Research', *Journal of Genocide Research* 8(3), 2006, p. 273.

NDH. Undoubtedly many of the Orthodox and Catholic inhabitants of the region had been Vlach-speaking until the early modern era and this ancient language, which is related to Latin and Romanian, is found across the Balkans, especially in Macedonia and Greece, and only died out in Istria in recent years. Nevertheless, the term 'Vlachs' to describe the Orthodox peoples of the Dinarics, particularly Krajina, was used in the 1940s and then revived by nationalists in Croatia in 1990s, to de-legitimize their presence in the region and to separate them from the rest of the Orthodox peoples who might define themselves as Serbs. Typically the Ustaša targeted Serb villages and killed all the inhabitants. Often victims were thrown into limestone ravines, some were made to dig graves and were then buried alive. In the Karst region, some sinkholes are very narrow at the surface, but deeper underground and these are known in Bosnian as *vrtače* or *ponore*. It was these sinkholes that were used to dispose of a large numbers of bodies.[26] Sometimes the villagers were ritualistically taunted and dehumanized in a way that often takes place in violence between neighbours or people who speak the same language. Part of the antipathy towards the Serbs must have been a direct ricochet from the First World War, when the Croats were almost all subjects of the Habsburgs. Serving on different sides in the war and then accepting the status of losers made men across Europe discernibly bitter. Croat nationalists and intellectuals had reified and hated the hegemony of Belgrade in the 1920s and 1930s. Vladimir Dedijer quoted an Ustaša murderer intent on killing his Serb acquaintances: 'I know who you are and how you are, but I can't help you; I can't help the fact that you are Serbs, that you belong to the people among whom the new laws of the state make no distinction. You are all guilty for what happened during the time of the former Yugoslavia, and you will pay for it, everyone of you, down to the last.'[27] These actions were executed in a hurry and a few survived the atrocities by feigning death or escaping. Young lads out in the fields sometimes witnessed atrocities

---

[26] These sinkholes pose a danger for smaller grazing animals like sheep and pigs, who frequently fall into them inadvertently in the Dinaric Karst regions.

[27] Dedijer, Vladimir *The Yugoslav Auschwitz and the Vatican: The Croatian Massacre of Serbs during World War II* (Buffalo, NY: Prometheus Books, 1992), pp. 155–164.

from trees where they were hiding and were able to escape and organize resistance.

Although Jewish communities had been fragmented and dislocated by the collapse of the Ottoman Empire, it was during the Second World War that they were systematically destroyed. The settlement of Jews in the former Ottoman lands goes back thousands of years, but a large number were Ladino-speaking Sephardi, who came to the relatively tolerant South-East of Europe after their expulsion from Spain by the Inquisition in the fifteenth and sixteenth centuries. The Jewish communities of Anatolia and the Balkans numbered over 300,000 individuals by 1900, with the greatest concentrations in cities such as Sarajevo, Dubrovnik, Istanbul and Salonika. The fourteenth-century *Sarajevo Haggadah*, a prayerbook used for the Feast of Passover with Hebrew calligraphy and brightly coloured illustrations, was saved during the Second World War. Museum curator Derviš Korkut hid the book after a Nazi general, Johann Fortner, came to the Vijećnica. In 1941, he had published an article that argued that anti-Semitism was foreign to Bosnia and that the Jewish cemetery in Sarajevo had never been desecrated.[28] Later elevated to the ranks of the 'Righteous Among the Nations' at Israel's Yad Vashem for sheltering a Jewish girl, Mira Papo, he also took a considerable personal risk in saving the prayerbook. The *Haggadah* was rescued again in 1992, although many other unique manuscripts were lost at this time including many of the Ottoman-era *defters* or cadastral records.

Ante Lokić, a prominent member of the Ustaša who had been born in Mostar, attempted to save the NDH in league with another prominent Ustaša, Mladen Lorković. Sensing in 1944 that the Axis powers were doomed to defeat, they attempted to get the Ustaša to switch sides. Pavelić regarded this as treasonable behaviour and both were imprisoned, but not executed until April 1945, just days before Pavelić fled for Zagreb in the wake of the Partisan advance. The architect and commandant of the concentration camp Jasenovac, in which more than 70,000 Serbs, Jews and other 'enemies of the state' were killed, was Vjekoslav Luburić, born in

---

[28] Baskar, 'Komišluk and Taking Care of the Neighbor's Shrine', p. 52.

Hercegovina, who was to become one of the most notorious war criminals of the Second World War in the Balkans. Luburić's father had been killed by the Yugoslav police in the 1920s and he had come to detest and resent Serbs and the Serbian monarchy. In the last months of his time in office, Luburić instigated a reign of terror in Sarajevo.[29] Like Pavelić, he also managed to escape at the end of the war.

Luburić had visited Germany and the extermination camps in the East of Europe to see what had been set up. In Jasenovac, more than half of the prisoners were Serbs, although Roma, Jews and political prisoners were targeted. Nominally in a work camp (*logor*), inmates were kept on starvation rations in insanitary conditions. Many died of water-borne diseases, others were killed by gas. Random acts of sadism were commonplace, as well as the use of knifes and saws to kill and mutilate prisoners. The Ustaša carried elaborate knives forged in their factory in Serin with ornaments, braid work and the letter U.[30] Many of their atrocities involved mass killings with knives and their pictures indicate that these killings were carried out with a carnivalesque air. One Ustaša from Široki Brijeg 'won a competition by cutting the throats of 1,360 Serbs with a special knife, for which act he was given the prize of a gold watch, a silver service, a roast sucking pig and some wine'.[31] As the Partisans moved slowly towards Jasenovac in April 1945, the Ustaša guard attempted to remove incriminating evidence and kill any survivors, 80 of whom escaped in the final days. Recent estimates of the numbers killed by the Ustaša regime at Jasenovac are more than 80,000.

The Partisans who liberated Jasenovac found piles of emaciated bodies and extensive evidence of widespread abuse and torture including photographs. The victorious fighters did not have to invent the crimes of the former regime since they left an evidence trail. Bosnians who had been active at a more minor level in the defeated Ustaša state, were subject to summary justice, long prison

[29] Greble, Emily *Sarajevo, 1941–1945: Muslims, Christians, and Jews in Hitler's Europe* (Ithica: Cornell University Press, 2011), p. 230.

[30] Dedijer, *Yugoslav Auschwitz*, p. 232.

[31] West, Richard *Tito and the Rise and Fall of Yugoslavia* (New York: Carroll and Graf, 1995), p. 92.

sentences and social ostracization. Historians attracted attention in the 1980s by revising down the numbers killed at Jasenovac. Future Croatian president Franjo Tudjman gained some notoriety as a revisionist. Initially the Communists had claimed that some two million people had been killed in the Second World War. Although the numbers killed are unlikely to have been as high as the total claimed by the Communists and were probably closer to one million, there is still a tendency to deny the extent of the destruction or to equate Jasenovac with the mass murder of Croat and Slovene soldiers who fought for the Axis at the end of the war. If there is a link between these events, it was at the level of anger experienced by the Partisans who liberated the camp and went on to commit atrocities in the weeks immediately after the war. Although the result of their furious anger cannot be excused, their persecution of their enemies should be understood in the context of fury, grief and elation at victory at a time when the Allies had also lost much of their compassion for the young men drafted into Axis armies.

Vjekoslav Luburić's brother-in-law Dinko Šakić, originally from Studenci in Hercegovina, became the last commandant of the Jasenovac extermination camp for seven months in 1944. Former prisoners remembered his white horse, black leather boots and the whip he carried with him. He escaped the wrath of the Partisans in 1945, moving to Spain and then to Argentina where he lived as Ljubomir Šakić and ran a textile factory. He and his wife Nada had three children and he met quite openly with Croatian émigrés for several years. He was tracked down by the Simon Wiesenthal Foundation after an interview on television was broadcast in Buenos Aires in 1998. He was tried and imprisoned in Zagreb and sentenced to a maximum of 20 years in jail in 1999 after having been found personally responsible for the death of 2,000 individuals at Jasenovac in 1941–1945. He died unrepentant at the age of 86 in 2008 in Lepoglava prison, where Tito, Pijade and Milovan Djilas had also been prisoners in different times. His trial gave the government of Franjo Tudjman a chance to repudiate any links with the Independent State of Croatia, although he was not sentenced until October 1999, by which time the president was terminally ill.

THE ČETNIK MOVEMENT

In eastern Bosnia, Ustaša authority was quickly challenged by Serb guerrillas known as Četniks. These Serbian monarchists were conscious of the past and again like their predecessor linked their own political movement with older struggles. The strength of this oral tradition can be seen during the Second World War, and the legends of the Romanija mountain, one of their strongholds near Sarajevo, lived on for decades after the war. The organization into self-defence *četas* (bands) by Serbs in the Independent State of Croatia after the first Ustaša atrocities in 1941 was often on a very rapid and spontaneous basis before the formal leadership of either Draža Mihailović or the Partisans could be accounted for. In many respects the Četnik formations simply represented a political group that wanted to restore the Karadjordjević monarchy. Their leader Mihailović had trained in Paris and was a loyal officer of the king. After the capitulation of the state, he refused to serve under the German occupiers or for quisling administration of Milan Nedić and went into hiding, gathering supporters around him. They adopted some of the old bandit traditions, grew long beards, lived in the woods and were overwhelmingly Orthodox. In Hercegovina, Draža Mihailović presented the atrocities of the 1940s in terms of local vendetta traditions,[32] thus distancing himself from any direct responsibility. Their headquarters was initially around Doboj in northern Bosnia, later moving to Ravna Gora in western Serbia. As the movement grew, its political character became clearer.

The lawyer Stevan Moljević, born in Rudo near the Serbian border, had advocated both getting rid of non-Serbs from what he defined as Serb lands and forcing Muslims to migrate to Turkey. As the war progressed, the Četnik movement came to represent a more extreme type of eliminationist nationalism and carried out vicious acts of genocide in eastern Bosnia. Former Mlada Bosna activist and army officer Jezdimir Dangić led a group of Četniks that terrorized the eastern Bosnian towns. Četniks kidnapped several Catholic nuns and threw their bodies into the river.[33] They became known as the

---

[32] Dulić, *Utopias of Nation*, p. 208.
[33] Dizdar, Zdravko and Sobolevski, Mihael *Prešućivani četnički zločini u Hrvatskoj i u Bosni i Hercegovini: 1941–1945* (Zagreb: Hrvatski institut za povijest: Dom i svijet, 1999), pp. 147–148.

'Drina martyrs' (*Drinske mučenice*) and were eventually beatified by Pope Benedict XVI. The so-called 'black troikas' of the Četniks would use knives during their terror campaigns, earning them the Partisan nickname of '*koljači*' (cut-throats). Ivan Kareić recalled the scene in Višegrad in February 1942: 'from early morning through the night, a crowd of people would stand and watch as corpses passed under the bridge over the Drina. [victims] who had been tied together and had their throats cut'.[34] During the war, the Četniks set up a primitive concentration camp at Kosovo kod Knina. It was probably the savagery of the Četniks and their reputation for gratuitous cruelty that lost them crucial support. Mihailović faced a number of problems as a guerrilla leader. He could not unite all the Yugoslavs, even though he wanted to restore the Karadjordjević monarchy. Many Četniks saw war primarily as an eliminationist opportunity, killing thousands of Muslims in eastern Bosnia.[35] The Četniks were also anti-Semitic and anti-Communist (although neither sentiment was particularly rooted in the Serbian peasantry). Their tactics could only ever damage the Germans and Ustaša. They could not resurrect an unpopular dynasty that had abandoned the country, nor could they unite all the anti-German forces. When the Partisans started gaining ground against the Germans, the Četniks collaborated with the latter, which meant that they were considered to be traitors by the Partisans.

The Communist Partisan leader Josip Broz Tito saw the Četniks as the most formidable opposition that the Partisans faced because they had firm roots in popular ideology (unlike the occupying Germans, Italians or even the Ustaša). Pro-Russian tendencies among the Serb peasants, a residue from the First World War and the long traditions of Orthodox connections could be turned into pro-Soviet sentiments, which is what the Partisans achieved. By the autumn of 1943, the Partisans had decisively weakened the Četniks, which allowed them to concentrate on the fascists.[36] The collapse of Italy in the summer of 1943 had also sapped the strength of the

---

[34] Dulić, *Utopias of Nation*, p. 205.
[35] Šehić, Nusret *Četništvo u Bosni i Hercegovini (1918–1941). Politička uloga i oblici djelatnosti Četničkih udruženja* (Sarajevo: Akademija nauka i umjetnosti Bosne i Hercegovine, 1971).
[36] Hoare, Marko Attila *The Bosnian Muslims in the Second World War* (Oxford: Oxford University Press, 2006).

Četniks. The ability of the Partisans to unite all Yugoslavia not only gave them a military edge over the Ustaša and Četniks, but also meant that they were able to exploit their victory in a moral sense for many years, giving them greater political durability. In contemporary Republika Srpska, the Četnik movement has been restored to the heroic status that the Partisans stripped it of. In Banja Luka, Draža Mihailović is now regarded as a kind of martyr and his followers as honest patriots.

THE PARTISAN REVOLUTION

In April 1941, when Yugoslavia collapsed, it had been a monarchy for just over two decades. The Allies and in particular the British hoped that the young King Petar would be restored to the throne. The key to the political problems the region had experienced could only by overcome by a force that could mould the Orthodox, Catholics, Jews, Roma and Muslims into a single community. King Aleksandar, despite his intentions, had failed to create that community. His life was cut short by terrorism, which made the infant Yugoslav state even weaker. Bitterness from the First World War had festered and then proliferated though the Ustaša movement, which had committed genocide in Bosnia. The horrific experiences of the 1940s should have made the feat of unifying the faith communities almost insuperable. In this context, the achievement of Tito and the Communist Partisans is all the more unlikely. The achievement of the Communists was to weld religious tradition and its core values with a progressive ideology that looked to a better future of education, social levelling, graft, personal emancipation and legal equality. In the shorter term, personal heroism, a cult of the leader and a very primitive sort of patriotism that depicted Bosnia as a victim of foreign invasion, were of the utmost importance.

It was clear from earlier wars that there was no lack of personal bravery in the Balkans. Catholics, often led by priests, reconciled to death by the promise of eternity. In Orthodox theology, sins cannot be forgiven and remain like a stain on the soul of the sinner. The onus falls upon the individual soldier to be brave rather than risk staining his or her soul with cowardice. General Alfred Krauss commended Captain Emil Redl with his brave Bosnians (*mit seinem tapferen Bosniaken*) during the Isonzo campaign.[37] Muslim combatants, believing that their day of death has already been decided by God, had a reputation for acts of astonishing bravery. The execution of heroic resistance fighters like Croat Stjepan Filipović, the commander of a Partisan brigade and a pre-war Communist activist, allowed the Partisans to galvanize innate heroism that existed in the region. Filipović was photographed defiantly declaring '*Smrt fašizmu, svoboda narodu!*' ('death to fascism, freedom to the people') and gesturing with his arms flung out just prior to his execution in May 1942, which inspired a generation. As atheists, the Communists cared much less about religious divisions in Bosnia than all of the other political forces at the time, seeing them all as equally archaic and irrelevant in building the new Yugoslavia. The Partisans represented a leftist version of Yugoslavism forged through the experience of war and a shared culture and Bosnia was at the epicentre of this struggle to make a new world. In some respects they were able to pass on the values of the fighters of 'gallant little Serbia' during the 1914–1918 war to other Yugoslavs who had been made to feel like the defeated and less than heroic remnants of former regimes by the Karadjordjević monarchy. All the peoples of the region would join the Partisan ranks, although Serbs from the NDH were overrepresented.

The Partisan movement grew out of the pre-war Yugoslavian Communist Party, founded in Vukovar in 1920, which was affiliated with the Soviet-led Comintern. It was declared illegal in December 1920 after significant industrial unrest in Tuzla and operated underground thereafter. A breakaway group Crvena Pravda (Red Truth) adopted terrorist tactics and tried to kill Aleksandar Karadjordjević in 1921. Like the other Communist parties of Europe, the Yugoslavs suffered from Stalinist purges in the 1930s and its leader Milan Gorkić was shot by the Soviet secret police, the NKVD, in Moscow in 1937. Josip Broz Tito succeeded him as party leader. Gorkić had been born in Sarajevo in 1904 after his Czech parents settled there

---

[37] Krauss, Alfred *Das 'Wunder von Karfreit': im besonderen der Durchbruch bei Flitsch und die Bezwingung des Tagliamento* (Munich: J.F. Lehmann, 1926), p. 63.

as part of an internal migration in the Habsburg monarchy. His birth name was Josef Čižinský, but like many activists he adopted a *nom de guerre*. In the early 1920s, before he departed for the Soviet Union, he was active in working-class politics in Sarajevo. Also active in the working-class movement in Sarajevo and elsewhere in Yugoslavia was future prime minister Djuro Pucar, originally from Kesići. Pucar was vital in formulating the Partisan strategy of armed resistance to the Axis and spent much of the war in the Banja Luka region.

The Partisans quickly grew into a mass movement with only distant links to the old Leninist party. After defeat in Užice and betrayal by former comrades such as Živko Topalović, who had turned to the Četniks, Tito turned westwards towards Bosnia and Croatia where his primary task was to create a united opposition to fascism. From their stronghold in Bosnia, the Partisans were able to take Serbia, although they took Belgrade in alliance with the Soviet Red Army. They used their knowledge of the terrain to full advantage. They also exploited local autonomies. The Partisans were able to organize disaffected Muslims in the Cazin region of western Bosnia. In 1943, they managed to persuade the local warlord Husein 'Huska' Miljković to defect from the Ustaša to their ranks. He was killed just a few months later by pro-Ustaša elements.

When it became clear that the Ustaša were not able to contain the threat from left-wing guerrillas, seven military offensives were launched against them by the Wehrmacht beginning with the Battle of Kozara in early 1942. They came close to destroying the Yugoslavs guerrillas on several occasions and each time the Partisans honed their tactics. Isolated from their allies including the Soviets until 1943, they suffered attacks by bombing, tank columns and infantry by adversaries who were better armed and equipped. They stole weapons whenever possible and carried out basic acts of sabotage such as altering road signs and blowing up bridges. Nazi atrocities had made the war look like one of basic survival and drove non-Communists into their ranks. After 1943 and the Nazi defeat at Stalingrad, the Partisans still suffered several more attacks as the will to break their strength became even fiercer. Fascist Italy collapsed in 1943, which meant that the Third Reich controlled most of the region via the Ustaša and other quislings until early 1945.

The Battle of the Neretva River in early 1943 became known as the fourth offensive, the Battle of the Sutjeska from May to June 1943 was the fifth. The final Nazi raid on Drvar from April to May 1944, was their seventh offensive. The Partisan leader Josip Broz Tito and his dog Tigar survived the attack on Drvar, which had become his headquarters, by hiding in a cave from which he was rope-lifted out. The Germans attacked the front entrance of the cave with heavy machinegun fire in the action that they called *Rösselsprung* (a reference to the knight on the chess board). Aleksandar Ranković held off the attackers and probably saved Tito's life, which may be the reason why he survived a purge in the 1960s.

The Axis powers found it particularly hard to break the intelligence communications of the Partisans. Women and children could also cut through conventional military intelligence networks, evading Axis control. The Second World War caused many boundaries to collapse: political, social and geographical. Breaking down some of the Ottoman legacy of segregation for women, Partisans travelled with their female fighters and accepted anyone – including hodjas and Orthodox priests – who swore loyalty to their cause. Even the Allies, in awe of the bravery of the Yugoslavs, could not always come to terms with such avant-garde tactics such as using female combatants. Many Partisan women wore fatigues and took the same risks as men. Strict moral codes of sexual constraint were imposed on the fighters. Photographs of Stana Tomašević in her uniform were known to resistance fighters across Europe. After the war, she became a close ally of Tito and a diplomat. She eventually married a Norwegian who had first seen her on poster that had been airdropped into his occupied country to fortify local resolve. It is clear that the Partisans did lift the spirit of people across the world. Historian E.P. Thompson, who visited Bosnia in 1947, remembered five years earlier 'the first news which came through to us from Yugoslavia, of how the peasants had taken to their wooded mountains, fighting without boots or equipment, and with only the arms which they tore from the enemy's hand'.[38]

---

[38] Palmer, Bryan D. *E.P. Thompson: Objections and Oppositions* (London: Verso, 1994), p. 53.

As the Communist Partisans began to fight back against the Nazis and their allies, they won a number of key Bosnian towns and united the peoples of the region behind their leader Tito, the great-grandson of a Habsburg-era serf and former Comintern agent, who created a local version of the cult of the personality. Bosnia was the centre for much of the fighting in the war and became central to Partisan legitimating myths and symbols after 1945. Amnesties for former Četniks who often deserted en masse to the Partisans helped the movement to grow in eastern Bosnia. The Partisan casualty rate was terrible as they scrambled around the hills of Bosnia with little regard for their personal safety. Probably 300,000 were killed from less than a million fighters. Franjo Kluz and Rudi Čajavec were Partisan pilots from Bosnia who defected from the NDH and died in combat. Both took immense risks flying over Ustaša columns. The Yugoslav Air Force was founded on the basis of their flights, which were launched in from an airfield close to Prijedor.

The Partisans created a rich culture, with a new and radical style for a future multi-ethnic Bosnia. They organized football and other sporting events drawing on the proletarian tradition of fitness clubs before 1941. They adapted the Soviet Red Army song *По долинам и по взгорьям* (*Through Valleys and Hills*) into *Po šumama i gorama* (*Through Woods and Hills*), which was ideal for the Bosnian context. 'Through the woods and hills of our proud country march the companies of Partisans … We will die before we give up our lands!' The peasants were a crucial source of support for these guerrillas and very strict codes of conduct towards the local population were ruthlessly imposed. Miscreants could be summarily executed. The political character of the second Yugoslavia was created at the Anti-Fascist Council for the National Liberation of Yugoslavia (*Antifašističko Vijeće Narodnog Oslobodjenja Jugoslavije*, AVNOJ), where the left-wing intentions of Tito's followers were spelled out. First assembled in November 1942, the council met in a small area of liberated territory around Bihać, which was subsequently lost. The second session, which met in Jajce the following November, was the political foundation of the new regime. Strict Leninist discipline was underscored by the secret police department OZNA ('Department for the Protection of the People') founded in May 1944 under the Serb Alekandar Ranković. Ordinary Bosnians realized that their private life had disappeared when they used the pun 'OZNA sve dozna' ('OZNA knows everything').

On the principle that the pen is mightier that the sword, propaganda was absolutely central to the Partisan strategy. Typewriters were always carried alongside guns. During their brief occupation of Užice, they had started to print *Borba* (*The Struggle*) and to graphically record the atrocities committed by their enemies. Their occupation there had been an interesting experiment in socialism and appropriation of the means of production, but they lost control and had to regroup in Foča. As a group they made many errors that lost them many combatants. The front during the war changed on many occasions. In her memoirs *Sjećanja iz Bosne*, Dr Nadžija Gajić-Sikirić described the impact of the rapid loss of ground by the Partisans. She was living in Oglavak where the local population supplied the Communists with milk and bread. The Germans attacked the town and a young barber from Prijedor who she had been speaking to just an hour before about his plans for marriage was dead in the street after being hit by mortar.[39] After Užice, the Partisan social experiment would be more limited in scope and they would concentrate on trying to win the struggle in Bosnia before returning to Serbia. However, in most conventional combat, the lines of territorial control tend to be contiguous. The Soviet Red Army pushed through Eastern Europe at the same time, taking cities from the Nazis in an almost linear assault. The Partisans took areas and lost them again, which means that Ustaša occupation was full of strategic and ideological holes.

The British Special Operations Executive (SOE) operated behind Axis lines from 1940 onwards. Much of their intelligence-gathering for the Balkans took place in Cairo and they also had agents in Istanbul. They sent a number of agents to Yugoslavia including Duane 'Bill' Hudson, a former mining engineer who had worked in Yugoslavia before the war and knew the language. Hudson had a deep empathy for the people of the region and witnessed the collaboration by the Četniks with the Italians as well as German reprisal atrocities. He sent radio messages to the British authorities and was shocked that the munitions dropped to the Četniks were

---

[39] Gajić-Sikirić, *Sjećanja iz Bosne*, p. 36.

used against the Partisans rather than the Germans. A second agent, Terence Atherton, who also knew Yugoslavia well having worked there before the war, was murdered in 1942 by a bandit. By the time the British gave their unequivocal support to the Partisans, the latter had already sustained enormous casualties and grown quite wary of outsiders including the Soviets.

SOE agents were important in moulding the British prime minister Winston Churchill's opinion of the Partisans and in shaping historiographical interpretations of the war in its aftermath. Bill Deakin, who had worked for Churchill as a research assistant before the war, was with Tito when he was almost killed by German aerial bombing. His memoir *Embattled Mountain*, widely regarded as a classic of war literature, vividly described the German fifth offensive at the Battle of Sutjestka in 1943. He watched Tito's Alsatian dog Luks shield its master and then die of its wounds. SOE agent Bill Stuart was also killed. Deakin was impressed by Partisan fortitude and humanity, particularly the honour with which they treated their wounded, who they would carry despite the military risk to the active combatants. Deakin worked closely with fellow SOE agent Fitzroy Maclean, a Scottish Unionist MP. Maclean was particularly impressed by Tito's leadership qualities and conveyed his support for the Partisans to Churchill. Having been in the Soviet Union in the 1930s, Maclean thought of Communists as doctrinaire and lacking in intellectual autonomy. Tito's confidence and resolve impressed him and he thought the Yugoslavs were very different from the Russians. It is likely that the Partisans exaggerated their capacity to fight and savagely attacked the Četniks for their collaboration with the Axis occupiers, and it was this view that was conveyed to Churchill via Maclean. Churchill decided to back Tito regardless of his politics. Allied support followed with sustained air drops of supplies from planes, which the Partisans used to attack the Serb Royalists as much as the Axis occupiers. Maclean also vividly captured his experiences in the memoir *Eastern Approaches*. He was to become a close friend of Tito's and later spent a great deal of time in Korčula, where he bought a property. Deakin and Maclean made up part of the official British delegation to Tito's burial in 1980, one of the largest state funerals in recorded history. Basil Davidson, later famous for his historical

Fig. 10 Statue of Josip Broz Tito in Sarajevo (by
Richard Mills)

research on Africa, was parachuted behind the Partisan lines in
1943, received the honour of Yugoslavia's *medalja zasluge za
narod*, awarded to those who had distinguished themselves in the
struggle to establish the new state.

Several things aided the Partisans. First and most fundamental was the leadership of Josip Broz Tito, apparently fearless and paternal. He managed to inspire his followers in an extraordinary manner and his charisma cast a spell over many Yugoslavs until his death in 1980. The Partisans relied on unswerving loyalty to a leader whose bravery was unquestionable. Communist propaganda emphasized the fact that Tito was in the heat of the conflict and the young king was far away in London, although from September 1944 Petar had urged the Yugoslav people to support the Partisans in radio broadcasts. Tito's own commitment to rebuilding Yugoslavia predated the war and he was heavily influenced by his Serbian Jewish prison cellmate, Moša Pijade. Moving headquarters helped people of all religions to fraternize and to begin to mould their distinctive culture. Many of their ranks were Serbs who had had other forms of security removed as their villages had been destroyed and their extended families murdered. The Second World War was a demographic tragedy for the Serbs and their new loyalty to the Communists was similar to the allegiance that orphans from the Russian Civil War had given to the Bolsheviks. When we look at the long term in Bosnian history, we can see the collapse of the League of Communists in Bosnia and Yugoslavia in 1990 not so much as an ideological crisis for the Serbs, but more as an emotional catastrophe. In the post-war era in Bosnia, church attendance from the Orthodox was much lower than among Catholics. There was also a renewal of Muslim piety in the 1970s. It was only as the fabric of Tito's state began to disintegrate that Serbs turned to the Orthodox Church in great numbers.

The Partisans promised a new order. Their use of female fighters intimated at equal participation after the end of the war. In Hercegovina, even among non-Muslims, women did not traditionally eat with the men in the villages and both men and women would refuse food until asked for a third time.[40] In this context, we can see just how radical the Partisans were. Their euphoria and comradely ties meant their morale remained high despite horrific losses. Most of all, it was the idea of a shared future – brotherhood and unity (*bratstvo i jedinstvo*) that was the formula that promised

---

[40] Dedijer, *The Beloved Land*, p. 212.

to remake Bosnia and Hercegovina for all its inhabitants. Special Operations Executive agent Basil Davidson described the mood among the Partisan Third Corps in Tuzla in September 1943: 'They had public discussions on the future of the Jugoslav State. Through their wire-less transmitter (situated in Russia, and in daily morse contact with Tito's H.Q.) they reached out to the rest of the country and to the Allies. They spoke of that period afterwards almost in idyllic terms; it was their first realization of what they might achieve in the future – and the fruits of liberty which cost as much as it cost them are very sweet.'[41]

[41] Davidson, Basil *Partisan Picture* (London: Bedford Books, 1946), p. 98.

5

Bosnia and the Communist experiment

ECONOMY AND SOCIETY

At the end of the war, Tito and his comrades at the top of the party took the historic decision, codified in the 1946 Constitution, to create a Bosnian republic drawing on an earlier move by the Partisans in 1943. Paradoxically, a system that was designed to contain nationalism actually ossified pre-existing categories. The Communist Partisans, like other Marxists, were highly influenced by Stalin's work on the national question and the Yugoslavia that they constructed as a federation of republics in 1946 was modelled closely on the Soviet Union. The future status of Bosnia-Hercegovina was debated until the Communists rejected the idea of it as an autonomous region and decided instead that it should be a separate republic with three constituent nationalities, all of whom were equal. Although the new Yugoslavian state was 'largely manned by the Serbs of Bosnia and Croatia',[1] as Stevan K. Pavlowitch has argued, the new Republican divisions were specifically designed to keep Serbia smaller and weaker in a confederation in which they represented 42 per cent of the overall population. Perhaps as significantly, the Communists created Slovenian and Macedonian republics for the first time and restored the old polity of Montenegro, which had in effect disappeared in 1918. The first prime minister

---

[1] Pavlovitch, Stevan K. 'Serbia and Yugoslavia: The Relationship', *Southeast European and Black Sea Studies* 4(1), 2004, p. 102.

of the new Bosnian Republic was Rodoljub Čolaković, a long-term Communist who had been involved in Crvena Pravda in the 1920s. Originally from Bijeljina, in 1937 he had travelled to Spain to fight for the Republicans. Between 1946 and 1955 he published five volumes of an influential 'memoir of the liberation war', *Zapisi iz oslobodilačkog rata*. He had honed his writing skills in the Comintern before the war and writing for *Borba*. Čolaković remained prime minister of the republic until 1948, when he was replaced by another prominent Partisan Djuro Pucar, nicknamed 'Stari' ('the old guy') even though he was only in his early forties during the war. Originally from the Bosansko Grahovo region, he was also an experienced activist before the war broke out and had spent time in prison. Until 1990, Bosnian politics was almost entirely dominated by former Partisans, which meant that the leadership became progressively older as the decades went on. But in 1945, they represented a new world and were minded to change the republic.

The new authorities did not try to piece together the new Bosnia with Sandžak or old Hercegovina, which had been ceded to Serbia and Montenegro in 1912 and 1878, respectively. This decision left thousands of Slavonic Muslims, who would later identify as 'Bosniaks', within neighbouring republics (or what Serb nationalists would dub a 'green highway' that led all the way to Albania). Sandžak had been a troublesome theatre of war for the Partisans and local Muslims had often supported the Third Reich following the collapse of Italy in 1943. The SS organized a Muslim militia in Sandžak and were led by a local *Volksdeutsche*, Karl von Krempler. Until their defeat, local Muslim militias led by Sulejman Hafiz Pačariz and Husein Rovčanin fought in German uniforms and terrorized the local population with violence and extortion. The decision to exclude Sandžak from Bosnia and keep it inside Serbia and the newly created republic of Montenegro meant that local Muslims looked to Sarajevo or to Belgrade or even further afield to Turkey for authority.[2] The new regime effectively redrew

---

[2] This search for authority and identity is beautifully conveyed in Hadžišehović, Munevera *A Muslim Woman in Tito's Yugoslavia*, translated by Thomas J. Butler and Saba Risaluddin (College Station, TX: A&M University Press, 2003).

the internal boundaries of the new Bosnian republic on the basis of the territory the Habsburgs had annexed in 1908. These were the borders that were considered immutable by the Bosnian government in 1992. But despite their adamant stance, they were of relatively recent vintage, at least in the East. By recreating these borders, the Communists wanted to avoid further territorial disputes and the cruelties that had accompanied both World Wars. They also wanted to contain any potential recrudescence of Croat or Serb nationalism and the Bosnian republic was considered to be a huge wedge between neighbouring republics. The Communists also decided that the port of Neum and about 20 kilometres of the Dalmatian coast, which had an overwhelmingly Catholic population, should be retained. Although its inclusion bifurcated the new Croatian republic, it did give Bosnia access to the sea.

Although just a few of the leading Partisans were from Bosnia, they all knew the area intimately from the long years of scrambling an existence on rocky pathways, living like mountain goats, sleeping rough in cold weather and dealing with the local people. Many had lost family and friends in its tragic hills and valleys, which were etched onto their collective consciousness.[3] The historian Vladimir Dedijer, who later played a key role in creating the cult of Tito's personality, remembered being 'pulled toward the dark forest' by his dead friend Lola Ribar and wife Olga, who lost an arm before finally succumbing to her wounds, awaking from terrifying dreams in tears.[4] The Sutjeska River in which the Partisans had washed their blood-soaked bandages, and the caves at Drvar, where Tito had narrowly escaped being captured, remained vital Communist sites of memory. Although the Ustaša extermination camps at Jasenovac and Stara Gradiška were inside the border of the Croatian republic, the latter was just within sight of the small town of Bosanska Gradiška on the other north bank of the Sava River. Tito and his followers could never quite escape from the bitter legacy of the war years, in which Sarajevo lamp-posts had been

---

[3] Bato Tomašević went to look for the remains of his brother Duško and eventually identified his skull by the filling in one of the molars. Tomašević, Bato *Life and Death in the Balkans: A Family Saga in a Century of Conflict* (London: Hurst, 2008), pp. 352–353.

[4] Dedijer, *The Beloved Land*, p. 338.

Map 7. Bosnia during the Communist era in Yugoslavia

used to hang Partisans[5] and icicles of blood had hung from the bridge at Foča: As Adil Zulfikarpašić put it: 'Under this terrible red [i.e., with frozen blood] canopy, the Drina rocked the dead bodies as if they were simply asleep.'[6] Instead, the Communists attempted to control the present and shape the memory of the past.

In many respects the Communists had faced an almost insuperable task in overcoming the mutual radicalization and distrust between the peoples that belonged in the new state. The wartime

[5] Gajić-Sikirić, *Sjećanja iz Bosne*, p. 33.
[6] 'Po tim strašnim crvenim baldahinom Drina je ljuljuškala mrtva tijela kao da ih uspavljuje', in Zulfikarpašić, Adil *Bošnjak* (with Milovan Djilas and Nadežda Gaće) (Zurich: Bošnjački institute, 1994), p. 75.

fighting had left hecatombs of dead and the unpalatable truth was that most of the dead had been killed by South Slavs and not the invading armies. Moreover their point of departure in their attempt to create 'brotherhood and unity' (*bratstvo i jedinstvo*) was not an easy one. Popular culture tended to reinforced notions about the absence of trust and the impossibility of friendship between peoples: 'You cannot use a pumpkin as a pot, you cannot have a Catholic as a friend' or 'you cannot measure the sea, you cannot trust a Turk'. Yugoslavs continued a more gentle tradition of alterity by telling Mujo, Suljo (or sometimes Haso) and Fata jokes about Bosnians. Most of the humour revolves around the gullibility or naiveté of the Bosnians.

After the war, people mixed together in all public places. For most of its existence, the Titoist regime in Bosnia targeted the young through education, leaving the elderly in villages to tend mosques and observe old customs. The party made it clear that it deemed the traditional dress of Bosnian women (Christian and Muslim alike), such as *dimije* (baggy trousers) and headscarves, a sign of oppression. Some Muslim heritage was destroyed under the guise of modernization and the very religious faced difficulties finding top jobs. Muslim cultural characteristics (such as modes of dress and speech) were branded old-fashioned and even rustic. Schools in Communist Bosnia were, however, integrated from the outset, teachers often taking on an extremely important role in shaping the new generation. The integration also helped to create real friendships at an early age, something that many Bosnians remember with great pride and nostalgia about this era. In 1949, the University of Sarajevo was founded, drawing on a rich tradition of medressas in the city as well as building upon several smaller colleges that existed before the war. As an institution it was totally integrated at its inception and students from all religious backgrounds mixed together on the campus. Both Alija Izetbegović and Vojislav Šešelj were alumni of the university. In the 1970s, universities were also established in Tuzla, Banja Luka and Mostar.

Whether the people living in the Bosnian republic ever came to see themselves as primarily Bosnian is debatable, although other Yugoslavs tended to regard them as 'Bosanci' regardless of religious background. Bosnians celebrated all the religious festivals

Fig. 11 Počitelj (by Matt Willer)

in their republic, rewarding themselves with an excessive number of medieval feast days. Muslims would visit their Serb friends at Orthodox Easter to give their respects, having been to the houses of Catholic friends earlier in the holy calendar. To some extent, this was a very superficial set of rituals. In Sarajevo in the 1980s, anthropologist Cornelia Sorabji observed that there was quite a profound level of ignorance among Muslims of one Sarajevo suburb about both Orthodox and Catholic culture. Adil Zulfikarpašić suggested that much vaunted Bosnian values of tolerance and respect were accompanied by a real lack of interest in the habits of other religions. Of course, the existence of difference did not necessarily equate to hostility, but did become a clear political problem once Communist hegemony had gone in 1990. To try to overcome mistrust, the Partisans had invented a myth, namely that the problems of the region were due to foreign invasion and threat and that the Yugoslav peoples had deep fraternal bonds that transcended their religious differences. At the end of 1942, Tito had founded a Young Pioneers movement, which lasted until the demise of his state. Its members, inducted at the age of seven and given little red and white uniforms, promised not only to spread brotherhood and unity but to cherish (*cijeniti*) all the Yugoslav peoples. Yugoslavs remained forcibly united by the policy of 'brotherhood and unity' until the 1980s.

Whereas the Habsburgs had ruled without the widespread consent of the Orthodox community, the new republics of Bosnia and Croatia were heavily dependent on the institutional loyalty and participation of former Serb Partisans of these regions and their kin. Whereas Serbs wore the *titova kapa* with its little red star, Muslims tended to prefer to wear black berets so it was possible to distinguish between them at a glance. Knowing that they had stronger support in the west of the country than in Serbia proper, where the revolutionary tide had been far weaker, the Communist formula of governance by loyal Serbs at least temporarily contained the further spread of Četnik loyalties. Nevertheless, these nationalist sentiments seem to have remained strong in the private sphere of the extended family, as did the memory of wartime atrocities. Scholars of nationalism have noted the importance of the dichotomy between these two spheres. Nationalists of the 1990s began to say things in public that they had previously reserved for their trust group.

After the war, the Communists dealt with their enemies with characteristic brutality. Rather than surrender to the Partisans, Croatian soldiers had killed themselves with their own grenades at Bihać. In September 1945, the last Ustaša chief of police, Erih Lisak, had returned to Yugoslavia to organize remnants of the fascists hiding in forests that were commonly known as *Križari* (Crusaders).[7] He was captured and hanged by the Communists after a mass trial in Zagreb in 1946. The remaining Križari tended to be isolated and poorly armed and most were captured in 1947 by Yugoslavian Security Services (UDBA) in a security operation known as *Gvardijan*. One leading crusader, Ljubo Miloš, was captured and executed in 1948. During his trial, Miloš – who came from Bosanski Šamac and had joined the Ustaša in 1941 at the behest of his cousin Vjekoslav Luburić – confessed in graphic detail to the crimes he had committed while dressed in a medical white coat in the Ustaša death camp. In 1950 there was what can only be described as a peasant uprising (*Cazinska buna*) against the regime in Cazin.[8] Local farmers had

[7] Tomasevich, Jozo *War and Revolution in Yugoslavia* (Stanford: Stanford University Press, 1975), p. 560.
[8] Kržisnik-Bukić, Vera *Cazinska buna 1950* (Sarajevo: Svjetlost, 1991).

opposed the collectivization of agriculture and were angry about the quotas that they had been set for delivering crops to the state. In neighbouring Kordun peasants also expressed similar hostility to the new economic regime. The discontent involved Serbs and Muslims working together and eventually calling for the restoration of the Karadjordjević monarchy, which sealed their fate in the eyes of Tito. Rebel families were relocated after the authorities managed to break the resistance and 17 peasants were shot by firing squad, including the leaders Serb Milan Božić and Muslim Ale Čović.

Ethnic Germans and Italians, from old Habsburg- or Venetian-era communities were expelled en masse and have never returned in any great numbers. There were a number of villages in the Bosanska Krajina region around Kozara that had been populated by ethnic Germans for decades, including the settlement of Windhorst (*Nova Topola*), which had been founded in 1879. The male population had been drafted into the Wehrmacht and many had left in 1942 for the Reich. The homes of expelled people were given to loyal Partisans as a reward for their wartime service, which bound them even further to the state. The Bosnian Serb Vaso Čubrilović was instrumental in the formation of this policy of extreme intolerance towards minority national groups. The weeks after the war were particularly fierce in terms of retribution. Enemy soldiers were executed, as were the soldiers of the Croatian Homeguards that were taken prisoner by the Communists. Johann Fortner, the Wehrmacht Senior Division commander who had failed to destroy the *Sarajevo Hagaddah* in the early 1940s, was extradited after the war from Germany and shot in Belgrade in 1947. The Quisling Serb Milan Nedić had also been extradited in 1946 and committed suicide before he could come to trial. General Franz Böhme, who ordered the mass executions of Serbs in 1941, committed suicide before he could be extradited to Yugoslavia. Draža Mihailović was shot after a show trial in 1946, but the memory of his Bosnian stronghold at Ravna Gora survived in the private sphere and many Serbs continued to revere him. Jezdimir Dangić, a youthful member of Mlada Bosna and the scourge of the Drina valley in the early 1940s, was handed over to Tito by the Soviets and hanged in 1947. The ideologue Stevan Moljević, who had guided much of the movement's actions until the January 1944 Sveti Sava meeting in Ba, was incarcerated in Serbia and passed away in 1959. He believed that much of Bosnia was simply Serbian territory, that the Muslims belonged elsewhere and it was their fundamental political duty to unite the Serbs to the West of the Drina with their 'compatriots'.

Like the Četniks and German military, Croat nationalists who had failed to escape in the last days before the Axis collapse were punished and systematically anathematized at every opportunity. Alojzije Stepinac, archbishop of Zagreb was put on show trial to highlight the collaboration between the Roman Church and the Croatian fascist Ustaša. Miroslav Filipović, a Franciscan from Banja Luka and a notorious Jasenovac sadist, was tried and executed in his vestments in 1946. When the Ustaša regime had crumbled in 1945, many of its supporters as well as those who feared the Partisans fled north from the capital Zagreb in columns desperate to get to British-controlled Carinthia, where they imagined their fate would be better. Many Ustašas had disguised themselves as Catholic priests. The Franciscan historian Dominik Mandić, from the Široki Brijeg region of Hercegovina, who was subsequently based in Rome, appears to have acted as an intermediary. Some seem to have skulked under the radar of the Allies in the Church of San Girolamo in Rome, eventually making it to Spain or Argentina.

In the last months of the war, Ante Pavelić had attempted to renegotiate the borders of the Independent State of Croatia with Mihailović effectively changing his 'everything up to the Drina' policy. However, rather than just representing a policy of despair in the moment of likely defeat, it is likely that Pavelić had vacillated about the Bosnian Drina border for some time. Although he was a follower of Ante Starčević in so far as his embrace of the Muslim Bosnians was sincere, he was less sure about where Croatia's boundary with Serbia should lie. If there are signs of Pavelić's hesitation in 1945, then there were clear signs that he had backed down entirely from the notion of Croatia's Drina border in exile by about 1954, which caused a rift between himself and Vjekoslav Luburić, perhaps the most notorious of the Ustaša sadists. Pavelić believed that an enlarged Croatia (which would include some of Bosnia) would be recreated as soon as the Soviet Union collapsed, which did of course eventually take place, but only well after his own death. Pavelić arrived in Madrid in 1957, after surviving an attempted assassination by the Communist secret police (UDBA) in Argentina. Spain was a friendly destination for Croatian extremists after 1945 and a number of other fascists lived there at the time including a small colony of Germans in Tarragona. Franco's Spain had been the only country outside the Axis to recognize the Independent State of Croatia in 1941.[9] Pavelić died from the complications from the bullet in his spine in late 1959. The Spanish press quietly reported his death as if he had been a respectable leader rather than a *génocidaire*. Luburić, who was barred from even attending his funeral, outlived the *poglavnik* by ten years, eventually being assassinated in 1969 in Carcagente (Carcaixent) near Valencia.

While in the Costa Brava, rather than lapsing into safe obscurity with his wife and young family, Luburić maintained networks of political contacts, including Franco's minister Agustín Muñoz Grandes who had led the Spanish volunteer *División Azul* on the Eastern Front in the Second World War. Like the Spanish, thousands of Croats and Bosnians had fought in Operation Barbarossa and at Stalingrad. He also met with a number of prominent Bosnian Muslims including Nahid Kulenović, son of the vice-president of the Independent State of Croatia, Džafer-beg Kulenović. Luburić and his followers were never able to abandon the idea of a Croatia that included the Muslims within its ranks. *Drina* was to become the title of his journal published in Madrid, in which Luburić wrote under the grand, but by now useless title of 'General Drinjanin'. This title in itself was a direct challenge to Pavelić's authority among the exiles. The journal published poems and other literary references to the lost border in Bosnia. Luburić was assassinated in 1969 during a particularly ruthless spate of killings by Tito's secret police, the UDBA. He was stabbed and the body concealed and only discovered some time later by his neighbours, by which time he had bled to death and his murderer had fled the country, most probably on public transport. His killer, Ilija Stanić, still lives in Sarajevo, but now claims that he represented a pro-Pavelić faction rather than the Yugoslav secret police. Luburić's funeral in Madrid was a lavish paramilitary affair with the dark sunglasses and gun salutes

[9] Hoare, *The Bosnian Muslims*, p. 19.

that later became popular with the Irish Republican Army. Nahid Kulenović was also assassinated by UDBA in Munich in 1969. The Croatian nationalist terrorism of the 1970s and 1980s largely stemmed from General Drinjanin's influence. In 1971, the Yugoslav ambassador in Stockholm, Vladimir Rolović, was shot by followers of Luburić including Miro Barešić.[10] Barešić was himself killed during the Croatian War in 1991. More daringly, in 1972 the so-called Bugojno group (*Bugojanska skupina*) tried to start an armed uprising codenamed Phoenix (*Feniks*) against the Communist regime, which was quickly extinguished. Four of the group were put on trial in Sarajevo and all but one was executed for treason. This gave Tito's regime a chance not only to discredit Croatian nationalism but to show that it had extinguished the spirit of 1971 at home if not abroad. The operation to quell *Feniks* was criticized by veteran Partisan and 'Španec' Čedo Kapor, who was expelled from the party for his forthright comments. 'It hurts me to see that the whole republic was mobilised to catch twenty people. As if they had ten planes and twenty aeroplanes each ... I think we could have done it with less parade and with a lesser cost.'[11] Most Croatian nationalists in exile never lost hope that an independent Croatia, which included Bosnia, would be reborn. They would meet in Canada, Australia or Argentina under portraits of Pavelić and sing the Second World War version of the national anthem *Lijepa naša domovino*, namely, '*Savo, Dravo, Drino teči...*' ('flow Sava, Drava and Drina') rather than '*Teči Dravo, Savo teči*' ('flow Drava and Sava').[12] By doing this they perpetuated the link between Croatian national identity, the Bosnian Muslims and the NDH. In exile, they even issued colourful, but essentially useless stamps of their 'homeland'. Most of these had folkloric themes, depicting places in Bosnia or even the extended map of the NDH unchanged or even extended to Sandžak. One of the Bugojno group's members, the paramilitary Blaž Kraljević, originally from Lisice, was assassinated in 1992 in the early months of the Bosnian War, most probably by a rival Croat paramilitary group.

[10] Hockenos, Paul *Homeland Calling: Exile Patriotism and the Balkan Wars* (Ithaca: Cornell University Press, 2003), p. 62.

[11] Andjelić, Neven *Bosnia-Herzegovina: The End of a Legacy* (London: Routledge 2003), p. 45.

[12] Krizman, Bogdan *Pavelić u Bjekstvu* (Zagreb: Globus, 1986), p. 363.

This may have happened because they wanted to break the long-standing relationship that the Ustaša had forged with the Muslims. Another, Ludvig Pavlović, was also killed in the Croatian War in 1991 after having spent many years in prison for his part in *Feniks*.

The Communists faced both profound internal and external challenges. If the Croatian fascists had faltered over where the precise borders should lie, then Bosnia also represented something of a theoretical challenge to the Leninism of Tito and his closest advisors, especially the homegrown expert of the 'national question', the Slovene teacher Edvard Kardelj. As a result of the strong Austro-Marxist heritage at the top of the party, they wanted to give each Yugoslav 'nation' a homeland. However, they were initially unsure as how to define the Muslims. In part this came from their general sense that Islam was the vestige of an Ottoman colonial legacy, that religious practice was old-fashioned and would wither with time and that the Muslims were South Slavs who had simply 'turned Turk'(*poturčiti se*) and could therefore turn back. Muslim Partisans often chose to take on Serb *noms de guerres*, which they then quickly abandoned in 1945. After the war, the Mladi Muslimani ('Young Muslims') movement was suppressed by the regime in the form of a show trial in Sarajevo in August 1949. Several were executed and the young Alija Izetbegović, who had served in the SS-Handschar Division, spent three years in prison. Muslim material culture was often levelled under the guise of modernization. Munevera Hadžišehović recalled that in Sandžak after the war in her hometown of Prijepolje '[t]hree Muslim graveyards, a *türbe* [tomb] and a mosque in the town were destroyed so that new buildings could be constructed'.[13] By the late 1960s the regime had become more decentralized. Muslim nationality was discussed at AVNOJ, but not introduced until 1971 with the census category 'Muslim in the ethnic sense', which became the building block for the more distinct 'Bosniak' identity that was forged in the 1990s. By this time, Bosnians seem to have internalized the notion of their very special interethnic harmony, although there are some signs of a new individualization by then, such as the building of mosques and churches. In 1971 in Croatia, most of the Central Committee

[13] Hadžišehović, *A Muslim Woman in Tito's Yugoslavia*, p. 112.

of the party were purged. Nevertheless the Communist regime felt the need to check Muslim 'autonomist' trends in the League of Communists as it had also dealt with what it saw as nationalism in other republics. In Bosnia in 1972, leading Muslim former Partisans Avdo Humo from Mostar and Osman Karabegović from Banja Luka were expelled from the party for their deviation from the party line, but quickly readmitted in the peculiarly Leninist tradition of self-purging and self-criticism.

Communist victory in 1945 brought with it the challenge of reconstructing the economy of a country, which had been totally devastated by war. Much of the infrastructure had been damaged, many lives lost and blighted farms were left without crops and animals. Bridges, roads and railway lines had been destroyed and more than one million people killed. Young people worked in brigades to reconstruct the country, often during the school or college vacations. In 1947, British historians Edward and Dorothy Thompson, future Labour politician John Stonehouse and cartoonist Gerald Scarfe, all drawn to Tito's revolution, worked on the Sarajevo Samac railway in a youth battalion. In 1941 there had been 150,000 sheep in Bosnia and by 1945 this number had dwindled to only a few thousand.[14] Factories, many of which dated from the Habsburg era and had been managed by Germans, were left without equipment and staff. Some rural areas were badly depopulated, including many Orthodox villages in Hercegovina. The survivors were frequently traumatized by the violence they had witnessed and exhausted by overwhelming personal loss. In his acceptance speech for the Nobel Prize in 1961, Ivo Andrić described Yugoslavia as 'a country which, at break-neck speed and at the cost of great sacrifices and prodigious efforts, is trying in all fields, including the field of culture, to make up for those things of which it has been deprived by a singularly turbulent and hostile past'.[15]

Nowhere else in Yugoslavia did the Communist experiment in 'brotherhood and unity' reach as deeply as it did in Bosnia. Bosnians

[14] Philips Price, Morgan. *Through the Iron Curtain: A Record of a Journey through the Balkans in 1946*, (London: Sampson Low, 1949), p. 63.

[15] Nobel Prize Library: S.Y. Agnon, Ivo Andric (New York: Alexis Gregory/ Helvetica Press, 1971), p. 121.

invested more in Yugoslavia in an emotional sense than almost any other republic and thus had more to lose. Former Partisans Džemal Bijedić, Branko Mikulić and Raif Dizdarević rose up the ranks of the Bosnian party to take part in national leadership. The last prime minister of federal Yugoslavia, Ante Marković, was born in small town of Konjic in Hercegovina. Political coercion went hand in hand with genuine cultural and economic change. Exogamous marriages, especially in Sarajevo, were a special feature of this era and friendships based on intimacy and not just respect broke down the old barriers. Key to the regime's policy of brotherhood and unity were the education, industrial, leisure, security, military and medical sectors. It was in factories, hospitals, schools, army barracks and football pitches that loyal citizens and Tito devotees were moulded. The Yugoslav People's Army (JNA) became the largest *per capita* army in Cold War Europe. With its mineral wealth and central location, Bosnia became the centre of Yugoslavia's armament industry. After the party, it was the only national institution of any size or political importance. Yugoslav army conscripts were sent far away to other republics to build up their sense of loyalty to the state as a whole, all schoolchildren learnt the principles of self-defence from an early age. Many football teams were reconstructed or merged with pre-war teams and had players from all religious backgrounds. Asim 'Hase' Ferhatović won widespread support as a striker for FK Sarajevo, a club that had been founded in 1946. School children were taken to all the historic sites, including the waterfall at Jajce and bridge at Mostar to increase their local patriotism. Tito took every opportunity to remind Yugoslavians to 'guard brotherhood and unity' with all their strength.

In 1964, the Belgrade-based production company Avala stirred up controversy with a film made to commemorate Serbia's victory in the first weeks of the First World War against the Habsburg monarchy. In the closing lines of the film, the celebrated actor Ljuba Tadić uttered an obscenity that is frequently used in Bosnian and Serbian languages, but had not been heard on film before. In some respects *Marš na Drinu* (*March on the Drina*) conformed to the style of Communist-era war films, of which there were many. It covered the period between the mobilization in late July 1914 to the first battle of the war on the Bosnian Frontier at Mount

Cer. Stanislav Binički's 1915 march that opened the film was composed to celebrate the Austrian rout at the Battle of Cer the previous year. The final stanza reminds Serbs of their sacrifice in that war: '*Krv je tekla, krv se lila, Drinom zbog slobode*' ('Blood ran, blood streamed beside the Drina, for freedom'). Much of the film is framed as a discussion about how the Central European adversary would attack Serbia, with a reflection on the nature of the terrain and the rivers. This reinforced the idea that the Drina was a symbolic boundary between Serbia and Bosnia, although it clearly was not an ethnic border per se. Major Kursula, played by Tadić, memorably explains to a blue-uniformed Czech prisoner of war who has helped them that 'it could not be that Serbia would be invaded just like that' ('*Ne može u Srbiju tek tako da se upadne*'). In the 1960s, such words could have been interpreted as inflammatory and nationalist. Viewers in 1964 would probably have thought primarily of the recent invasion of the Third Reich and the epic struggle to oppose an army of superior manpower. However, by evoking the First World War, the question that the Communists had desperately dodged in 1945 was implicitly addressed, namely that Yugoslavs had fought for the enemy and against their 'brothers'. The 'noble lie' was challenged by the reality. The atrocities of the Habsburg army in the villages of the region are hinted at, some of which were carried out by other South Slavs. Serb suffering during the First World War was also depicted in the *Vreme smrti* (*Time of Death*) published by Dobrica Ćosić in 1972, which interspersed the actions of fictional characters with the real events. It became a popular work of fiction, helping to perpetuate very negative opinions and memories.

Bosnia was perhaps the most conformist of all the Communist Yugoslav republics, but not without subtle forms of protest. The writer Meša Selimović was born in Tuzla and studied in Belgrade in the 1930s where he increasingly came to identify with a Serbian literary tradition. His most well-known book, published in the Bosnian capital in 1966 was set in Ottoman Sarajevo in the eighteenth century and entitled *Derviš i smrt* (*The Dervish and Death*). The novel is an experiment in existential philosophy; each chapter begins a quotation from the Koran. Selimović had been a Partisan in the Tuzla region during the Second World War and the heroic actions of his comrades were described by Basil Davidson. After his brother was accused of theft, he was summarily executed by the Partisans despite Meša's passionate intervention. The main narrator of the novel, Ahmed Nurudin, also failed to save his brother's life. It was made into a film in 1974 and is still regarded as one of the greatest Bosnian novels. As a novel about an arbitrary and cruel system of justice, it could be also read as a commentary on Tito's Yugoslavia.

Bosnia has a long tradition of mining and has high natural reserves of lignite and bauxite as well as lead and zinc composites.[16] Silver ore mining in Srebrenica was recorded in antiquity and during the Habsburg era, the town became a centre for salt mining. In the Middle Ages, metal work from hammered silver was prized in the Adriatic region and known as '*al modo de bossina*'.[17] Salt mining in Tuzla also has a long history. The name of the town is derived from the Turkish word for salt and it was known by the Bosnian name for salt (*Soli*) in the Middle Ages. The iron ore mine of Ljubija near Prijedor opened in 1916 and still operates. In 1920, there had been a strike by miners (*Husinska buna*) fuelled by conditions close to slavery in the mines, which the Communists were heavily involved in. One of the leaders, Jure Kerošević, was hanged after a trial in Tuzla. During the war the Partisans sang *Konjuh Planinom* (*The Mountain of Konjuh*), which remembered their dead comrades of 1920. Communists revived the memory of their struggle after 1945, designating 21 December as 'Miners' Day'. Like many cultural forms of the left in this era, it was based on the notion of the sacrifice of an earlier generation of proletarians, but mining remained dangerous. In June 1965, 122 miners were killed after a methane gas explosion in Kakanj and in 1990, 180 miners perished in the same way in Dobrnja-Jug. Bosnia was hit by natural disaster in 1969, when an earthquake destroyed a church in Banja Luka.

There is no doubt that the regime valued its most loyal workers, who were paid above-average salaries and enjoyed perks such as holidays by the Dalmatian coast in newly designed hotels. This helped to forge an extraordinary generation of shock workers,

[16] *La Bosnie et l'Herzégovine*, p. 321.
[17] Lovrenović, *Bosnia: A Cultural History*, p. 65.

Fig. 12 Bosniak miner Alija Sirotanović on the 20,000
dinar note

including Arif Heralić and Alija Sirotanović – whose images both
adorned Yugoslav banknotes. Heralić came from Zenica and was
a blast furnace worker in the steel mill, exceeding his production
norms and extolling the regime. Tito often came back to Bosnia and
once visited Sirotanović when he worked in the Breza coal mines.
Sirotanović, who usually sported the Muslim black beret, was a
humble man, living without electricity for much of his life. His support for the regime was expressed in simple, if rather uncontro-
versial slogans such as 'it is necessary to work'. He broke Alexei
Stakhanov's production record in the 1940s and was awarded the
prestigious 'Hero of Labour' award. Much later he accepted a Fića
car as a token of Tito's esteem, but asked for little else. The Fića car,
made in Kragujevac by Zastava came off the assembly line between
1955 and 1985. It was one of the best-known cars in Yugoslavia,
based on a popular Fiat model.

As a town, Zenica represented a very particular kind of Bosnian
Communist modernity. The Bosnian National Theatre was founded
there soon after the war in 1950 and in 1977 moved to a stunning
new modernist building designed by Jahiel Finci and Zlatko Ugljen.
Although the town's industrial potential was first realized by the
Habsburgs after the 1870s, and an industrial plant modernized by
Krupp in 1936, its population shot up after the Second World War.
Its proximity to Sarajevo gave it extra significance as a producer of
raw materials. Through the distinctive self-management (*radničko*

samoupravljanje) system, Bosnian workers received political and cultural education. Although self-management tended to encourage parochialism and competition between republics and it deterred investment,[18] it was a central part of the post-1950 state ideology and subject to hagiographic veneration by local and international writers. As an economic system, self-management evolved in the period of shock after the 1948 break with Cominform. Yugoslavia had initially been close to the Soviet Union, even if the origins of the split with Stalin can probably be traced back to the Popular Front politics and the Spanish Civil War. A considerable number of Yugoslavs fought in the Iberian conflict, affectionately known thereafter as 'naši Španci' ('our Spaniards') or simply 'Španec' ('the Spaniard') and the experience of guerrilla warfare had tactical significance in the 1940s.

Early Yugoslav propaganda focused on the fraternal co-dependency between Stalin and Tito. Both men were pictured side by side in posters, with local Bosnian leaders added for balance. The shock of Yugoslavia's expulsion from the Communist fold ricocheted throughout the Bosnian republic, but eventually led to even greater devotion to Tito. Without Leninism, the regime had little steer, as most of the leading Partisans were sincere Marxists. According to Milovan Djilas, Tito was initially sceptical about the idea of self-management of factories, but soon overcame his initial doubt. Through the new industrial system, Bosnians demonstrated an aptitude for hard work and innovation. Many also travelled to other republics for jobs and adopted the new customs and cultures of their adopted republics. In the factories of Slovenia, Bosnian women learned to read and write to a much higher standard than had previously been enjoyed in their old homes.

Bosnia's economy had been based on trade, mining, agriculture and pastoralism for centuries. Tito's regime also had ambitions to create an industrial base to fortify the state (and this ambition had been one reason for Yugoslav dissatisfaction with their position in Stalin's bloc). Through self-management, many workers took real

---

[18] Jančar, Barbara 'Ecology and Self-Management: A Balance Sheet for the 1980s', in John B. Allcock, John J. Horton and Marko Milivojević (eds.) *Yugoslavia in Transition* (Oxford: Berg, 1992), p. 342.

Fig. 13 Industry in Zenica (by Richard Mills)

satisfaction in what they had achieved, experiencing a kind of 'factory patriotism' that was also common in revolutionary Russia. Yugoslav Marxists even began to believe that they were overcoming the old problem of labour alienation and indeed there was considerable pride in local production. Other industries grew in Bosnia, including Aluminij in Mostar and the Rudi Čajavec factory in Banja Luka, which made televisions. Vitex and KTK in Visoko produced textiles and leather respectively, drawing on a long Ottoman artisan tradition in that region. In the Communist period, KTK was the largest leather goods manufacturer in Yugoslavia. A large hydroelectric plant had been constructed near Mostar. Cigarettes were produced in Fabrika duhana Sarajevo, often named after Bosnian rivers such as 'Drina lights'. The improbable sight of a smoking cowboy on a poster was a bizarre juxtaposition with everyday life during the siege, but after 1970 the factory started to produce the famous *Sarajevski Malboro*. Alcoholism was apparently widespread even among Muslims and perceived as a problem of modernization. Medical professionals were deeply influential and wrote for high-circulation newspapers about its causes and incidence.[19]

The cult of Tito's personality had grown in part because the remote and dangerous geography of the Partisan war favoured the spread of myths. It had also grown because of his indisputable personal courage and the fact that he had led the struggle by taking huge risks. His legend as their 'white violet' comrade (*'Druže Tito, ljubičice bijela'*) outlived him and he was feted whenever he made public appearances in the republic, usually with the cries of 'hero'. After the war, Drvar became the centre of a flourishing timber industry. After the dictator's death, the devoted town renamed itself Titov Drvar. Many other towns, street and public places were named after the dictator and some names survived the 1990s. Tito's style became increasingly kitsch as his taste for white uniforms and waistline expanded. His friendship with movie star Richard Burton and his glamorous wife Elizabeth Taylor flourished after soirées on Tito's yacht, the *Galeb* (*Seagull*), which he even sailed up the Thames. In 1979, on *Dan mladosti* (the day of youth) Koševo Stadium in Sarajevo was filled with formation dancers eager to celebrate his birthday. They sang 'Tito is our sun, Tito is our heart' (*'Tito je naše sunce, Tito je naše srce'*) as they formed into a red and white corpuscles. 'Party, youth, army, the people!', they chanted as their elderly leader looked on. At times the shape of the dance routine reached genuine aesthetic heights, especially when they formed into the shape of the Sutjeska memorial. Koševo Stadium, nowadays also known as Asim Ferhatović Hase Stadium, was to be the sign of Olympic triumph only five years later. More tragically, its reserve stadium was to be a site of mass burial of the war dead during the siege. Sarajevan Zdravo Čolić released a song *Druže Tito mi ti se kunemo (Comrade Tito, We Swear Our Allegiance to You)* in 1980, which was previously sung at young pioneer events. The words were based on the pioneer pledge and it was to become perhaps the most important patriotic song of the late Communist era.

---

[19] Savelli, Mat 'Diseased, Depraved or just Drunk? The Psychiatric Panic over Alcoholism in Communist Yugoslavia', *Social History of Medicine* 25(2), 2012, pp. 462–480.

After the dispute with the Soviets and their satellites in 1948, the Yugoslavs had been forced to look elsewhere for their international contacts. After the 1955 Bandung Conference in Indonesia and the first Non-Aligned Movement summit in Belgrade 1961, Yugoslavia created a new and rather distinctive position in the world for itself. Exchange of information, students, technical expertise and Islamic radical contacts were all results of this experiment in a third way, although many suspected that the sympathies of the movement were essentially pro-Soviet. Tito's friendship with the Egyptian leader Gamal Abdel Nasser and President Sukarno of Indonesia gave Bosnian Muslims a greater sense of cultural importance. They were often picked to serve as Yugoslav ambassadors in Muslim countries and regained some of the status in society that they had lost in 1918. As a result of political and cultural pressure, Bosnia-Hercegovina became one of the most solid pillars of the Communist regime. Eccentric Hungarian artist Csontváry Kosztka Tivadar had painted Bosnian scenes on huge canvases in the early twentieth century. His painting of the waterfall at Jajce, which captures the essence of one of the region's tourist attractions, appeared on a 1973 postage stamp issued in Yugoslavia's fraternal Communist neighbour Hungary.

The loss of Trieste (which the Partisans left in 1945 and was confirmed in 1954) was an incalculable economic and cultural blow for Yugoslavia. However, there remained a free flow of ideas, but more importantly a flourishing black market. Bosnians would often make the train trip to Trieste and return laden with luxury goods. By the late 1980s, rampant inflation meant that Yugoslav dinars were quickly converted to deutschmarks and the markets of Italy offered cheaper prices than shops in Sarajevo or the other Yugoslav centres. After the 1960s, thousands of Bosnians worked abroad as *Gastarbeiter* and used their savings to build extensive homes in the countryside, many of which were burnt down or trashed during the war in the 1990s. It seems that they suffered dislocation without reproaching Tito himself, whose reputation in Bosnia remained very steady. Exile brought hard currency and luxury goods to Bosnia, but also served to erode the traditional family at a time of other social change. Men endured long and often lonely periods away from home and women bore the brunt of domestic responsibility.

Some families left Yugoslavia altogether at this time. In his auto-biography, Swedish international footballer Zlatan Ibrahimović recalled how his Croatian mother Jurka worked 14 hours a day as a cleaner in Malmö while he sometimes earned pocket money beside her by emptying waste paper baskets. He also speculates that his Bosnian father Šefik, originally from Bijeljina, had married to gain a Swedish residency permit.[20]

Until the mid-1980s, Bosnians still felt a level of optimism about the future. Tourism increased after the 1970s. In 1973, Djulada Seidović from Doboj visited the island of Hvar on a trip paid for by his trade union. 'This is my first time at the sea,' he told a reporter. 'Up to now I had only seen it on TV.'[21] Traditional Islamic material culture could provide exotic Ottoman-themed day trips for Adriatic holidaymakers coming inland. The high levels of iron in the water near Srebrenica ensured that the spa complex at Banja Guber flourished as a tourist destination. Bosnia enjoyed a remarkable cultural efflorescence in the later Communist period. The Tuzla-born basketball player Mirza Delibašić helped the Yugoslavs take gold at the Moscow Olympics in 1980. Ismet Rizvić captured the optimism of the time with his pictures of Počitelj, where an artists' colony flourished. The poetic realist painter Safet Zec, originally from Rogatica, moved to Sarajevo and captured much of the beauty of the city in his work.

Films, books and poetry about the Second World War enjoyed special favour. When Richard Burton appeared as Tito in *The Fifth Offensive* (*Sutjeska*) in 1973, the ageing dictator turned up to the film shoot watching 'himself' rather impassively. Perhaps the most famous Partisan film *Valter brani Sarajevo* (*Walter Defends Sarajevo*), directed by Hajrudin Krvavac, had appeared the previous year and remains a highly regarded film especially in the Far East. Emily Greble has suggested that the film reinforced a myth about Partisan resistance in the city, which was rather different from the

[20] Ibrahimović, Zlatan, *I am Zlatan Ibrahimović*, (Harmondsworth: Penguin 2013).
[21] Duda, Igor 'Workers into Tourists: Entitlements, Desires, and Realities of Social Tourism in Yugoslav Socialism' in Hannes Grandits and Karin Taylor (eds.) *Yugoslavia's Sunny Side: A History of Tourism in Socialism (1950s–1980s)* (Budapest: Central European University Press, 2010), p. 65.

nuanced reality of collaboration and coercion. The talented film director Emir Kusturica had early success in 1981 with *Sjećaš li se Doli Bel? (Do You Remember Dolly Bell?)* set in Sarajevo. He then took on a film script about the period of the Tito–Stalin split in *Otac na službenom putu (Father is on a Business Trip)*, which was released in 1985. The film follows the life of a Sarajevo Muslim family and their Orthodox friends as they deal with repression in the aftermath of the row with Cominform. Bosnians, like other Yugoslavs had been punished if they showed any sympathy for Stalin and the Soviets. Some had even endured spells in the notorious Adriatic prison Goli otok, a camp where prisoners were forced to work on the quarry in intense sun. Kusturica's film dealt frankly with the themes of punishment, betrayal and forgiveness.

The traditional *sevdalinka* songs of the Ottoman period were adapted into catchy popular music by singers of Muslim heritage. Silvana Armenulić (1939–1976), who was born Zilha Bajraktarević and originally from Doboj, was adored across the region. She had possibly the best known hit of the era with the song *Šta će mi život, bez tebe dragi?'(What Good Would My Life Be Without You, Darling?)*. Her career was cut short by death in a car accident in 1976. Like Sirotanović, she was a model Muslim for the regime to promote. Tito and his wife Jovanka both liked singing and invited her to perform for them. Politically loyal, talented, glamorous and married to a Serbian tennis star, Radmilo Armenulić, she represented a specific kind of Yugoslav Muslim modernity. But behind the glamour was private anxiety. When the Radmilo and Silvana married, they argued with their disapproving parents, a fate that often accompanied couples from so-called 'mixed' marriages. Her style remained understated if not traditional, but she fell out of favour with the media authorities after refusing to pose in swimming gear on Belgrade television in 1972. If Silvana dressed in a way that explicitly rejected the old ways, then much more could be said about the style of singer Lepa Brena (Fahreta Jahić) who played upon her Muslim heritage to full effect in videos but dressed in revealing clothes. Also married to a Serbian tennis player, Brena was one of the last 'Yugoslavs' of the 1980s. Her 1989 song *Robinja (Slave Girl)* was a huge hit and saw her writhing in chains in captivity in 'Oriental' Istanbul. Another song from the same album,

Jugoslovenka (*Yugoslav Girl*), sung as duet with the Bijelo Dugme singer Alen Islamović, celebrated the diversity of the expiring country. It quickly became an unfortunate and controversial dirge, although it was her express intention to convey patriotic loyalty. At the time, Bosnian popular culture, still steeped in Titoism, was beginning to look out of step with the rest of the country.

The city of Sarajevo was celebrated by many artists, including singers Kemal Monteno and Zdravko Čolić in the early 1970s. Čolić was chosen to represent Yugoslavia at Eurovision in 1973 and although his song *Gori vatra* (*A Fire is Burning*), written by Monteno, was popular at home, it did not do particularly well in the contest. Sarajevo was also the first home of the iconic group Bijelo Dugme. The rock group, whose musicians were variously Croat, Muslim or Serb, was affirmatively Yugoslav at a time when nationalism was in fashion in other republics. Until their demise in 1989, the rockers mimicked, but managed to improve on, most of the musical trends of the era. Their guitarist, Sarajevo-born Goran Bregović, whose compositions have adorned Emir Kusturica's films, has since been a major factor in the spread of Balkan folk music outside the region, often playing to packed stadiums in Germany and Turkey. He has since composed parts of the soundtrack for films such as *Arizona Dream* (1993) and *Borat* (2006). Traditions from Bosnian music have been preserved in the popular work of Dino Merlin, another contestant on Eurovision from Sarajevo, who composed a stirring version of the national anthem. Haris Džinović has adapted Roma styles of music for popular consumption through the region. In 1982, he released a popular album *Kao Cigani* (*Like Gypsies*) with his band Sar e Roma.

Combining the products of pastoralism with the Ottoman celebration of vegetables, traditional Bosnian food remains an exceptionally high-protein diet firmly rooted in the past. Cooks still use the universal cooking pot or *Bosanski lonac*. *Burek*, a filled filo pastry dish, is made with green vegetables, cheese or meat and is cooked in a metal pot called a *sač* (from the Turkish word *saç*) that is placed on top of the coals in an oven. *Ćevapčići* and *somun* (bread baked in the embers) are prepared well beyond their original in homelands and are popular with locals and tourists alike. They have now become standard fast food in the former Yugoslavia.

When Bosnian migrants protested in the Slovenian capital about the denial of planning permission for their mosque in the 2000s, they jokingly threatened to withdraw their sale of food to the citizens of Ljubljana: 'no *džamija* for us, no *burek* for you' was the slogan on one poster. The beer Sarajevsko, a legacy from nineteenth-century industrialization, was popular across Communist Yugoslavia. The huge Klas bakery fed much of Sarajevo and was targeted early on in the 1990s siege. Although it was produced in the neighbouring Croatian republic, the inventor of the popular 'gold dust' seasoning Vegeta, Zlata Bartl, was from Dolac.

When it was announced that Sarajevo would host the Winter Olympics, new hotels including the ochre yellow Holiday Inn designed by architect Ivan Štraus were built and the skiing facilities spruced up. Always an odd choice, given that the Republic of Slovenia had much better facilities, it was a triumph for the Bosnian capital. Television viewers saw the official mascot, the little wolf Vučko, announce the broadcasts and the red snowflake logo appeared everywhere as Yugoslavia went for gold in the men's skiing. One of the newly built resorts at Pale later transmuted into the Bosnian Serb military headquarters in the spring of 1992, an incongruity captured by Paweł Pawlikowski when he filmed Radovan Karadžić trying to take a phone call in a decommissioned cable car. The prosperity that Yugoslavia enjoyed was desperately short-lived as a consequence of the regime's extravagant borrowing in the previous decades. The impact of economic decline was felt very acutely in Bosnia in the 1980s, with high levels of unemployment, low wages, rampant inflation, strikes and fiscal instability. Many Bosnians lost faith in the regime's financial institutions and began to hoard the more stable deutschmark. By 1986 young people were experiencing an average of three-year wait for a job and the situation was worse for graduates.[22] The establishment was also tarnished by scandals. In the post-war period, the north-west region of Bosnia went from being poor to domination by the food company Agrokomerc. This firm started off with poultry and other meat products and rapidly grew in size, supplying much of the Yugoslav food market by the 1980s. It employed several thousand at its peak.

[22] Jančar, 'Ecology and Self-Management', pp. 351–352.

Its charismatic director Fikret Abdić became embroiled in a financial scandal in 1987, which led to the resignation of the influential Muslim Communist politician Hamdija Pozderac.

Problems with the Communist hold over the minds of people became clearer after the spectacular success of the apparitions of the Virgin Mary in Medjugorje, a small Franciscan parish that incorporates the hamlets of Bijakovići, Vionica, Miletina and Šurmanci. Several young people from the parish claimed to have seen and heard Mary, Mother of God, on 24 June 1981 on a hill called Crnica. The first to see Mary (or *Gospa*, as they call her) was Ivanka Ivanković, who had lost her mother Jagoda in the May of that year. Through the apparitions, she claims to speak to her deceased mother several times a year. The other visionaries – Vicka Ivanković, Jakov Colo, Ivan and Mirjana Dragićević and Mirjana Pavlović – have all continued with a committed religious life with an emphasis on the power of prayer, although not all still have the visions. Many of the elements of the story mirror Marian cults elsewhere in Europe (Knock, Lourdes, Marpingen and Fatima), although Medjugorje is the only Catholic shrine in Europe where multiple seers have emerged. The Franciscans had promoted visionaries in the recent past and often been embroiled in arguments with the wider Catholic Church. The blessed Gabriele Allegra promoted the work of an early twentieth-century mystic from Via Reggio in Italy called Maria Valtorta. Secular priests from Hercegovina, as non-Franciscans are known, often blamed the order of friars for the encouraging maverick religious trends.

St John's Eve, 23 June, had traditionally been illuminated by hill-top bonfires and was an important turning point in the religious calendar. The festivities have been linked to pre-Christian rituals of fertility, visions and portents of renewal. It was also the time of year when Bosnian and Serbian peasants captured the insect *kermes vermilio* for its crimson dye.[23] According to two British travellers in the 1870s in Sarajevo, on 24 June 'the sun is said to dance at dawn on the top of the hill Trebovich: on that day, and on St. Elias's and St. George's days, the Mussulman [Muslim] population turns out of doors, and the whole side of Trebovich, especially

²³ Belamarić, 'Cloth and Geography', p. 286.

the neighbourhood of the Moslem saint's tomb, is bright with red turbans and jackets and groups of women in white veils'.[24] In Podmilačje, there was a traditional pilgrimage of all religions from across Bosnia on St John's Eve. The sick and those in need of spiritual comfort would arrive at the Church of St John in Podmilačje, which was subsequently destroyed during the 1990s. Medjugorje already had a stone cross that had been erected there in 1933. Some claimed to have seen columns of light rising from the cross and an annual pilgrimage had followed. The faithful at Medjugorje have also described seeing the sun 'dancing', suggesting that the region enjoys some interesting patterns of light. Just before the apparitions, there had been a dramatic storm and local women, fearing the devil's hand, had gone out and doused the streets with holy water. Within days of the news of the apparitions, the parish was flooded with visitors, mostly women, anxious to experience the miracle themselves.

The parish priest Jozo Zovko was away on a retreat in Zagreb when the apparitions happened. When he returned, he himself experienced a vision in which he was instructed to protect the children. The apparitions then started to take place within the safer confines of the local church hall. The authorities were initially very hostile to the phenomenon and Zovko was blamed and arrested. One of the children's Franciscan tutors, padre Slavko Barbarić had earned a Master's degree in child psychology in Rome. Suspicion was cast on the veracity of the visions and the bishop of Mostar, Pave Žanić, appointed a special commission of 15 theologians, psychologists and psychiatrists to examine the case.[25] The children were attached to monitors during their ecstasy, but the results were inconclusive. Although most of the commission decided that the apparitions were not genuine, a cult was created which saw the arrival of millions of tourists in the 1980s, a pilgrimage that continues to this day. Žanić also blamed female susceptibility for spreading the cult beyond the locality.

[24] Muir Sebright Mackenzie and Irby, *The Turks, Greeks and Slavons*, pp. 8–9.
[25] Perica, Vjekoslav *Balkan Idols: Religion and Nationalism in Balkan States* (Oxford: Oxford University Press, 2002), pp. 111–112.

Tourism boosted the economy of this dry, relatively remote spot in what George Arbuthnot had called 'a perfect sea of rock',[26] and relatives of the visionaries made money selling refreshments and souvenirs. Many locals built extensions on their houses, seeing the miracles as an alternative form of revenue to working in German factories. Perhaps one real miracle was the fact that tourists taking holidays on the Croatian coast would be tempted to leave the crystal clear waters of the Adriatic for the dry lands of the Hercegovina karst. The appearance of Mary, Mother of God, in this small town was also fortuitous in that it already had an improbably large church of Sveti Jakob that could absorb a large number of visitors. It was consecrated in 1969, but built in the 1930s during the royal dictatorship. Initially hostile to the Mary phenomenon, the Communists relaxed when they realized the Catholic lira would be amply spent in the town. Nevertheless, the apparitions strengthened the bond between Hercegovina and the rest of the Catholic world, in turn strengthening the hold of the Franciscans once again. Medjugorje soon came to resemble other holy places, with a large golden mile selling postcards, novelty figurines and rosaries. In the summer nights the air is still filled with the dulcet sound of nuns singing and strumming guitars. A Hollywood film, *Gospa*, was made about the town's story in 1995 in which Martin Sheen played the priest Zovko. Mary's message to the teenagers, rather poignantly, was one of peace and piety. She also predicted the return of Christianity to Russia. The chosen group have continued to spread the word in international Catholic forums since 1981. Her very popularity hinted at the weakness of alternative narratives and appealed in particular to the Catholics of Hercegovina as well as many Croats over the border.

Local Serbs took a much dimmer view of the apparitions. Just days before the apparitions in June 1981, the graves of the slaughtered priests at the Žitomislić Orthodox Monastery had been opened and given a ceremonial reburial. They were particularly concerned that a revival of Catholic piety in a region that had strong Ustaša sympathies in the 1940s would dishonour the memory of the local Orthodox who had been buried in mass Karst

---

[26] Arbuthnot, *Herzegovina*, p. 30.

graves nearby. In the late summer of 1941, more than 650 women and children from the village of Prebilovci were massacred by the Ustaša. The men had retreated to the surrounding hills, believing that they would be the target of the attacks. The majority of those killed were thrown into the Golubinka karst pit near Šurmanci while they were still alive. Most perished, although some survived by hiding until the Ustaša men had departed. Tito's regime avoided full and frank discussion of the war and atrocities, preferring a narrative that blamed foreign invaders for sowing the strife. After the war, the local Partisans sealed up the pit and commissioned a monument to the dead. After the fall of Communism, renewed openness in public debate led to a fraught examination of the war-time massacres and symbolic reburials of their bodies, often led by the Orthodox Church. In 1990, Radovan Karadžić descended into a Karst pit near Medjugorje to help to exhume the remains of the dead. The relatives of the victims then passed the bones between each other in a long column. The entire event was blessed by the Orthodox Church and broadcast on television. Even before the Bosnian elections in the autumn of 1990, the stage was set for significant political radicalization.

For much of the early and mid-twentieth century, nationalist writers had included the Bosnian Muslims within the Croatian nation. Rather than stressing their separate Muslim heritage, they were often regarded as the purest of the Croats. In exile, extreme nationalist Vjekoslav Luburić and his followers perpetuated the idea of a Croatia that included the Muslims: 'The Drina [idea] brought together hodžas and priests, generals and rank and file soldiers, workers and intellectuals, young and old. This was a programme for all Croats, because it was neither regional, religious or tied up with rank.'[27] At the same time, negative images of Islam were perpetuated in Yugoslav culture. Ivan Aralica's epic novel *The Horseman* (*Konjanik*) revisited the nineteenth-century Croatian literary trope of the *hajduk* and Turk and evokes largely negative relations between religious communities in the hinterland of Zadar in the eighteenth century. The east of Bosnia, especially the Drina River, has far less surviving significance in mainstream

[27] Krizman, *Pavelić u Bjekstvu*, p. 341.

Croatian nationalism, which scaled back its territorial ambitions to Hercegovina. Dobroslav Paraga and his associates still called for 'Croatia to the Drina' after 1992, but overt anti-Islamic prejudice of the kind that Pavelić and Luburić would not have recognized is more common among Croat nationalists nowadays.

In 1986, the Communist regime put Andrija Artuković on trial in Zagreb after his extradition from the United States. Artuković was a significant Ustaša ideologue, having been an early follower of Pavelić. Born in Klobuk in Hercegovina in 1899, he had followed a Franciscan path of Catholic radicalization after a seminary education in Široki Brijeg. He had been put on trial and imprisoned under the Karadjordjević regime from 1935 to 1936 and had even been publically defended by a youthful Milovan Djilas. He served as minister of the interior and justice under the Ustaša regime and was implicated in the policies of anti-Semitism and genocide. After the war, he spent some time in a leafy Dublin suburb, attending mass every day, before moving to California and living under the pseudonym Alois Anich. The Yugoslav authorities lobbied for his return for decades, even issuing an expensive pamphlet condemning him. He was sentenced to death in 1986 but the sentence was not carried out due to his frail health and he died in prison in 1988. Through the trial, the Yugoslavian government was able to revive a collective distain for the crimes of the Ustaša regime.

A clear precondition for the growth of extreme ideologies is the gap between expectations and reality, and nationalism became something of an alternative career for underemployed Yugoslavs after the death of Tito. In 1982, a writer who grew up in Slivlje in Hercegovina, Vuk Drašković, published an epic novel *Nož* (*The Knife*), which would be heavily criticized by the Communist authorities, but praised by many literary figures. Its hero, Alija Osmanović, finds out that he had been adopted and raised by Muslims who had slaughtered his family during the war. The theme of a painful concealment of historical truth struck a chord that Drašković would articulate over the following decades as he became a leading Serb nationalist. At the same time, dissidents were being punished in Bosnia. In 1983, Alija Izetbegović and several other activists were imprisoned in Sarajevo for their putatively extreme Muslim beliefs. Although he served fewer than five years of a much longer sentence, his long-term health was badly damaged. The following year the Sarajevan Vojislav Šešelj was also jailed for overt Serb nationalism. Across Yugoslavia and the rest of world, concerned individuals signed petitions for his release and his case drew the attention of Amnesty International. Popular nationalist fears were stirred up by the media, the Orthodox Church and by academics, articulated in the draft Memorandum of the Serbian Academy of Arts and Sciences of September 1986, a sophisticated critique of the Communist legacy as well as a strident 'defence' of the Serbs within the Confederation including Bosnia.[28]

In January 1990, the League of Communists that had ruled Bosnia since the 1940s effectively disintegrated after an emergency meeting in Belgrade. The timing was not auspicious for Communist activists, who had recently witnessed the gentle collapse of fraternal parties in neighbouring countries and the more ominous execution of Romanian dictator Nicolae Ceauşescu on television. The events that precipitated the collapse of the Congress largely came from Slovenian impatience with the Milošević faction and were only indirectly related to events in Bosnia. It was to be in Bosnia that this political crisis was to be felt most profoundly. When Slobodan Milošević found support among Kosovo Serbs and ousted his former boss Ivan Stambolić in Serbia in 1987 on a nationalism pretext, the latter warned him that he was risking the future of the country. The Partisans and their Communist epigoni had feared the recrudescence of the nationalism for years. Its revival was always their mortal fear and always evoked as the worst-case scenario for Yugoslavia. By the 1980s, their recitation of the same mantras had attracted the satire of Slovene journalists and the derision of angry Serb nationalists who poured their scorn on the 1974 Constitution in the form of the Serbian Memorandum. After the rise of Milošević in Serbian, nationalists were able to flaunt their views far more openly. On the Serbian television programme *Minimaxovizija* in 1991, Vojislav Šešelj told the audience that Bosnia was a Serbian land, adding that 'I should know because I am from Bosnia'. When he then threatened to take

---

[28] Dragović Soso, Jasna *Saviours of the Nation? Serbia's Intellectual Opposition and the Revival of Nationalism* (London: Hurst, 2002), pp. 176–195.

out the eyeballs of Croats with rusty spoons (so that they would die of tetanus) the audience laughed heartily (perhaps because they thought he was joking or even because they were unused to hearing such things in the media). By this time the phenomenon had gone beyond a mere revival of Četnik ideas and had reached huge proportions. By the late 1980s, Serb megalomania had begun to poison community relations in many towns. In the overwhelmingly Muslim town of Kozarac, Dušan Tadić, who became the first person to be convicted of war crimes from the 1990s war, helped to found a local branch of the Serbian Democratic Party in 1990. Tadić and his wife Mira had once had many friends in the town but they turned against their former friends, including the policeman Emir Karabašić who had been a pallbearer at his father's funeral. A similar process of violent radicalization occurred across the republic, encouraged by the overt provocation of the supporters of Slobodan Milošević.

From the mid-1980s, newspapers in Serbia had begun to publish stories about violent and sexual attacks on Serbs by Albanians in Kosovo, myths that may have helped to lay the foundations for the events of the early 1990s in Bosnia, where sexual violence against Muslim women was extremely widespread. With their fear of Islamic encroachment, especially after the Iranian revolution of 1979 and the traumatic legacy of earlier genocides, ordinary Serbs were vulnerable to cynical nationalist politicians. Yugoslavia's Muslims were attacked en masse by Serb nationalists such as Miroljub Jevtić, who attempted to link the rise of Islamic 'fundamentalism' in the wider world but particularly Iran with a religious revival of Islam in Bosnia. In April 1990, the Croatian Democratic Union (HDZ) had been elected in the neighbouring republic. Its leader Franjo Tudjman had gained some notoriety for the publication of a revisionist history in 1989, which significantly revised the number killed at the Jasenovac extermination camp downwards. Yugoslav Communist-style discursive moderation rapidly disappeared with the recrudescence of fascist rhetoric.

Slobodan Milošević's supporters travelled the length and breadth of the country, often supplying free buses and hospitality to Serb nationalists. The rallies were generally made up of a mixture of patriotic songs, speeches and vows to protect Serbs everywhere. Some would turn up to rallies with placards with provocative anti-Islamic slogans: 'Oh Muslims, you black crows, Tito is not around to protect you' or 'I'll be the first, who will be the second to drink some Turkish blood?'[29] In 1990, a psychiatrist Jovan Rašković published a book called *Luda zemlja* (*Mad Country*) in which he argued that the Serbs as a people had been traumatized by the genocide of the 1940s. He discussed how the Serbs had an instinct for leadership, but with aggressive tendencies. Croats, according to Rašković, were suffering from a castration complex and were afraid of being abused, whereas Muslims were fixated in the anal phase and valued people only by their property and had a tendency towards accumulating goods. He founded the Serbian Democratic Party in Croatia in 1990. He then contacted a professional colleague in Bosnia, Radovan Karadžić, and urged him to found a similar party in Bosnia. Karadžić toured Bosnia with Rašković in 1990 talking to audiences about the Serb plight. The emotional and fervent response at nationalist rallies suggested that the collective trauma about the Second World War had not evaporated. Serb nationalists leaders offered more than a way of challenging old grief. Far more significantly they broke a Communist monopoly on heroism, persuading their followers that they were Serb knights whose valorous pedigree could be traced back to 1914, the Balkans Wars, to the armed bandits of the Ottoman period and even to the Middle Ages.

Political parties had begun to form across Yugoslavia since the summer of 1989. By 1990, Bosnia had three new significant parties, which effectively undermined decades of interethnic cooperation in the League of Communists. The Croatian Democratic Union (HDZ) was allied to Tudjman's party, the Serbian Democratic Party (SDS) was closely linked to fraternal parties in neighbouring republics and the Party of Democratic Action (SDA) was essentially Muslim-led. The elections at the end of November 1990, in which Bosnians voted for ethnically based parties, effectively left the republic divided into political zones, with only Tuzla and Novo Sarajevo with no nationalist majority. The SDA leader Alija

[29] Cigar, Norman 'The Serbo-Croatian War, 1991' in Stjepan Meštrović (ed.) *Genocide after Emotion: The Postemotional Balkan War* (London: Routledge, 1996), p. 57.

Izetbegović had been pardoned and released from prison in 1988. Although his rival Fikret Abdić received more votes in the presidential elections it was Izetbegović who was to take up the role of president. As a political figure, he divided the Bosnian nation. Many regarded him as a principled and erudite man whose moderate views about Islam in Europe offered real political opportunities. In 1970 he had published the *Islamic Declaration*, a discourse about the place of his religion in a modern secular world. For nationalists, he was little different from Muslim extremists. His hometown of Bosanski Šamac, also the birthplace of the late Serbian president Zoran Djindjić, is now within the Bosnia Serb entity. It is now usually referred to simply as Šamac.

Within months of the election of Tudjman in Croatia, parts of the neighbouring republic simply became ungovernable as the Serb minority started to take over the areas in which they were to be found in any numbers. The Bosnian elections had created potential ethnic zones at a time when the Croatian Serbs had set up an autonomous region in Krajina. Autonomy was supported by the army (JNA) who tacitly supplied weapons to the rebels. Four similar Serbian autonomous regions were formed in the summer of 1991 centred on Banja Luka, Trebinje, Romanija and Bijeljina just at the time as the fighting had begun in the neighbouring republic. These were to be the centres of insurgency in 1992 against Izetbegović's democratically elected government after the declaration of independence. Despite witnessing the war in Croatia in 1991, many of Bosnia's political leaders could not imagine a parallel deterioration in their own state. In other words, despite the genocides of 1940s and the terrible devastation of 1914–1918, they were staggered by the rapid deterioration of decades of good intercommunal relations. For them, 'real existing socialism' had meant the absence of open ethnic conflict or hostility. Most of the rest of Eastern Europe continued to experience relatively good interethnic relations after the collapse of Communist regimes. The violent situation in the Western Balkans was absolutely exceptional in post-1989 Europe.

The strength of the revival of Serb nationalist ideas in the 1980s suggests several things. First, that the genocide of the 1940s did have a profound impact on the Serbs of Croatia and Bosnia. Jovan

Rašković, who worked in a hospital in Šibenik as a psychiatrist for many years, observed that the Croats as a group did not appear to suffer from collective guilt about the Ustaša genocide. Asymmetrical memories of the 1940s may have exacerbated a sense of indignation among Serbs especially as their role as guardians of the new moral order receded when the League of Communists lost its hold on Yugoslavia. Second, it suggests that Četnik supporters were never as definitively crushed as Croatian fascists had been inside the state. Whereas the Habsburgs had ruled without the widespread consent of the Orthodox community, the Yugoslav republics of Bosnia and Croatia were heavily dependent on the institutional loyalty and participation of former Serb Partisans and their kin. Knowing that they had stronger support in the west of the country than in Serbia proper, where the revolutionary tide had been far weaker, the Communist formula of governance by loyal Serbs at least temporarily contained the further spread of Četnik loyalties. Nevertheless these nationalist sentiments seem to have remained strong in the private sphere of the extended family, as did the memory of wartime atrocities. Finally, the nationalist revival and the strategy of ethnic cleansing suggests that a model of 'extirpation' of Islamic communities had survived in the collective memory in some form. The survival of Muslims in Bosnia until the 1990s was historically exceptional and due largely to the Habsburg legacy. It has been tempting for commentators to see the wars of the 1990s in terms of 'de-Ottomanization'. It was to be the recrudescence of Četnik ideology in the 1980s and in particular the explicit revival of the plans to divide Bosnia and Croatia, that was to fatally break the 40-year pact between western Serbs and the Communists. Serb nationalists offered more than a way of channelling old grief.

Rising Serb nationalism left Bosnia looking like an isolated remnant of brotherhood and unity. Serb activists began the process of destruction of their actually existing lives in the Bosnian and Croatian republic, which rapidly increased after the formation of ethnically based political parties in 1990. The spirit of the Log Revolution in Krajina, during which the local Serb authorities in Knin rejected rule from Zagreb and blocked the local roads with felled trees, soon spread to neighbouring Bosnia. Within the SAOs in Bosnia, pre-existing moral standards were later suspended as people helped to round up and execute their neighbours with whom they had previously had good relations. This surge of Serb nationalism had left Bosnians, and the Muslims in particular, in a vulnerable position, hovering between Islamic piety, Bosnian *convivencia* and 'brotherhood and unity'. In the context, their lack of stridency and national assertiveness could be seen as a weakness or, at the very least, political unpreparedness. Ben Lieberman has examined what he calls 'cognitive dissonance', which leads individuals to take violent actions against neighbours or friends, with whom they had previously shared the daily life occurrences of sporting events, education, hospitality and even exogamous relations.[30]

The policy of brotherhood and unity worked insofar as a lot of Bosnians and indeed other commentators believed in this new status quo, but it created a false sense of permanence and stability. The Yugoslav League of Communists (*Savez komunista Jugoslavije*, SKJ), formed from the Communist Party (KPJ) in 1952, had the reputation as one of the most liberal Leninist parties in power during the Cold War era and in 1985 readers of the *Rough Guide* book series were informed: 'Known as *Milicija*, Yugoslav Police are generally easy going and helpful.'[31] Historian of Soviet Communism Geoffrey Hosking even felt that Josip Broz Tito had demonstrated that 'it was possible to institute a different kind of socialism'.[32] President Izetbegović gambled the future of a unified Bosnia on two false premises. First, he did not anticipate the widespread collusion, either through fear or willing participation, of Bosnia's Orthodox population in war crimes. Second, he believed that the international community would shore up his government and safeguard the independence of the newly recognized state, despite the ominous arms embargo imposed the United Nations in the summer of 1991. It is clear from Izetbegović's statements in the early

---

[30] Lieberman, Benjamin 'Nationalist Narratives, Violence Between Neighbours and Ethnic Cleansing in Bosnia-Hercegovina: A Case of Cognitive Dissonance?' *Journal of Genocide Research* 8(3), 2006, pp. 295–310.

[31] Dunford, Mark and Holland, Jack *The Rough Guide to Yugoslavia* (London: Routledge and Kegan Paul, 1985), p. 8.

[32] Hosking, Geoffrey *A History of the Soviet Union* (London: Fontana, 1985), p. 325.

months of 1992 that he placed notions of democracy and the law at a very high level, but was unable to match principle with reality. His lack of pragmatism and adherence to principle won him great devotion and respect, but meant that his government could not cope – either militarily or philosophically – with the insurgency in its first and most aggressive phase. Izetbegović's indignation with the flagrant disregard for principle was soon replaced by another extreme reaction (i.e., by a sense that if the Bosnian government did not fight back against the rebellion, the Bosnian Muslims would be exterminated as a people). Both reactions to the situation in which he found himself were driven by ideology. The latter response helped to fuel a sense of collective tragedy that has been very hard to overcome since 1995.

An inability to think about the borders of Yugoslav republics and to imagine beyond the previous decades afflicted the political classes across Yugoslavia and indeed the international community. The exception to this was nationalists who looked at the regional map very differently and always historicized. In 1991, Croatian nationalist Anto Valenta published a study entitled *Podjela Bosne i Borba za Cjelovitost* (*The Division of Bosnia and the Struggle for Unity*) in which he advocated an exchange of population, creating Croat, Serb and Muslim 'regions' (*regije*) from the former Socialist Yugoslavian Republic, whose borders had been decided upon historical grounds in 1945. According to Valenta's theory, 194,000 Serbs would leave the central Muslim regions, to be 'replaced' by the same number of Muslims who would leave the Serbian entity. Hypothetically 170,000 Croats would then leave the central part of Bosnia to be exchanged for 170,000 Muslims coming in from the Croat region. He also advocated the exchange of some 95,000 Serbs and Croats respectively from their regions. The book included several maps marked with arrows to illustrate his point.

The continual demonization of fascism under Tito had meant that most Yugoslavs would not even permit themselves the right to think about the shape of the republics differently. It was simply seen as being in very bad taste. Often this lack of political imagination about the borders of republics had some tangible benefits in the sense that some potential conflict was avoided. Montenegrin nationalists have steadfastly refused to consider the bay of Kotor with its Catholic population as 'Croatia', but violent political reaction on this issue was never a serious threat. The 'violence as a first resort' by Serb nationalists after the declarations of Bosnian and Croatian independence was widely regarded as illegitimate by non-Serb actors, including the international community, from the very outset. The experience of the Kosovo Albanians in the early 1990s does suggest that, had the Serbs opted for non-violent protest against the Tudjman and Izetbegović governments, they would have been similarly ignored.

Debates about the sexual abuse of a Kosovo Serb farmer Djordje Martinović by Albanians was turned into a media circus. Newspapers discussed the Muslim penchant for 'deviant' behaviour after the farmer claimed he had been attacked with a broken beer bottle by his Muslim neighbours. It later emerged that the injury was in all likelihood self-inflicted. The damage that this incident did to ethnic relations was much more long-lasting. Although a causal link between discourse and violence cannot be proved and we cannot say with absolute certainty that paranoia about Kosovo in the 1980s led to widespread rape of Bosnian Muslims in the 1990s, we do know that particular views of Muslims were commonplace in popular culture at that time. After the Martinović case, everyday life became a discursive battleground between ethnic groups in which people lost their inhibitions about naming. This discernible rise in the use of offensive language was reinforced by old stereotypes about innate character.

Vojislav Šešelj certainly tapped into a current in Serbian nationalist discontent. By 1990, the Drina had long since been abandoned by most Croatian nationalists as a plausible boundary. Šešelj shifted the border of Serbia westwards by rhetorical flurries, denying the right of Muslims to live even beyond the Drina border. His rhetorical style is a cynical cocktail of past events, lines half quoted from other Serbs (especially Jezdimir Dangić and Vuk Drašković) and urgency: 'Brother Četniks, the time has come to retaliate against the Balije. The Drina is not a border between Serbia and Bosnia, but rather it is the very spine of Serbia [*kičma srpske države*]. Every place that

Serbs live is Serbia. Arise, brother Četniks, especially you that live on the other side of the Drina for you are the bravest and show the Balije, Muslims and Turks the green corridor[33] and the road to the East.'[34] The ethnographer Ivan Čolović, a rare critic of nationalism who continued to write in Belgrade in the 1990s, argued that imagining the Drina as such a vital part of the body politic made it essential to control.[35]

The river had been the theme of the unofficial Serb national anthem *Marš na Drinu*. In later years, the song was used to threaten and frighten Bosnians. In 1991, Radovan Karadžić and Šešelj attended a Serb nationalist meeting on Romanija on *Djurdjevdan* to the sound of *Marš na Drinu* crackling in the background. For several days before the main mosque in Zvornik was blown up in 1992, the sound of the *Drina March* was broadcast from the minaret. It was in the context of Serbian radicalization and the outbreak of war in Croatia that Bosnia lurched towards independence in 1992. One theme running through this period of the disintegration of Yugoslavia is that of preparedness and unpreparedness for conflict. In their bitter cynicism, nationalists, both Croat and Serb, were prepared to exploit this. International unpreparedness for the conflict in the former Yugoslavia often took the form of an obtuse lack of understanding about the nature of the federal system. Combined with an essentially racist discourse that characterized peoples in the Balkans as violent by nature, intervention often left the unprepared even more vulnerable. When Bosnian Muslims did attempt to protect themselves against aggression, they were – at least in the notorious case of the armed defenders of Srebrenica in 1993 – disarmed as if they were the primary aggressors. Genocide studies has often focused on questions of why, when and how people commit violence. These kind of existential questions that delve into psychology are undoubtedly extremely valuable. We have learnt a lot about

---

[33] *Zelena transverzala* was a term used in Sarajevo in the 1980s to refer to the green belt in the city. For nationalists it has the connotation of a belt of Muslim territory from Bosnia through to Sandžak, Kosovo and Albania.

[34] 'Svedok o izjavama Šešelja 1992', *B92*, 4 February 2009.

[35] Čolović, Ivan *Politics of Symbol in Serbia: Essays in Political Anthropology*, translated by Celia Hawkesworth (London: Hurst 2002), p. 33.

human behaviour *in extremis*. However, in the midst of a political crisis, to ask this kind of question – why are humans violent? – is entirely the wrong response. By the time the Bosnian government and its supporters had overcome the shock at the behaviour of some of their compatriots, they had lost their country. Lack of concerted international intervention in the early years of the conflict made sure that they never truly got it back.

6

Bosnian independence, war and genocide

FROM POLITICAL CRISIS TO WAR

In the period of the dissolution of state between the spring of 1990 and 1992, some of the Yugoslavian republics found themselves in a more straightforward position to move towards independence than others. Although Croatia had been 'silent' for many years before the elections in 1990, some important issues with regard to the national question had been determined by the active diaspora community. In other words, most Croatian nationalists in 1991 were not overtly seeking a slice of Bosnia: the breakdown in Bosnian–Croatian relations occurred later in 1993. Slovenians had prepared for independence at all levels of society and this political transition had few important enemies by July 1991. Bosnia found itself singularly badly prepared for the end of Yugoslavia and, in particular, a Serb nationalist insurgency instigated from outside the republic. From early 1992 until the winter of 1995 Bosnia was mired in the worst military conflict in Europe since the Second World War. The immediate causes are to be found in the revival of a Četnik programme among a small stratum of Serb intellectuals that quickly reignited popular nationalism. Bosnian Serbs went from being good Yugoslavs to enemies of their neighbours within a matter of months. Many of these nationalists were from outside Bosnia and their aims were significantly abetted by Slobodan Milošević in Serbia. The more long-term causes of conflict were the malaise in the economy, residual notions of 'self-defence', the chasm between the city and countryside and the absence of strong, unifying political leadership when the League of Communists collapsed.

In many respects, the situation in Bosnia came to resemble the deteriorating circumstances in Croatia in 1991. The declared independence of the neighbouring republic had led to intense fighting in contested regions that bordered on Bosnia. Krajina was occupied by local Serb insurgents, Slavonia was fought over town by town and the inhabitants in Adriatic towns were terrorized by attacks from the sea. By the beginning of 1992, there was partition and short-term peace, but this came at a very high price for Croatia's President Tudjman. Some areas of the republic had been badly damaged by fighting in the previous months. The town of Vukovar looked like a Central European city from 1945, with its historic buildings scarred by shelling and mortar. Many of the Croat men of the city had been slaughtered in a nearby abattoir, an ominous prequel to Srebrenica. With an almost flagrant desire to taunt the international community and the hapless residents of the city, Dubrovnik, a UNESCO Heritage Centre, was repeatedly pounded in the long deadly autumn of 1991. On 23 October 1991, a young Bosnian girl Zlata Filipović recorded in her diary that 'a real war' was going on in Dubrovnik and that she had watched the shelling on the television with her parents, but that the city was 'cut off from the rest of the world'.[1] In the autumn of 1991 the war spread over the Bosnian border just briefly when Ravno, a village in Hercegovina close to the Croatian border, was devastated by an attack by the Yugoslav People's Army.

The massacre of civilians and the destruction of so many priceless buildings in the Bosnian War were predictable given that the adversaries were often the very same men. Indeed from the onset, the International Criminal Tribunal for the Former Yugoslavia, which was established in 1993 to investigate allegations of war crimes, formulated the idea of a 'joint criminal conspiracy' that linked the two wars. By 1992, Serbs had been rewarded for the ethnic cleansing of Croatia by granting them a *de facto* republic, a state within a state. This had come at the price of more than 11,000 deaths in

---

[1] Filipović, Zlata *Zlata's Diary: A Child's Life in Sarajevo* (Harmondsworth: Penguin 1994).

just a few months and the cities were full of refugees from Krajina and eastern Slavonia. Serbs living in Zagreb had been driven out by widespread intolerance and intimidation. Bitterness had become almost endemic across Croatia. In the summer of 1991, the United National had banned the import of weapons to the region, which penalized those forces that were not already fully armed. The democratically elected leaders of Bosnia found themselves unable to defend their state by a superior show of force against a heavily armed insurgency. Eventually the Bosnian government was able to arm and found some support from Islamic Mujahedeen, even reversing many of the defeats of 1992.[2]

Bosnia lurched towards war in circumstances in which many political errors were committed on all sides. In most modern democracies, politics is divided along left–right grounds and public discussion tends to revolve around how to distribute national wealth. In Bosnia, the elections had divided Bosnians into distinct ethno-religious parties that claimed to represent all their co-religionists regardless of any other ideology. Communist-era brotherhood was entirely replaced by the concept of power sharing. The character of the Serb insurgency and the willingness to use force as almost the first resort was clear from the previous months of fighting in Slavonia and Krajina. Radovan Karadžić as the leader of the Serbian Democratic Party (SDS) played a self-important role in this. In his infamous speech in the Bosnian parliament on 15 October 1991 he honed his role as 'God of War' (as he had been dubbed by the Croatian press): 'I want to repeat for the hundredth time that the Serbian Democratic Party does not create the will of the Serbian people, it interprets it.' He continued that independence from Yugoslavia would set the Muslims on a 'highway to hell' (*autostrada pakla*) because they could not defend themselves. This rhetorical challenge, which was played back at the Hague Tribunal on 29 October 2009, was intended to make him look like a moderating influence but it can also be juxtaposed with things that he is reported to have said around the same time. In October 1991, in a telephone conversation that was tapped, Karadžić talked about the breakdown of law and order in the event of Bosnian independence

[2] Hoare, Marko Attila *How Bosnia Armed* (London: Saqi, 2004).

as he imagined it. In a recording of the tape that was played at the Tribunal he said: 'They [i.e., Muslims/supporters of the Bosnian government] have to know that there are 20,000 armed Serbs around Sarajevo. That's insane. They will – they will disappear. Sarajevo will be a "karakazan", a black caldron, where 300,000 Muslims will die … That people will disappear from the face of the earth.'[3] The duplicity of Karadžić's personality was described by poet Semezdin Mehmedinović in his *Sarajevo Blues*: 'in all of our meetings he seemed to present very reasonable suggestions … He seldom spoke when we hung out in a group at cafes, he just listened. When he did join a conversation, his words were calm and reassuring, perhaps because of his years as a psychiatrist.'[4] Karadžić repeatedly made the point that Serb radicalization was so great that it could not be fully controlled by him. The fighting in Croatia in the previous months should probably have confirmed this to a Bosnian audience.

President Alija Izetbegović was visibly angry with Karadžić in the Bosnian parliament on 15 October and his response was to move ever closer to independence. He subsequently fell out with the JNA general Sefer Halilović very early on in the crisis, which led to bitter recrimination. In late February 1992, Halilović had argued for a more robust defence of Sarajevo. The Bosnian government called a referendum on independence on 29 February 1992, which was boycotted by almost one-third of the population of the republic. Bosnian Serb assembly members implored the Serb population not to take part. Of the electorate who did vote (between 64 and 67 per cent of those entitled to vote), more than 99 per cent opted for full independence from what remained of Yugoslavia. Even though the Serbs wanted to remain in Yugoslavia, this is unlikely to have been a state of 'brotherhood' as the Kosovars found out in the 1990s. The referendum revealed just how deep the chasm and incommensurability between those who wanted to leave Yugoslavia completely and those who wanted to remain had become. Bosnia had been a

---

[3] The International Criminal Tribunal for the Former Yugoslavia. Case number IT-95-5/18-T, the Prosecutor versus Radovan Karadzic, 27 October 2009, ICTY, The Hague.

[4] Mehmedinović, Semezdin *Sarajevo Blues* (San Francisco: City Light Books 1998), p. 14.

part of other states since the Middle Ages and this move would have been a profound break with historical tradition. It had leaned either westwards towards Central Europe or eastwards towards Belgrade and Istanbul. It was sandwiched between potential aggressors and its army had not yet been properly formed.

Despite internal divisions and the fact that they had failed to carry the support of the majority of the Serb population with them, the Bosnian government went ahead, declared independence and promptly faced widespread and highly organized Serb resistance. A Serb, Nikola Gardović, had been shot during a wedding in the *baščaršija* on 2 March 1992 at the time of the referendum and is often considered the first casualty of the war. Most Bosnians were more inclined to peaceful politics at this stage. On 6 April 1992, 20,000 unarmed people marched in Sarajevo as a protest against nationalist politics, demanding that Bosnia remain 'as one'. They reflected a growing sense of belonging that contrasted with Serb nationalist radicalization. In the 1991 census, most people had stated that their language was *bosanski*. They expressed anger not only towards the Serb nationalists but to politicians from other parties who had failed to curtail the radicalization. The author and actor Josip Pejaković had a microphone and was televised 'imploring the viewers at home to come into the streets. "We have been left to ourselves ... we must show them that we can come to an agreement ... we must come to an agreement, as we always have. Come to the government buildings, do not be afraid. You miners ... you hungry masses, come! We won't give up Bosnia! We won't!"'[5] The crowd then took up the chant. Tragically, as they were demonstrating, they were fired upon by a handful of snipers in the Olympic era Holiday Inn. Two young women – Suada Dilberović, a 23-year-old medical student from the University of Sarajevo and 34-year-old Olga Sučić – were killed. The Vrbanje bridge where they were shot was subsequently renamed in their honour. There is a small stone memorial beside the bridge and their deaths are frequently remembered to this day with fresh flowers. This event demonstrated that

---

5 Mujanović, Jasmin 'Princip, Valter, Pejić and the Raja: Elite Domination and Betrayal in Bosnia-Herzegovina', *South-East European Journal of Political Science* 1(3), 2013, p. 116.

unarmed democrats could be defeated by a small show of force and the point was to be repeated thousands of times over in the following years.

As independence was declared in Sarajevo and the new state was recognized internationally, a parallel 'Serb Republic of Bosnia and Hercegovina' was formed on 7 April 1992 (and was called Republika Srpska from August onwards). From this point on the Serbs created a separate state with its own institutions. The Yugoslav National Army (JNA) left Bosnia and Hercegovina in April 1992, by which time most of its weaponry was in the hands of the Bosnian Serbs. Backed by an armed wing of the SDS, a Bosnian Serb Army (VRS), commanded by former Communist general Ratko Mladić was quickly formed. Manoeuvres over the military draft in early 1992 had meant that the JNA was heavily staffed by Bosnian Serbs within the republic, which gave the Serbs an initial military advantage. Many Serbs argued that independence was illegal without the support of all three of the 'constituent' nations of Bosnia. They also asserted that they would have been in a majority had they not been suffered from genocide and the loss of about half a million Orthodox people in the Second World War. This point was continually reinforced by Serb propaganda.

Just as Zagreb had remained with the government during the Croatian War, the capital Sarajevo remained a stronghold of the Bosnian government and was subjected to one of the longest sieges in modern warfare. After the Serbs who opposed independence had held a parallel referendum on their own autonomy, they then began a genocidal campaign of terror in the areas that they held. They rapidly took over the northern and eastern parts of the country. The Serb strategy of war crimes was not an irrational outburst of ancient hatreds, but a military plan primarily intended to create a land bridge from Serbia to Krajina. At the trial of Radislav Krstić at the ICTY, the former Yugoslav army adviser Radovan Radinović said how important it had been to join 'Serb lands' together: 'without the Central Podrinje, there would be no Republika Srpska, there would be no territorial integrity of Serb ethnic territories'.[6] In the

---

[6] Wagner, Sarah E. *To Know Where He Lies: DNA Technology and the Search for Srebrenica's Missing* (Berkeley, CA: University of California Press, 2008), p. 26.

first few weeks of the war, the boldness of the plan became apparent. As a town close to the border with Serbia, Bijeljina was the first town to be systematically targeted. Željko Ražnatović, known to his men as Arkan, led a tightly organized band of paramilitaries known as the Tigers into the city. Many were experienced troops, directly involved in atrocities in Vukovar in 1991. They murdered vulnerable and unprotected civilians, especially those involved in political parties, and left their mutilated bodies on display, a tactic later dubbed 'elitocide' by British journalist Michael Nicholson. Just a few months after the end of Communism and within days of the first free elections in Croatia, Arkan had led his knife-carrying supporters who then rushed onto the pitch at Maksimir Stadium in Zagreb. The 13 May 1990 riots between fans of Dinamo Zagreb and Red Star Belgrade have often been seen as a prelude to the war.[7]

For several days before, local Serbs in Bijeljina had stayed away from work, collectively aware that the city would be targeted. Many people also panicked and fled. Paramilitaries allowed pictures to be taken before executions, but also killed dozens of foreign journalists that summer, many of them Austrian. The armed Serbs protected by the reconstituted JNA, moved swiftly across eastern and northern Bosnia with astonishing speed. Those Muslims and Croats who did not make it to larger towns were rounded up and put in makeshift detention camps in buildings that had been schools and barracks. Thousands of sexual attacks took place on men, women and children. Prison camps at Manjača, Prijedor and Omarska were set up to taunt, scare and starve Muslims in an attempt to break their resolve. War tourists arrived from Switzerland or Germany and tortured their former neighbours. The houses of those that had fled were burnt or gutted. Floorboards were lifted in the search for booty, fruit orchards torched and gardens dug up. Landmines were laid to punish those who dared to return and widespread looting also took place. White goods appeared on the Belgrade black market and opportunistic looters reported seeing the bodies of Muslims

[7] Slapšak, Svetlana, Milošević, Milan, Cvetićanin, Radivoj, Mihailović, Srećko, Curgus Kazimir, Velimir and Gredelj, Stjepan *The War Started at Maksimir: Hate Speech in the Media: Content Analyses of Politika and Borba Newspapers, 1987–1991* (Belgrade: Media Centre, 1997).

Fig. 14 Monument to fallen Serbian soldiers in the Bosnian
War in Bijeljina (by Richard Mills)

floating in the rivers. When Arkan's wife Ceca Ražnatović appeared
on Belgrade television years later wearing a necklace, a viewer phoned
in and described its inscription precisely. It had been stolen from her
in Bijeljina.[8]

Within weeks, armed Serbs had taken over almost 70 per cent of
the country. Civilians remaining in Serb-occupied territories by the late
spring of 1992 either fled to government-held areas such as Sarajevo
or to the eastern towns, which were entirely surrounded until 1995.
Towns such as Goražde, Srebrenica and Žepa became virtual ghettos,
often without transport links, medical supplies or basic foodstuffs.
Paramilitary groups formed across the region. Vojislav Šešelj, originally from Sarajevo, proclaimed himself the head of the Četniks, and
it was often commented that his followers were drunken, dirty and

[8] Higginbotham, Adam 'Beauty and the Beast', *The Observer*, 4 January 2004.

poorly disciplined.[9] His supporters were distinctive in the 1990s as they grew long, often unkempt beards and stank of alcohol. According to popular culture, they frightened and threatened people, but were generally inefficient killers. Far more devastating in terms of loss of life were organized groups, including the *Beli Orlovi* (White Eagles), led by Dragoslav Bokan, and Mirko Jović's *Vitezovi* (Knights) inspired by sharper images such as those in martial arts films. In Hercegovina the Croat *Jokeri* (Jokers) unit dressed in black and white and with Ustaša insignia. Changing outward appearance seems to have been a highly significant part of the transition from 1980s to 1990s Bosnia. Michael Sells observed that paramilitaries transformed themselves into different figures and actually wore ski masks or painted their faces: 'Before he put on the mask, the militiaman was part of a multi-religious community … Once he put on the mask, he was a Serb hero; those he was abusing were *balije* or Turks, race-traitors or killers of the Christ-Prince Lazar.'[10] Men who dressed up became 'knights' rather than neighbour-killers and rapists. In part this was because nationalism was built on a number of historical myths. Ivan Čolović has argued that the 'discourse of warlike ethnic nationalism places contemporary events … outside the co-ordinates of historical time … [offering] a mythic, anti-historical perception of time'.[11]

SARAJEVO UNDER SIEGE

The siege of Sarajevo had a military and strategic purpose, but it was also intended to break the spirit of the democratically elected government and its supporters. Ratko Mladić had reportedly told his troops to shoot slowly and to shell the city until the inhabitants were 'on the edge of madness'.[12] In 1992, the director Paweł Pawlikowski made the film *Serbian Epics* on the mountain of Romanija, when he pictured the Russian poet Eduard Limonov firing on Sarajevo

---

[9] Vulliamy, Ed *Seasons in Hell: Understanding Bosnia's War* (London: Simon and Schuster 1994), p. 46.

[10] Sells, Michael. *The Bridge Betrayed: Religion and Genocide in Bosnia*, 2nd edn (Berkeley, CA: University of California Press, 1998), p. 77.

[11] Čolović, *Politics of Symbol in Serbia*, p. 13.

[12] Du Preez Bezrob, Anne Marie *Sarajevo Roses: War Memoir of a Peacekeeper* (Cape Town: Struik Publishers, 2006), p. 61.

for 'sport', while in the background a guslar sang and lambs were roasted on spits. Romanija was linked to resistance and banditry and these rituals served to historicize the struggle. In the same film, Karadžić explained the strategy of encircling the city to Limanov. He gave a version of the history of the region and discussed his own poetry. 'Notice how many mosques they have ... After Turks came, after Kosovo battle, Serbs who didn't accept Islam have been pushed to the mountains, out of valleys, out of good land.' He continued, 'there is a poem of mine about Sarajevo ... "I can hear disaster walking, city is burning out like a *tamjan*" [incense in an Orthodox Church] ... many other poems have something of prediction, which frightens me sometimes'. Although a Montenegrin with Četnik heritage, Karadžić had moved to the city as a youth and worked as an UDBA informer while he was a student. In his professional life, he had been a psychiatrist and coached a football team before becoming involved in Serb nationalist politics.

Karadžić and his supporters were frequently seen as men who wanted to destroy urban civilization. The Bosnian government used an idea of barbaric backwoodsmen versus the urbane sophistication of the town-dwellers and this notion of 'mountain men' was also picked up and used by Western journalists during the siege. However, many of the soldiers were from Sarajevo and had had fairly normal lives in the city before 1992. Borislav Herak, a soldier who gained notoriety after he confessed to murder and rape, had previously worked in a textile factory. He continued to tune into local radio despite being on the other side after he quit the city in May 1992. Herak's father stayed behind and warned his son not to join the Bosnian Serb army. 'I told Boro many times, "Never pick up a gun" ... But he didn't listen. He just said, "That's okay, old man, you just stay here and wait for the Serbian shells to kill you".'[13] Perhaps part of the appeal of fighting in the VRS or for paramilitary groups was that the standard rules of war had been discarded. Men could rape women and were clearly told that they could do this in revenge for Serb women who were being attacked by the other side. They could steal other people's possessions and

---

[13] Burns, John 'A Killer's Tale – A Special Report', *New York Times*, 27 November 1992.

commit acts of vandalism without punishment. They behaved not so much like mountain men but like violent automata. When they talked about the war much later, many expressed a detached kind of solipsistic regret for what they had done and suicide remains high among Bosnians.

Sarajevo divided into hostile neighbourhoods, which quickly became frontlines. Apartment blocks on opposite sides of the same street formed the frontline. Buildings were repeatedly pounded and many of them still have the mortar pockmarks. Although the government and supporters clung onto power north of the Miljacka, the southern suburb of Grbavica became the frontline. Non-Serbs living outside the areas of government protection were subjected to horrific treatment. Women were raped, attacked by gangs, tied to tanks and motor vehicles and sometimes shot. Others perished from blood loss after sustaining internal injuries. Some Serbs managed to tip off their neighbours in the suburb, but many remained part of a conspiracy to scare, 'punish' and eliminate their neighbours. Government positions were pounded with mortars until 1995. Nests of snipers were set up in the surrounding suburbs and hills targeting civilians and some passages and tramlines were particularly vulnerable. Grbavica football stadium was on the frontline and significantly damaged. A tunnel was constructed that lead Sarajevans to the airport beneath Serb-held territory, which meant shifting tonnes of soil. It was constructed very rapidly and acted as a lifeline to the city. Controlled by the Bosnian army, who required people to submit official documents, hundreds of thousands of civilians made their way out of the city this way. It took a couple of hours to walk to the airport on foot. The tunnel was vulnerable to flooding, but also allowed arms and food supplies to reach the population. Travelling to Sarajevo airport remained very perilous and, in January 1993, deputy prime minister Hakija Turajlić was killed.

Thankfully most of the books and manuscripts from the Gazi Husrev Beg Foundation Library were hidden, smuggled out by the resourceful and courageous staff including the night watchman, the cleaner and the head librarian who all dodged scores of bullets in order to preserve what they regarded as the people's heritage. They concealed books in banana crates in the safer cellars of a mosque. The art historian Marian Wenzel smuggled the library's catalogue out of the country and delivered it to the Al-Furqan Islamic Heritage Foundation in London, who subsequently gave the museum staff an award for their courage.[14] The collection in the Vijećnica did not fare so well. It was gutted and about two million of priceless and irreplaceable books and manuscripts destroyed. 'Sarajevans describe how the air was filled with flakes of paper covered in elegant Arabic calligraphy that turned into ash as they fell.'[15] Observers who struggled to put out the blaze believed it was the interior rather than the exterior of the building that was predominantly targeted. By destroying much of the extant manuscripts of the republic, the aggressors were not only trying to destroy culture, but also cadastral records. Many firefighters died in the attempt to save the Habsburg landmark. The Haggadagh that survived the expulsion from Spain of the Ladino community and occupation of Sarajevo by the Ustaša only survived the siege by being locked up in a vault. Since the war, it has been exhibited permanently.

Journalists reported on the Bosnian war, setting themselves up as important moral authorities in a situation of international inaction. Ed Vulliamy, a passionate lobbyist for human rights, later served as an expert witness at The Hague. Maggie O'Kane was stunningly bold in her methods and made pioneering interviews with nationalist extremists. Roy Gutman was the first person to write about prison camps in detail. As journalists clustered in the Holiday Inn without running water in the taps, they shared the risks of the city. Many of their memoirs have a genuine literary quality and convey the frustration of those years very well. War reporting was not without some controversy. A British newspaper, *The Daily Mirror*, ran a headline: 'Belsen 92: the picture that shames the world'. The picture was of emaciated prisoners in one of the *ad hoc* detention centres that had been set up by the Serbs. Comparisons between the predicament of the Bosnian Muslims and the victims of the

[14] Walasek, Helen, 'Marian Wenzel 18 December 1932–6 January 2002', *Bosnia Report*, nos. 27–18, May 2002.
[15] MacDowall, Andrew 'Sarajevo: City Commemorates End to 'a Century of Conflict', but Divisions Still Run Deep', *Observer*, 28 June 2014.

Fig. 15 Mortar damage in Sarajevo (by Richard Mills)

Third Reich seemed apt, although it is not always clear that this has helped outsiders to understand what actually happened.

The courage and tenacity of ordinary Bosnians during the war years is a tale of wonder. Sarajevo streets were repeatedly hit by bombs and shelling left thousands dead and many more with grievous injuries. Loss of limbs was a frequent result of mortar bombs. The Markale marketplace in the centre of the city was a favourite target and, because of the concentration of shoppers, scores of people could be killed with one bomb. Sarajevans accepted death and injury with sublime grace. Muslims referred to the sense of community as *merhamet*,[16] which could perhaps be translated as collective philanthropy. Those who had been killed or injured received an enhanced level of respect from the community. Muslim military martyrs known as *šehidi* were buried in Sarajevo's cemeteries with

---

[16] Weine, Stevan M. 'Redefining *Merhamet* after a Historical Nightmare' in Joel M. Halpern and David A. Kideckel (eds.) *Neighbors at War: Anthropological Perspectives on Yugoslav Ethnicity, Culture and History* (Pennsylvania: Penn State Press, 2000), p. 404.

dedicated monuments to them. Nermin Tulić, a theatre director who lost his legs in the bread queue bombs, subsequently appeared in his wheelchair in the 2003 film set in Sarajevo *Ljeto u zlatnoj dolini* (*Summer in the Golden Valley*). He has spoken movingly about how his family helped him after his injury.

Life inside Sarajevo, quite apart from the mortal threat of bombs and bullets, was far from easy. The presence of UN peacekeepers led to a sharp increase in prostitution and corruption. Criminal gangs controlled the city trade through a black market in valuables and mafia style organization. Some such as Ismet Bajramović (nicknamed Ćelo 'the bald forehead') attained an allure of criminal glamour after they were interviewed by foreign magazines. The men who built the tunnel out of Sarajevo were paid a packet of cigarettes a day instead of wages; such was their value on the street. Cosmetics were also a valuable commodity as women struggled to preserve their appearance despite adversity. Many recollected how they would dress smartly to defy the aggressor and chose their best clothes to wear when they went out to market. Pride became an important mechanism in the preservation of the new normal. Within the city, intolerance towards Serbs who had chosen to stay was tangible although divisions were not always clear cut. Although most insisted on calling the insurgents 'Četniks', Serbs in the city were harassed and reproached. There had been significant intermarriage in the city before 1992 but none of these relationships survived the war, and divorced couples would move to either side of the divided city. Gavrilo Princip's great-nephew Mile fought in the siege of Sarajevo, while Mile's aunt Svetlana remained in the besieged city. Life on rations, precarious emergency healthcare and the lack of real interaction with the outside world whittled away at people's spirits. UN rations were not considered to be adequate to support an active life, although they aimed to provide over 2,000 calories per day mostly in tinned and dried food. One scene in the 1997 film *Savršeni krug* (*A Perfect Circle*), which is about the siege, revolves around recovering tins of corned beef that had been concealed inside the toilet cistern. Ribald jokes about the lack of privacy during blackouts were commonplace. Yet somehow people adapted. Ivana Maček's wonderful *Sarajevo under Siege* (2009) based on her wartime fieldwork as an anthropologist, describes how one young man whose family were eating oats joked about the extra B vitamins that had improved their hair and nails. Maček describes the lengths that some would go to in order to make a decent cup of coffee. 'One of the more fascinating scenes I witnessed was a group of young men in front of the Youth Theater beside a very battered Fiat 550 [the smallest car that existed in the former Yugoslavia, nicknamed Fića]. The car had no wheels and the engine compartment at the back was opened. The men were connecting an espresso machine to the engine.'[17]

Many turned to writing to reach their own people and the outside world. Teenager Zlata Filipović wrote a poignant diary in which she nicknamed the sniper that fired on their district 'Jovo' (a common Serbian name). She was often compared to Anna Frank by contemporaries, although she survived the war. Izet Sarajlić wrote mordant, biting poems about the siege, the injuries to the people queuing for bread, the absence of protest and support from 'former Yugoslav friends'. In *Teorija distance* he reminded his readers: 'I am one of those who think that on Monday, one should talk about things that pertain to Monday. It may be too late by Tuesday.'[18] Miljenko Jergović wrote a series of memorable short stories in the collection *Sarajevski Marlboro*, published in 1994. His style is heavily laden with symbolism and explores the pain of broken relations with neighbours through the metaphor of an apple tree and the death by mortar of a young beautiful 'doll' from Foča. *Sarajevo, ljubavi moja* (*Sarajevo, Love of Mine*) was Schlager-style ballad written in early 1970s and popular throughout Yugoslavia. Originally written by Kemal Monteno in 1973, its words took on even more poignancy in the 1990s and it became an anthem for the besieged city during the 1990s war, even sung by American folk singer Joan Baez when she arrived wearing a flak jacket in 1993: 'We grew up together you, the city and I … Under Mount Trebević we dreamt as to who would grow up faster and who would be the most beautiful. The growing boy fell in love then

[17] Maček, Ivana *Sarajevo under Siege: Anthropology in Wartime* (Philadelphia: Penn State Press, 2009), pp. 72, 79.
[18] Sarajlić, Izet 'Teorija distance' in *Sarajevska ratna zbirka* (Sarajevo: OKO, 1995), p. 10.

and he stayed here, connected to his city. All roads lead me to you
... Sarajevo, love of mine!' *Sarajevo, mon amour* was the French
title of General Jovan Divjak's 2004 memoir about the wartime
defence of the city. Sarajevo had always been loved by its citizens
and the war served to magnify this affection. Many preferred to
stay and risk death rather than lose their city

DESTRUCTION OF THE ENVIRONMENT AND CULTURAL ARTEFACTS

During the war, theft and looting became widespread. Gardens
were dug up of those Muslims who had made money in Western
Europe and might have hidden it. Stolen goods appeared for sale
in markets outside Bosnia for a fraction of their purchase value.
Nevertheless much of the handling of other people's property during the wars of the 1990s was gratuitously destructive. Food rotted
in the fridges of unoccupied damaged houses while the carcasses
of pets rotted in the yards. In the beginning of 1992, the Bosnian
landscape was dotted with mosques and churches, many of which
were of international architectural significance. Often well-tended
and cleaned by local women, mosques were filled with carpets, tiles
and silverwork. They were surrounded by characteristic Muslim
graveyards or *türbe*. In the course of the war, dozens were simply
destroyed. The Ferhat Pasha and Arnaudija mosques in Banja Luka
were blown up by the new nationalist authorities in 1993. Both had
been built in the sixteenth century, commissioned by Ferhad-paša
Sokolović, a relative of the Ottoman grand vizier. The Atik mosque
in Bijeljina was built in the reign of Suleiman the Magnificent and
dominated the town centre. The late journalist Gaby Rado sent an
extraordinary report from Bijeljina about the destruction of the
mosque, which was broadcast on ITN in the United Kingdom. Five
mosques were demolished in March 1993 during the night by a militia called the Panthers led by Ljubiša Savić. When the citizens of the
city awoke, diggers were levelling the sites. All telephone lines had
been cut off immediately before the explosions. According to Rado
'most local Serbs appeared shocked by what had happened'. It was
also reported that an Orthodox priest in the town wept during the
service on hearing the news. The eighteenth-century Mehmed-paša

Kukavica mosque in Foča was destroyed even earlier in 1992 along with the town's medressa.

In a desperate attempt to save the old bridge at Mostar and to keep their lifeline going, the defenders of the city had covered the stone structure and strung old tyres over the sides to protect the masonry. The bridge came under sustained mortar fire and was finally breached on 8 November 1993. The following day, the rest of the bridge fell quite suddenly and the stone masonry crashed into the Neretva River, which caused a large silty wave of stone. Much of the original masonry was recovered from the river by divers and was used when the bridge was rebuilt in 2004. Although the new bridge is a fine structure, it has lost the patina of the old Ottoman bridge. The bridge was destroyed by the Croatian Defence Council (HVO), clearly unaware that the original bridge had been constructed by Catholic stonemasons from Korčula and Dubrovnik under the direction of Muslim architects.[19] The HVO also destroyed the nearby Orthodox monastery of Žitomislić, which has since been rebuilt. In 1996, the novelist Jasmina Musabegović dedicated the novel *Most* (*The Bridge*) to the famous landmark. Along with the visible signs of Islamic life in Bosnia, such as the architecture, every other aspect of what it meant to be a Muslim at that time was also threatened.

SREBRENICA: GENOCIDE DISGUISED AS WAR

It took more than three years for the initial gains made by the VRS to be rolled back. The north-western town of Bihać, which became a United Nations safe area in 1993, proved to be the hardest town for the Serbs to take. Although close to the Serbian Krajina – and vital if the Serbs were to create a land bridge from Knin to Bjeljina – it was quite some distance from Serbia. The towns of Velika Kladuša and Bihać are geographically much more closely linked to Croatia than Sarajevo or Mostar. Despite its proximity to Croatia, Bihać had a large concentration of Muslim inhabitants. It was also difficult to take because of its geographical position nestling beside the Una River. There were some autonomous political trends and the town had been the power base of entrepreneur Fikret Abdić

---

[19] Goldstein, Ivo *Croatia: A History* (London: Hurst, 1999), p. 24.

before the war. As the rebel Serbs were pushed out of Krajina and failed to take Bihać despite huge losses, their military tactics became more desperate and the army demoralized. They turned their attention to easier prey. The inhabitants and refugees in Srebrenica had been marooned without access to adequate medicine and nutrition for more than two years by the time the town was encircled and overrun in July 1995. Morale was low among the inhabitants and Dutch UN soldiers. Sanitary conditions were terrible as large families shared limited facilities.

The capture of Srebrenica by the VRS in July 1995 depended on several factors. General Mladić knew the moment to inflict a decisive defeat on the Bosnian government and its supporters would never come again and he dealt first with his own men. Calling them 'brothers', Mladić walked among the men exhorting them to have courage. His direct and personal leadership style won him great devotion among his own troops. Then he dealt with the UN peacekeepers. The Dutch soldiers who had arrived at this posting in January 1995, had not got on particularly well with the local people (the misogynistic and anti-Islamic graffiti that they left behind still shame them years after the event). The UN were extremely poorly equipped and high command ignored their calls for airstrikes. In the context, they felt unsafe and unprepared to risk their lives. Mladić made assurances and taunted the UN commander Lieutenant-Colonel Thomas Karremans with alcoholic toasts to a long life and cynically exploited the Dutch unwillingness to stand up to the VRS.

In any other circumstances, Ratko Mladić is unlikely to have become a *génocidaire*. Although his father was killed by the Ustaša when he was an infant, he grew up in a small village on good terms with his Muslim neighbours, a fact he has himself acknowledged. He often talked nostalgically about the Yugoslav Communist period. Mladić had a good JNA career and would have been familiar as an officer with UN Conventions on the treatment of prisoners of war. In 1991 in Croatia, he already used tactics that bled into crimes against humanity. Unlike Karadžić, who had an elective affinity for extreme views, Mladić was a relatively ordinary man. He was adored by many Serbs and drew his military pension until 2005. By the time he was apprehended in

Vojvodina, he was poor and infirm. To date, he has not expressed any remorse.

In the late afternoon of 11 July, the VRS moved into the deserted town. It was an exceptionally hot day, over 35 degrees Celsius in the afternoon. Ratko Mladić appeared on television on 11 July 1995, telling viewers that Srebrenica was now 'Serbian' and that it was his gift to the 'Serb nation'. He continued that recalling the uprising against the 'Turks' (a reference to the early nineteenth century), the time for revenge had now come. At the Hotel Fontana in Bratunac on the evening of 11 July 1995, the Dutch representatives arrived with a schoolteacher Nesib Mandžić, an unofficial Bosnian Muslim representative to meet with Mladić. The consensus of the UN and Bosnian Muslim participants in the meeting was that General Mladić was putting on a threatening show calculated to intimidate them. The noise emitted by the dying pig has often been compared with a human voice. As the meeting began, the cries of a pig being slaughtered just outside the window could be heard in the meeting room. Mladić then placed the broken signboard from the Srebrenica Town Hall on the table.[20]

The Dutch had expected airstrikes that morning, but there was no attempt to save the town and they clearly felt abandoned and overwhelmed. In their desperation, most of the Muslims fled to the UN base at nearby Potočari where they believed that they would be safer. Several thousand people from the besieged enclave attempted to walk on foot to Tuzla through the hills and forest. The UN only allowed 5,000 people into the camp so the remaining refugees camped in nearby farms and other unoccupied buildings. The soldier Raviv van Renssen had been killed some days earlier by a grenade thrown by a Bosnian Muslim, who was angry because he expected UN troops to stay and defend them. The Dutch has been badly demoralized by Raviv's death and had lost some of their remaining sympathy for the Muslims as a result. On 12 July, buses arrived from Bratunac and the women and children were separated from the men. More than 20,000 women left Srebrenica in buses and were never reunited with their male relatives. Men were roughly

---

[20] The International Criminal Tribunal for the Former Yugoslavia, http://uhk.bilgi. edu.tr/.../prosecutor_ vs_radislav_krstic.doc.

ordered into nearby buildings where the executions began and were witnessed at this stage by the Dutch. The VRS then attempted to round up the men who had fled to the hills, pounding them with artillery. Captured men were taken to a nearby Bratunac and then on to warehouses, schools and deserted buildings in the wider region where they were targeted with grenades and shot en masse.

The UN troops were allowed to leave the enclave and were warmly greeted by Mladić who offered Karremans wrapped gifts. They had been forced to leave their weapons behind in Potočari. Delighted to leave Bosnia, they left without knowing fully what had happened in the 'safe area'. At a drunken victory party in Zagreb, they were congratulated by defence minister Joris Voorhoeve as they danced in a *kolo* (ring dance) to a brass band version of Gloria Gaynor's song *I Will Survive*. The Dutch army and government have received substantial criticism for their actions at Srebrenica. The publication of a report in 2002 by the Instituut voor Oorlogs-, Holocaust- en Genocidestudies led to the resignation of the prime minister Wim Kok. The report's authors deemed that the Dutch failed in its mandate, but also criticized the lack of UN response to Karremans' request for airstrikes. Goražde had not fallen precisely because the UN troops based there had interpreted the UN mandate differently. It is also clear that the Dutch underestimated the genocidal intent of the VRS, but they were hardly alone in that respect. Mladić had repeatedly lied to the Dutch and assured them that the refugees, if they surrendered their arms, would not be killed. The international community had tolerated years of attacks on unarmed civilians across Bosnia with offensive explanations about the barbarism of local people and their innate propensity to commit acts of violence. There was a studied resistance in recognizing that the point of the war was to destroy a democratically elected government and to take as much of the country as possible. The VRS were prepared to kill as many people as necessary to do this.

Serb attitudes towards the Muslims of Srebrenica had hardened after the attacks on the village of Kravica on Orthodox Christmas Day, 7 January 1993. Although most of the casualties were military, Bosnian government forces led by Naser Orić had killed a number of civilians in the village and destroyed properties. This battle attained an important symbolic significance for the VRS as the war progressed and hardened divisions. Mladić knew that his troops were angry about the terrible losses sustained at Bihać. Of the 22,000 Serb casualties in the war, most were military. Like some of the pals brigades in the First World War, the losses were not spread across the Serb community. According to a former student of mine who left Bosnia in 1992 to avoid the war, all the Serbs from his high school class in Bugojno were killed trying to take Bihać. Rape and abuse of prisoners had demonstrably not improved Serb morale and they were defiant in spite of international hostility and isolation. The impact of the war had taken a toll on Mladić, whose public statements became more bizarre and duplicitous as the war progressed. His daughter Ana killed herself in Belgrade in 1994, apparently in response to learning about her father's role in the siege of Sarajevo.

In the following days after the assault on Srebrenica, thousands of Muslim men were executed and dumped in the surrounding killing fields. Most were shot one after another, offering little resistance as they presumably feared mutilation and torture. Dražen Erdemović, an unemployed Croat from Tuzla married to a Serb, who joined the VRS for complex reasons related to personal finances, believed he had personally killed about 90 men. Crippled with guilt, he confessed to a journalist and his former army colleagues tried – unsuccessfully – to assassinate him. Brought to The Hague, he recounted the Srebrenica genocide under considerable duress, often on the brink of tears. His testimony at The Hague presented the war from the perspective of 'ordinary men': 'I wish to say that I feel sorry for all the victims, not only for the ones who were killed then at that farm … I have lost many very good friends of all nationalities only because of that war, and I am convinced that all of them, all of my friends, were not in favour of a war. I am convinced of that. But simply they had no other choice. This war came and there was no way out. The same happened to me.'[21] Erdemović was given a new identity after his release from prison.

Very few of those involved in the crimes of the 1990s did express remorse and often used the courtroom as a theatre to justify their

---

[21] The International Criminal Tribunal for the Former Yugoslavia, www.icty.org/x/cases/erdemovic/tjug/en/erd-tsj961129e.pdf.

narcissistic worldviews and criminal behaviour. The dentist and SDS politician from Krajina, Milan Babić, hanged himself in 2006 and asked his Croat brothers for forgiveness in his last testimony. Among the leading politicians, he has proved to be exceptional. Since he surrendered himself for trial at The Hague in 2003 charged with crimes against humanity, Vojislav Šešelj has often been in contempt of court by swearing and insulting individuals such as the judge Carla del Ponte and the politician Javier Solana. Originally elected in 1990 for the Serbian Democratic Party, Biljana Plavšić was regarded as rhetorically one of the most extreme nationalists. Formally a prolific researcher in plant biology at the University of Sarajevo, her speeches were peppered with inferences about Serb genetic superiority and Bosnian Muslim inferiority after 1991. During the war she was a senior politician in Republika Srpska. She surrendered to The Hague Tribunal in 2001 and used the courtroom to make a dramatic speech about the error of her previous ways. Sentenced originally to 11 years after being found guilty of crimes against humanity, she published a memoir *Svedočim* (*I Testify*) and was released early. After her release, she repudiated her contrite testimony.

In some respects the massacre at Srebrenica, which was deemed to be genocide by the International Criminal Tribunal in The Hague, has had a greater impact on internal and international politics than any of the other crimes against humanity committed during the Bosnian War or indeed since the Second World War in Europe. It exposed the anti-Islamic attitudes of some of the Dutch troops and eventually led to the resignation of a government in the Netherlands. The impact of the Srebrenica catastrophe was felt beyond the Balkans and the Netherlands. The credibility of the UN as peacekeepers was fatally weakened, which may have helped to pave the way for defiance of the United Nations by the military alliance led by the United States that invaded Iraq in 2003. Only when overwhelming military force was offered to the Serbs in 1994 and 1995 by NATO and by the Croatian army in Serb-held Krajina did the attacks on the Bosnian government start to falter. The local UN commanders handed the people of the town over to their enemies in what became one of the most tragic episodes in a long history of international ineptitude. The 8,000 men and boys who had been defined as 'combatants' were murdered and dumped in nearby fields in flagrant and cynical disregard for international law. In the run up to the Bosnian and Croatian Wars, Serb extremists had made a choice. Rather than scupper these new states at a slow pace of subversion (as the Albanians attempted to do in Kosovo after 1989), they adopted a strategy that resembled the eliminations of the Balkans Wars, but this time with modern weapons. And like the Ustaša, they struck rapidly and killed or drove out populations at lightning speed. Many remain unrepentant. The slogan 'Nož, žica, Srebrenica' ('knife, wire, Srebrenica') has been used regularly as a taunt by extreme nationalists.

PATTERNS OF VIOLENCE

Although I have argued that the war in Bosnia was essentially one of strategy and initiated to gain as much territory as possible, it was accompanied by a very high level of violence, far in excess of what would have been needed to simply win the war. First, there was the use of irregular soldiers. Paramilitaries were deployed throughout the war. The fear that their terrible violence engendered was often enough to frighten people out of their towns and villages with stories of atrocities committed spreading very quickly. Many were not from Bosnia and were attracted to fight because they were extreme nationalists, zealots, sadists or all of those things at the same time. Second, sexual violence and crimes of intimacy in which people hurt those they had once been on good terms with were also widespread. In 1986 Bosnian Muslim Sinan Sakić had a hit song about unrequited love *Pusti me da živim* (*Let Me Live*).[22] When Sakić performed it live, the audience would cheerfully sing along to the chorus, but it was used to taunt inmates in the Omarska camp before they were tortured.

In the 1980s Bosnia did not look like a country on the verge of civil war. As the economy was weak, many had travelled to cities outside the republic to get work. Serbs had headed for Belgrade, Croats to Zagreb and all to the factories of Germany and Scandinavia. Most people still treasured brotherhood and unity and

---

[22] 'Bosnia – 20 years on', *Observer*, 8 April 2012.

Fig. 16 Damage to buildings in Mostar (by Matt Willer)

had genuinely warm relations with people of other faiths. Old ethnic barriers had broken down in the cities, especially Sarajevo, and there was widespread exogamy and atheism. Many of the old ethnic markers had gone by the 1960s. Young women of all backgrounds had worn whatever was in fashion, be that miniskirts or drainpipes, and had long since abandoned headscarves. Younger men had also adopted global fashions and went out with friends of other religious backgrounds to drink coffee or beer. Schools and universities were totally integrated and taught courses such as the 'History of the Yugoslav Peoples'. Neighbours visited each other on religious holidays and took time off work to honour each other's customs.

Many Bosnians, possibly the absolute numerical majority, completely ignored wartime radicalization and propaganda. Tito's granddaughter, medical doctor Svetlana Broz, collected a remarkable series of stories about neighbours who helped each other during the Bosnian War in her 2004 collection about 'complicity and resistance', *Good People in an Evil Time*. Zorica Baltić a Serb from Mostar was not only helped by her Croat neighbours Andelko Filipović and Ivica Federcija, but was also admitted to a Mostar hospital by a Muslim doctor, Meliha Imamović, head of the psychiatric ward, in order to hide her.[23] One Muslim in Sarajevo told Ivana Maček: 'When an anti-tank shell hit ... my apartment, [a] Serb neighbour was the first one to come and help, to clean it up. He, and another neighbour who left with his family. Two fine people. Not because they helped me, I thought the same also earlier.'[24] Serb General Jovan Divjak left the JNA and led the defence of Sarajevo, which he considered to be his moral and human duty. Attempts to extradite him to Serbia in 2011 were foiled by the Austrian authorities and he receives a hero's welcome wherever he goes in the Bosnian-Croat Federation. Nevertheless political crises can serve to whittle away at universal human values and distort the behaviour of individuals once deemed normal. Duško Tadić, a Bosnian Serb who tortured his Muslim neighbours, including his former best friend, clearly had a nationalist worldview before the war started, but this may only have been ignited by propaganda in the preceding months as he joined the Serbian Democratic Party in Kozarac. As long as a sense of real difference was retained in the domestic sphere, there was always potential for division. In April 1992, a Serb soldier Miloš fighting in the siege of Sarajevo told journalist Ed Vulliamy 'Their women are bitches and whores. They breed like animals, more than ten per woman ... Down there they are fighting for a single land that will stretch from here to Tehran, where our women will wear shawls, where there is bigamy.'[25] In the privacy of the home, negative words for Muslims were used, such as *balija*, which spilled into the public sphere. Religious faith is not just a series of practices but involves the maintenance of distinct worldviews and values. Even if these values are only nurtured at home and not by the state, they will persist. Furthermore, there was a deep and perhaps not always conscious sense of historic difference between Serbs and Bosnian Muslims, which was complicated by a widespread belief that they had once come from the same families.

[23] Broz, Svetlana and Laurie Kain Hart (eds) *Good People in an Evil Time: Portraits of Complicity and Resistance in the Bosnian War* (New York: Other Press, 2004), pp. 35–37.

[24] Maček, Ivana 'Predicament of War: Sarajevo Experience and the Ethics of War', in Bettina E. Schmidt and Ingo W. Schröder (eds.) *Anthopology of Violence and Conflict* (London: Routledge, 2001), p. 215.

[25] Vulliamy, *Seasons in Hell*, p. 49.

The old customs and habits of Muslims, such as rituals of cleanliness, reinforced their own sense of separateness and even superiority to their Christian neighbours. The notion that Islam was a spiritual gift that enhanced their way of life implicitly meant that other people were less well-favoured. Islamic radicalism outside Bosnia after 1979 had also given this community a new sense of difference. Catholicism had flourished in Hercegovina after the 1870s and grew in confidence at the same time as Croatian nationalism was developing. The revival of religiosity in the 1980s in Medjugorje gave the people of that region a sense of distinctness. This led to a sense of their political distinctness and undermined a sense of belonging to Bosnia-Hercegovina. The Orthodox people had been oppressed under the Ottomans and the Habsburgs had failed to win them over. The ancestors of many of Bosnia's Serbs had been the old *rayah*, the poor and dispossessed people whose faith was a consolation. The destruction of so many Orthodox villages during the Second World War by both Bosnian Croats and Muslims had reinforced a mistrustful Serb worldview. Brotherhood and unity was a state policy enforced by the police and army. Andrei Simić has argued there was an 'invisible psychological wall'[26] between neighbours that covered alienation, fear and suspicion of other constituent nations.

The high incidence of rape became a focus of international attention and opened up a significant debate about the relationship between war and sexual violence. It also had an impact on the international judicial processes. In 1996, The Hague Tribunal prosecuted rape as a crime against humanity for the first time. Bosnian Muslim women were widely targeted and, as rape was not as widespread phenomenon in the Croatian War of 1991, this high incidence in Bosnia – in the tens of thousands – begs the question as to whether these women were targeted primarily because they were Muslim. Tone Bringa noted during her fieldwork that Muslim women were generally more devout than men and more likely to fast and make

---

[26] Simić, Andrei 'Nationalism as Folk Ideology: The Case of the Former Yugoslavia' in Joel M. Halpern and David A. Kideckel (eds.) *Neighbors at War: Anthropological Perspectives on Yugoslav Ethnicity, Culture and History* (Pennsylvania: Penn State Press, 2000), p. 115.

traditional ablutions.[27] Rape victims had infections of staphylococcus and other bacteria that originate in dirt and faecal matter after being raped. According to them, the rapists were dirty and smelt bad and in some cases already had blood on their bodies.[28] Here the violation of Muslim habits of cleanliness was intensified by the blood, filth and stench, especially traumatic for the women bought up surrounded by traditional rituals of purification.

The link between violence, sexuality and the Muslim–Christian border in the Balkans was forged as the influence of the Ottoman Empire and Islam waned decades before the Bosnian War. One of the best known of these texts was Gottfried Sieben's *Balkangreuel* (*Balkan Cruelty*) published in Vienna in 1909. Pirate editions followed in English and Czech and the book was reprinted as a series of postcards. The lithographs typically depict mass rapes of (naked) Christian women by Balkan Muslims in fezzes. In many of the lithographs, the rapists are already assumed to have killed the local men whose bodies are also in the pictures. In one, the mass rape takes place in an Orthodox church while the bound priest looks on helpless. There was an extant record of rape of Orthodox women and – although it had been centuries earlier – it had been preserved in folklore. The blind poet Filip Višnjić, who was an informant of Vuk Karadžić and upon whose verse he based a lot of his writing, spoke of the rape of Serb women in Bijejina in the early nineteenth century. Tešan Podrugović, a guslar born in Kazanci in Hercegovina also spoke to Karadžić about the rape of his family.[29] Serbian nationalism twisted and augmented a sense of historic wrong, giving the war years some of its most distinctive narratives in which the victimizers egregiously claimed to be victims even after they had committed the most heinous crimes. The Karadjordjević monarchy had of course favoured the Orthodox Serbs, but the genocide committed against them in the Second World War had left a legacy of bitterness and distrust especially in those areas where Ustaša atrocities had been

[27] Bringa, Tone *Being Muslim the Bosnian Way* (Princeton, NJ: Princeton University Press, 1995), p. 166.

[28] Gutman, Roy *A Witness to Genocide: The First Inside Account of the Horrors of Ethnic Cleansing in Bosnia* (Shaftesbury: Element, 1993), p. 71.

[29] Koljević, Svetozar, *The Epic in the Making* (Oxford: Clarendon Press, 1980), pp. 311–13.

widespread. The Serbs also carried the mantle of the Communist regime for many years. Their status as former Partisans had given many a sense of moral leadership over other Bosnians. The nature of the violence in the former Yugoslavia in the 1990s is very well-known. Many of those who carried out atrocities wore costumes, grew long beards and appeared to act out a historical part. Ivo Žanić argued that the symbol of the gusle has remained vital in nationalist imagery and was revived in the 1990s. He reproduces a photograph of Radovan Karadžić proudly holding a gusle at the birthplace of his forebear Vuk in 1992.[30] Serbs would often say what seemed like very odd things, while referring more vaguely to the *longue durée* and injustice against them as a community: 'Everything, from the assault by the Turks on Europe and the bombardment of Belgrade to Communist takeover of the government in the heart of Serbia all amount to a single conspiracy forged by the papists, Sultan Murat, Franz Josef and the Albanians against the [Serb] nation.'[31] Victims were subjected to ritualized violence, forced to drink alcohol, made to urinate in the mosque or had crosses carved into their flesh.[32] In 1992 in Omarska Prison Camp, Dušan Tadić, ordered prisoners 'to drink water like animals from puddles on the ground',[33] jumped onto their backs and beat them until they were unable to move. As the victims were removed in a wheelbarrow, Tadić discharged the contents of a fire extinguisher into the mouth of one of the victims.

Very often the violence in Bosnia seemed meted out ritualistically as a kind of collective punishment. Even the clothes that Muslim women wore were sometimes disturbed. Returning to her apartment at the end of the war, Lamija Hadžiosmanović told journalists for the BBC's *Storyville* that she had found one of her dresses had

---

[30] Žanić, Ivo *Prevarena povijest. Guslarska estrada, kult Hajduka i rat u Hrvatskoj i Bosni i Hercegovini 1990–1995. Godine* (Zagreb: Durieux, 1998), p. 390.

[31] Hladnik-Milharčič, Ervin and Standeker, Ivo 'Tako v nebesih kot na zemlji', *Mladina*, 7 June 1989, p. 8.

[32] Sorabji, Cornelia 'A Very Modern War: Terror and Territory in Bosnia-Hercegovina' in Robert A. Hinde and Helen E. Watson (eds.) *War: A Cruel Necessity? The Bases of Institutionalized Violence* (London: I.B. Tauris, 1995), p. 83.

[33] The International Criminal Tribunal for the Former Yugoslavia, www.un.org/icty/indictment/english/tad-1ai950901e.htm.

been shot at and was full of bullet holes. At The Hague Tribunal, Tone Bringa suggested that war criminals had gone to some trouble to desecrate Muslim clothes and that '*dimija*, which are these baggy trousers that Muslim women wear ... had been stuffed with hay and hung up'.[34] There were many witnesses to gang rapes, sometimes the women's male relatives. When a woman was raped in front of her father, one of them shouted to him that he was going to marry her.[35] Rapes often took place in hotels. Soldiers would arrive with women and check in without paying, which indicates widespread collusion with the practice. The conflation between spaces that had once been used for leisure and wartime torture was commonplace. Srebrenica was a spa before the war and people recuperated there by taking the iron rich waters. The once beautiful spa hotel near Višegrad, Vilina Vlas (named after a local species of fern), was used to imprison Muslim girls and women who were repeatedly raped and tortured.[36] The hotel is still open to visitors and recent promotional material stresses that the Vilina Vlas is a place of healing and calm, apparently without irony. In Republika Srpska, life went on as football teams were reconstituted,[37] libraries were restocked with Serbian classics and people lived beside the ruined homes of their former neighbours. In 1996, Belinda Giles made a documentary entitled *Trying Tadić*, although one would probably have to have a good grasp of the English language to understand the implicit double meaning in the title. She interviewed a number of people from the Kozarac, including Mira Tadić who complained that the Serbs had been stuck in the ruined town while the Muslims were living off international aid. When Dubravka Ugrešić wrote in one of her marvellous rhetorical flourishes that people do not die of shame, her comments were surely grounded in real existing nationalism.[38]

[34] The International Criminal Tribunal for the Former Yugoslavia, www.un.org/icty/transe16/990713it.htm.

[35] Gutman, *A Witness to Genocide*, p. 74.

[36] Bećirević, Edina 'Hotel Vilina Vlas, Višegrad – nekad i sad, sjećanje na žrtve silovanja', *Duh Bosne* 7(1), 2012.

[37] Mills, Richard 'Fighters, Footballers and Nation Builders: Wartime Football in the Serb-held Territories in the Former Yugoslavia, *Sport in Society*, 16(8), 2013, pp. 945–972.

[38] Ugrešić, Dubravka *The Culture of Lies* (Pennsylvania: Penn State Press, 1998), p. 188.

INTERNATIONAL INTERVENTION

At the outbreak of fighting, Bosnian President Izetbegović appealed to the international community to help him defend the state. Despite widespread sympathy for civilians who faced death by sniper on a daily basis, the international community initially did very little to help, insisting on separating the so-called 'warring factions' rather than imposing a military and political settlement. International ineptitude arguably made the fate of Bosnia worse and delayed government military successes. Often international inaction came down to an obtuse inability to distinguish between victim and victimizers. One British journalist John Keegan described the war as 'a primitive tribal conflict, of a sort known only to a handful of anthropologists'.[39] George Bush stated that the war in Bosnia was 'a complex convoluted conflict that grows out of age-old animosities'.[40] Communist Yugoslavia was one of the safest countries in the world with a murder rate lower than Western Europe, so the idea that violence was inevitable and the political crisis too complex to understand or prevent is empirically indefensible.

In the early weeks of the war in Bosnia, Muslim civilians had fled to the eastern towns to avoid being rounded up into camps, where they would face rape, torture and murder. After Mitterrand's visit on 28 June 1992, the airport was reopened, but the city remained effectively encircled. A United Nations Protection Force (UNPROFOR) intervened in June 1992 and the fighting almost stagnated. The UN's mandate in Bosnia was limited to humanitarian aid and its troops, distinctive in their blue helmets, delivered aid to beleaguered areas. During the conflict 320 UN soldiers were killed. Health organizations, including the Red Cross and Red Crescent, were deployed to help with the mounting casualties. In October 1992, the Bosnian Serbs delivered a significant blow to the government by capturing Jajce, a military setback that highlighted the failure of cooperation between the Muslims and Croats. The Serbs held the town until September 1995. An Orthodox church in Jajce had been blown up just a couple of weeks before the town was

---

[39] Simms, Brendan *Unfinest Hour: How Britain Helped to Destroy Bosnia* (Harmondsworth: Penguin, 2001), p. 234.

[40] Quoted in Gutman, *A Witness to Genocide*, p. xxxi.

captured by the Serbs. Jajce, an old Bosnian capital, had been the last Christian city to fall to the Turks in the fifteenth century.

The predicament of the encircled cities was well-known outside Bosnia as intrepid reporters relayed tales of desperation to the outside world. In 1993, UN general Philippe Morillon had been forced to concede a policy of protection towards the town of Srebrenica in eastern Bosnia. The safe area policy was his response to duress, but also an act of genuine compassion for those trapped by war. He announced to the people of Srebrenica (in English): 'You are now under the protection of the UN.' Under the safe area policy subsequently introduced by the United Nations, the people of Srebrenica were disarmed, which left them completely dependent on those outside the town for military defence. In effect, it was a policy that kept people alive so that they could be shot at again the next day. Sarajevo, Žepa, Srebrenica, Goražde, Tuzla and Bihać were also defined as UN 'safe areas' but were statistically some of the most dangerous places on the planet.

There were several important attempts to broker peace treaties. In early 1992, the Bosnian crisis still belonged very much within the remit of the European Economic Community (EC). Portuguese politician José Cutileiro worked with the former British foreign secretary Lord Peter Carington in the February before the war broke out. Designed to recognize different centres of power within the state, the plan proposed devolution of power between the constituent nations and increased regional autonomy. Sensing that the plan would significantly undermine the strength of the state, Izetbegović withdrew his signature. Experienced politicians Cyrus Vance, who had been Jimmy Carter's secretary of state, and David Owen, a former British foreign secretary, devised a plan in 1993, which proposed dividing Bosnia into ethnic 'cantons'. When the latter arrived in Sarajevo he warned the citizens not to expect a military solution and not to 'dream dreams' about Western intervention. He often talked about 'stitching' Bosnia together again. This plan looked likely to succeed until it was opposed by Ratko Mladić at what must have been his most hubristic moment. Ironically he had broken down on the way to the negotiations and was helped back on the road by UN officials. General Mladić opposed the signing of the Vance–Owen Plan theatrically by unfolding a map of just how much the Serbs would be giving up if they signed at a meeting of leading Bosnian Serbs in Pale. This intervention was a turning point in the relationship between the Serb insurgents and Serbian president Slobodan Milošević that rapidly deteriorated thereafter and the later often demonstrated open scorn for the Bosnian Serbs. Cyrus Vance resigned after this set back and was replaced by former Norwegian foreign minister Thorvald Stoltenberg. Both he and David Owen devised a plan that would have divided Bosnia into ethnic territories, which was again rejected by Izetbegović in August 1993.

Although the Vance–Owen Plan intended to create a regional solution to the crisis, it may have speeded up the ethnic cleansing of some regions to make Serb and Croat claims stronger. International negotiations came to very little, although some of the most experienced politicians of the age set their minds to ending the war. At worst, they prolonged the agony and flattered the vanity and hubris of the Bosnian Serb leadership. In the winter of 1991 Croats who sought greater autonomy had formed the Croat Union of Herceg-Bosna (*Hrvatska Zajednica Herceg-Bosna*). Relations between the Bosnian government and Croat politicians broke down in the summer of 1993, which led to the creation of a Republic of Herceg-Bosna in August, a short-lived state within a state headed by Mate Boban, who had close links with the nationalist wing of the Croatian Democratic Union. One of the first Croat leaders to recognize that the gains made by Serbs would probably be permanent, he met with Karadžić in Graz in 1993 to discuss the partition of the state into ethnic blocks. Emboldened by plans to divide the state, Croat Defence Council troops (*Hrvatsko vijeće obrane*, HVO) began targeting Bosnian Muslims in Hercegovina in 1993, particularly in the town of Ahmići, in which more than 100 civilians were killed. Strategically positioned between Croat-dominated towns in the Lašva valley, the town was razed, its buildings destroyed and bodies were left on the street by the time the UN arrived. Camps were set up in Heliodrom and Gabela in which Muslim prisoners of war were abused and some died as a result. The city of Mostar was very badly damaged and bifurcated by heavy fighting.

Many Bosnian Muslims did not feel that any less threatened by the nationalism of Croats than that of Serbs. By 1993, hundreds of Sunni Muslim fighters or *mudžahedini* had arrived in Bosnia to fight for the Izetbegović government. At the same time, specifically, Muslim brigades in the Bosnian army were formed. The press in Belgrade and Banja Luka ran reports of atrocities by these fighters, often graphically illustrated. In 2006, General Enver Hadžihasanović was sentenced to three and a half years for 'for failing to take necessary and reasonable measures to prevent or punish several crimes committed by forces under their command' at the International Criminal Court in The Hague. Prosecutor Ekkehard Withopf stated at the trial that most of the killings were carried out by foreign Muslim fighters, but the accused failed to prevent the deaths. Withopf stated that one captured Serb had been killed by 'a beheading that can only be described as a ritual beheading'.[41] Colonel Amir Kubura, chief of staff of the 7th Muslim Mountain Brigade of the Army of Bosnia and Hercegovina (ABiH) 3rd Corp was also sentenced in The Hague on the same charge. Some *mudžahedini* subsequently developed links to the Islamic militant group Al-Qaeda, while other remained in Sarajevo and settled there.

NATO jets shot down four Serb aircraft over central Bosnia in February 1994 for allegedly violating the UN no-fly zone. This was a decisive turning point in the war because the use of force proved to be more effective than humanitarian intervention. United States president Bill Clinton was particularly determined to broker a peace between the Croats and Muslims. The Washington Agreement in 1994 effectively ended the war between these groups. The Contact Group (which involved the Russian Federation, France, Britain, USA and Germany) had started to move towards a settlement that effectively meant partition of the state. The Bosnian War ended in late 1995, but peace came at a very high price. The events of the previous summer were decisive in ending the armed conflict. News about the Srebrenica genocide reverberated around the world and the Bosnian Serbs lost key support from diaspora groups. This was further exacerbated by a bomb aimed at the Markale market stalls in Sarajevo on 28 August that killed 37 people and maimed dozens more. The collapse of the Serbian republic in Krajina just a

---

[41] The International Criminal Tribunal for the Former Yugoslavia, www.icty.org/x/cases/hadzihasanovic_kubura/trans/en/031202IT.htm.

Map 8. Bosnia since Dayton

couple of weeks earlier and the exodus of thousands of Orthodox Serbs from Croatia looked like a significant change in Serb fortunes. NATO renewed its bombing raids attacks on Serb positions. At the end of August, Slobodan Milošević announced that he would represent the diplomatic interests of the Serbs of Bosnia, effectively marginalizing Ratko Mladić and Radovan Karadžić. Although the Bosnian army had made significant military gains in the previous weeks, Alija Izetbegović clearly feared that his government would be isolated from Franjo Tudjman if they continued to fight. A ceasefire was brokered in October 1995 and the fighting never resumed.

The representatives of the Bosnian people eventually signed the Dayton Peace Treaty, which brokered primarily by the American secretary of state Warren Christopher and the United States special envoy Richard Holbrooke. The discussions took place in the first three weeks of November 1995 in the unlikely setting of Wright Patterson Air Force Base in Ohio. Mladić and Karadžić were excluded on the grounds of their indictments for war crimes. The relatively inaccessible location as well as the dogged style of some of the diplomats can be credited with the speed with which the final agreement was reached. In his 2011 memoir *To End a War*, Richard Holbrooke wrote: 'The fourteen weeks that form the core of this story were filled with conflict, confusion, and tragedy before their ultimate success.'[42] The peace involved deciding the territorial boundaries of the two new 'entities' that were created. The Muslim-Croat Federation would cover 51 per cent of the republic while the Serbian Republic covered 49 per cent, which meant that some of the recent military gains by the Bosnian government were reversed. Against the fervent wishes of the Bosnian Serb representative Momčilo Krajišnik, Milošević rather momentously agreed that the Serbs would withdraw from Sarajevo. After having been attacked by the 'cowards on the hills', Milošević said they deserved to keep the capital because they had fought for it and stayed despite the years of danger and privation. At this stage he himself had not been indicted for war crimes. The bifurcation of Bosnian territory in 1995 had no historic roots and drew a line on the map rewarding the depopulation by the Bosnian Serb army. It created a very lop-sided state and, although the territorial division was almost 'equitable', most of the population lived in the Muslim-Croat Federation. Although the creation of a Serb republic within Bosnia might have seemed like the culmination of ambition, the Serbs lost their historic populations in Croatia in 1995 leading to widespread recriminations within the nationalist ranks.[43] In 2006, Montenegro also opted to leave a Federation with Serbia. The loss of Kosovo in 2008 further shrank the geographical areas in which Serbs now live as a majority.

The city of Brčko was placed under international arbitration. The surviving safe area in eastern Bosnia, the enclave of Goražde was to be connected to Sarajevo and a commitment was made to improve the existing road. The presidents of Bosnia, Croatia and Serbia were

---

[42] Holbrooke, Richard *To End a War* (London: Random House, 2011).

[43] Sekulić, Milisav *Knin je pao u Beogradu* (Bad Vilbel: Nidda Verlag, 2000).

key signatories as were the heads of state of France, Germany and the USA and the British and Russian prime ministers. Known for his passionate eloquence, the Bosnian prime minister Haris Silajdžić remarked: 'We cannot revive the 17,000 children dead in Bosnia. But we can get justice here and that justice means a fully functional Bosnian state, integrity, sovereignty, justice and democracy.'[44] In effect, Bosnia-Hercegovina became a partitioned state with some common parliamentary institutions but a state that may eventually evolve into two entirely separate countries. The implementation of the treaty has been administered by a European Union high representative, a unique arrangement that has now been renewed beyond its original mandate.

[44] Brogan, Patrick 'Goals Set Out For Peace in Bosnia', *The Herald*, 2 November 1995.

7

Conclusion: 'unmixing' Bosnia and Hercegovina

THE IMPACT OF WAR

Exactly 50 years after the apogee of the Independent State of Croatia, the Bosnian Serb Republic created by Radovan Karadžić and Ratko Mladić was at the peak of its territorial extent. The Serbs had pushed through Bosnia expelling, raping and murdering the local populations. By 1993, they controlled approximately 70 per cent of Bosnia and Hercegovina. As a consequence, Mladić was reluctant to sign the Vance–Owen Plan precisely because for him this would have represented territorial rollback. The year 1993 probably represented the peak phase of Serbian nationalism and expansion. In 1995, the Bosnian Serbs agreed to the partition of the state and reluctantly accepted the loss of Sarajevo and its environs as the tide of the war had turned against them. To create greater Serbian or greater Croatian states, both the Ustaša and Bosnian Serbs had committed or attempted to commit genocide. For a historian, the common denominator linking the 1940s to the 1990s is not simply the readiness of some political agents to commit war crimes including mass murder, but also the inherent instability of Bosnia as a state. The root cause of violence was the Serbs' discontent with borders of the successor states. Serbs revived old fascist plans for ethnic cleansing from the Second World War during which Bosnian Muslims had been attacked by Serb nationalists. Undoubtedly distrust of Muslims existed at the level of Serb popular culture as well as a hatred of the Ustaša and Croatian nationalism, but this itself was not the primary cause of the fighting. The war was one of intricate strategy to gain as much territory and people for any future Serbian state(s) as possible and frequently coordinated by nationalists from within Serbia itself. This strategy failed in Kosovo, Krajina and Croatia but worked in Bosnia, where violence was 'rewarded' by the Dayton Treaty.

During the war, international media insisted on describing 'warring factions' and frequently discussed 'violent' Balkan mentalities as though no other national groups had ever committed such acts. Muslims living in Serbia were generally left alone during the entire Bosnian War, which indicates that the war in Bosnia was one of the strategies intended to gain territory rather than a revival of 'ancient hatreds'. The Serbs wanted to remove Croats, Bosnian Muslims and Kosovars from key regions and were prepared to kill them en masse in the process, a strategy revealed most starkly in eastern Bosnia in the summer of 1995, when ethnic cleansing developed into genocide. In their attempts to destroy the Muslims within the regions of Bosnia that they claimed, the Serbs committed acts that were designed not only to kill individuals, but also to destroy morale and break community cohesion, such as gang rape and torture.[1] Genocide in Bosnia also tested the generations in post-1945 Europe who were determined to prevent another Holocaust. Prompted in part by the tragedies of the 1990s, there has been a growth in interest in comparative genocide and the way in which events can meaningfully be compared. The case of Bosnia has provoked debate in other areas, including the role of sexual crimes in war, obfuscation and genocide denial among extreme nationalists, nationalist agency in international conflict, the shortcomings of the international community (with particular reference to the United Nations), the nature of reconstruction and peacekeeping and the role of international law, especially the ICTY.

The break-up of Yugoslavia cost well over 130,000 lives and led to the displacement of millions. Most of the casualties were in Bosnia. Most of the casualties were Muslims, although more than

---

[1] Kennedy-Pipe, Caroline and Stanley, Penny 'Rape in War: Lessons of the Balkan Conflicts in the 1990s' in Ken Booth (ed.) *The Kosovo Tragedy: The Human Rights Dimension* (London: Frank Cass, 2001), pp. 67–84.

Fig. 17 Srebrenica (by Matt Willer)

25,000 Serbs and about 8,000 Croats also died. Bosnia's Muslims were also heavily displaced and an estimated two million left either temporarily or to rebuild their lives elsewhere. In the years after the peace, Bosnians attempted to find and bury their missing dead often with the painstaking work of the international community. An award-winning 2012 film, *Halimin put*, by the director Arsen Ostojić was based on the story of Zahida and Muharem Fazlić who searched for the remains of their missing adoptive son Emir. Exhuming the dead of Grbavica or Srebrenica meant identification of remains through dental records, clothes and shoes. A large percentage of the recorded war crimes took place in the Drina region and the river was again used as a place to dump bodies. In June 1992, Muslim prisoners were shot and then thrown off the bridge at Višegrad. In 2000, pathologists working for the ICTY found 131 bodies after grave sites in the Drina were exhumed.[2] Through this process the micro-history of the war has become much clearer.

---

[2] The International Criminal Tribunal for the Former Yugoslavia; IT-98-32/1-T 12910, 20 July 2009, www.icty.org/x/cases/milan_lukic_sredoje_lukic/tjug/en/090720_j.pdf.

Hida Sulejmanović only found out where her oldest son Senad had died years after the event. He had died in a paddock not far from Srebrenica and had probably been killed by shrapnel. Not all of his remains were found. As his mother said 'fifteen years of rain and snow moved away his bones'.[3]

The majority of the fatalities in the Bosnian War were male combatants, but the war negatively affected the lives of women and children. Children born to rape victims often faced confusion about their identity, a theme sensitively explored by director Jasmila Žbanić in her award-winning 2006 film *Grbavica*. Their mothers in turn feel stigmatized by rape and often suffer complex psychiatric disorders. Alen Muhić was adopted by a Muslim family in Goražde, but children at his school taunted him by calling him 'Pero' (a Serb name). His adoptive mother Advija stated that he went through 'hell' after he discovered the truth about his conception.[4] The presence of foreign troops has been linked to a growth in the sex trade. American Katheryn Bolkovac went to Bosnia in 1999 as part of a UN International Police Task Force, employed directly by a private military contractor, DynCor. After the body of a Ukrainian woman was found floating in the River Miljacka, she carefully documented abuse of women at an Ilidža nightclub called *Florida*. When she went to the club, she remembered: 'It was exactly as you see in the film ... huddled, they're holding each other ... on these bare, stained mattresses ... too afraid to talk. One of them pointed to the river outside. "We don't want to end up floating."'[5] She emailed top UN officials, but was dismissed from her post on spurious grounds. Bolkovac then successfully sued DynCor for wrongful dismissal after she exposed the link between sex traffickers and NATO-led Stabilization Force (SFOR) and International Police Task Force employees in 2001. Since 2003, the United Nations had had a zero tolerance policy on sexual abuse by its employees.

[3] Halilovich, Hariz *Places of Pain: Forced Displacement, Popular Memory and Trans-local Identities in Bosnian War-torn Communities* (Oxford: Berghahn, 2013), p. 226.

[4] Jahn, George 'Bosnian Children Born of War Rape Start Asking Questions', *Seattle Times*, 31 May 2005.

[5] Diu, Nisha Lilia 'What the UN Doesn't Want You to Know', *Telegraph*, 6 February 2006.

At Dayton, a new Bosnian currency – the convertible mark (*konvertibilna marka*) – was created replacing the Bosnian mark, which was used in place of the Yugoslav dinar after 1992. One mark is divided into 100 feniga. Since 2002, the currency has been pegged to the euro. Successive governments in Bosnia have faced the problem of reconstructing an economy badly damaged by fighting. The economy had relied on networks and informal exchanges that were badly disrupted. The thrifty resourcefulness of Bosnians, which has been described as 'artistry', was tested to the utmost. People from villages with plots of land would previously bring fresh produce to the towns for their relatives and exchange them for consumer goods, but this was not always possible after more Bosnians lost their links to the land. Some local councils found ingenious solutions to the economic downturn. Tuzla has the only salt lake in Europe and leisure facilities were built so that people who could not afford to take holidays in the Adriatic could swim and sunbathe. In early 2014, there were austerity protests that were dubbed the 'Bosnian Spring' in some newspapers. It was in Tuzla that the unrest began as demonstrations against political corruption and lack of economic progress since 1995. The credibility of politicians had been badly damaged in 2013 when the incumbent president of the Federation, Živko Budimir, was arrested after being accused of taking bribes for pardons. He was subsequently released without charge.

Another important way that the events of the early 1990s were recorded was through the meticulous record taking of the International Criminal Court for the former Yugoslavia. Bosnian pressure groups have regularly lobbied outside the court buildings in The Hague. The court transcripts are available in English on the United Nations website and provide an invaluable ledger of the war years. But the International Criminal Court may only ever deal with a tiny percentage of the real criminals who were responsible for the demise of Yugoslavia. Some have already died of natural causes, others are ordinary men or women who may hope to live out their lives as ordinary citizens and escape prosecution. The massacre at Srebrenica has had a greater impact on internal and international politics than any of the other crimes against humanity committed during the Bosnian War or indeed since the Second World War in Europe. It exposed the anti-Islamic attitudes of some of the international troops and the credibility of the United Nations as peacekeepers was fatally weakened. The ICTY court deemed that the slaughter of an estimated 8,000 men and boys as 'combatants' at Srebrenica in July 1995 was genocide. General Radislav Krstić was subsequently sentenced to 46 years in prison at the The Hague Tribunal for his role at Srebrenica. A key aspect of proving 'genocide' is the question of intent. The UN Convention of 1948 defines genocide as the 'intent to kill a national, ethnical, racial or religious group in whole or in part'. This dichotomy between the Bosnian Serbs and the responsibility of the Serbian state is highly problematic, just as the role of Mlada Bosna as agents of Serb nationalism exposed the uneasy relationship between Serbs inside and outside the boundaries of the state.

Radovan Karadžić's open engagement with journalists and very public association with the plan for genocide in the Bosnian Serb parliament made him a priority for indictment. For many years, he evaded detection. Initially he was based in Republika Srpska with a small coterie of loyal supporters. After the later 1990s, he disappeared. There were constant rumours and urban myths about his whereabouts. Mount Athos, the male-only Greek Orthodox monastery was one favoured destination and Herceg Novi in Montenegro another. Eventually in 2008, he was unmasked as an alternative healer Dragan Dabić living in Belgrade, his identity concealed by a full beard and long hair. In 2011, Ratko Mladić was finally apprehended in Serbia. He had drawn his military pension until 2005, but his later years on the run had obviously been damaging to his health. He was very weak by the time he was arrested and offered no resistance to the Serbian authorities. There was a sense that the ICTY could begin to complete its mandate after having apprehended all those who had been indicted and the full record could be written in court. Among Bosnian Serbs, there was a marked reluctance to abandon the man they often regard as a hero and a general to whom they feel they owed their towns. The people of Srebrenica defended the Bosnian Serb leader openly and defiantly in televised interviews. If they felt regret for the genocide at Srebrenica, this was not expressed. Mladić demonstrated extreme contempt for the relatives of his victims in the Dutch courtroom.

The capture of Ratko Mladić in 2011 almost completed the list of indictees. The survivors of the Srebrenica genocide have been an important pressure group in Bosnian politics since 1995 and kept consciousness about war crimes in the news. The village of Potočari, just east of Srebrenica where many of the victims were killed, has become an important memorial to the dead. Thousands of symmetrical white headstones stand at the memorial, recalling some of the First World War burial sites in Northern France. Tourists frequently visit the site and services are held there every year on the July anniversary.

Bosnia's landscape continues to be scarred with unexploded incendiary devices and taped off areas with the warning '*pozor mine*' ('beware landmines'). In 1997, the Bosnian government signed the Ottawa Treaty, which aims to stop the use of anti-personnel mines in military combat. However, they still have to cope with the legacy of in excess of 100,000 unexploded mines across the country. More than 500 people have been killed since the end of the war, many of them children, by stepping on unmarked mines. More than 100 of those killed were bomb disposal experts who work in very difficult terrain in which bombs are concealed under tree stumps or in grass and can be detonated by weights of just a few kilos. Extensive flooding in May 2014 loosened the soil in some areas and exacerbated the problem further and half a million had to be evacuated from their homes. It also destroyed crops as three months of normal rainfall fell in just a few hours but a quarter of a million people were left temporarily without clean drinking water. Swollen river banks also threw up more mass graves of people shot in 1992. However much Bosnians want to move on from the war years, many find it difficult to find inner peace with relatives still missing, presumed dead. Urban poverty and lack of investment has meant that people are still reminded of the war every day as they walk through the streets. Much of the urban architecture in Bosnia is Communist-era and the external plaster is often still marked with war damage. In Sarajevo a street of great trees (*ulica velikih drveta*) was constructed to remember the dead of the war, among them Srdjan Aleksić, a Serb who died defending his Muslim friend

Fig. 18 Yugoslavian Republican leaders Milan Kučan, Alija
Izetbegović, Kiro Gligorov, Franjo Tudjman and Slobodan
Milošević on 11 April 1991 (© Petar Kujundžić/Reuters/
Corbis)

in Trebinje. Bomb craters in the capital have since been painted
red and are known as 'Sarajevo roses'.

In 2003, Alija Izetbegović died three years after stepping down
from the presidency. In many respects he had become the personifi-
cation of the Bosnian statehood in the 1990s. Having endured nine
years in prison in total under the Communists, in 1948 and again
in 1983, he seemed to have the spiritual calm that many Muslims
feel that their religion offers them. Unlike many Bosnians, he had
strong personal roots in Turkey as his grandfather Alija had married a woman called Sidika from Scutari. During the years of war,
Turkey was one of the most steadfast friends to the Bosnian government. The rebuilding of Mostar's old bridge was undertaken by
an Ankara-based company, Er-Bu, that specializes in Ottoman construction techniques. A museum dedicated to the life of Izetbegović
was opened in the suburb of Vratnik in 2007, which involved reno-
vation of Ottoman-era watchtowers (*Kapi-kula Ploča* and *Sirokac*)

that were first build in 1739. It overlooks a cemetery for *šehidi* (martyrs).

Since the end of the war, Bosnia has had to renegotiate its sometimes fragile relations with neighbouring countries. Some countries, such as the United Kingdom, have had both an embassy in Sarajevo and a separate office in Banja Luka. Slovenian troops formed part of SFOR in Bosnia in 1996–1998 and relations between the two republics have been good. In 1999, the Serbian president Slobodan Milošević became the first serving head of state to be indicted for war crimes. Many regarded him as the primary instigator of the crisis in the Balkans. The judgment against him would have been an important landmark in legal history, but his death while on trial in 2006 prevented his case from being concluded. Relations with Serbia generally improved after the fall of Milošević in 2000. In 2007, the Serbian state was cleared of charges of genocide at The Hague Tribunal after the Bosnian state brought charges against it. Montenegro, Croatia and Slovenia all rapidly extended recognition to the former Serbian province of Kosovo following its declaration of independence in February 2008 and the established diplomatic representation in the capital Prishtinë. Serbia was strongly opposed to independence for Kosovo and this sentiment extended to the Republika Srpska so, despite some sympathy in the Federation, Kosovo has not yet been recognized by Bosnia and its passports are not valid, which sometimes complicates travel for people who until 1992 belonged to the same country. Montenegro became an independent state itself in 2006 and worked to ensure good relations with its neighbour. It also has quite a high Muslim population (estimated to be over 17 per cent of whom almost 9 per cent are classified as *Bošnjaci* or Bosniaks). Relations with Croatia have also been relatively smooth. In 1998, Alija Izetbegović signed the Neum Agreement with Franjo Tudjman that allows Croatian vehicles to pass through Bosnia territory on the Adriatic coast unimpeded. The Croatians have discussed the construction of a bridge that would link the peninsula of Pelješac with the main land (and therefore bypass Bosnian territory entirely). Green activists have been concerned with the impact of such a bridge on the local marine ecology (which is rich in shellfish), but this is unlikely to impede its eventual construction.

Like many regions of modern Europe, Bosnia and Hercegovina has suffered the profound consequences of population politics designed to change borders and eliminate certain groups and peoples. Jews who sheltered in the Ottoman lands after their expulsion from Spain were wiped out in the early 1940s by the Nazis. Orthodox people who had come to regard themselves as part of a Serb nation, were targeted and killed during the First and Second World Wars. After 1995 and the end of the Bosnian War, many Serbs left areas of historic settlement. 'De-Ottomanization' between the 1870s and the 1930s led to the emigration of many thousands of Muslims. In the 1940s, many were killed by Četniks and the entire demographic structure of Bosnia and Hercegovina was altered by genocide and population transfers in the 1990s. The Catholics of Hercegovina, fiercely independent and tied primarily to the Franciscan Order for centuries, came to view themselves primarily as unredeemed Croats by the twentieth century. Extreme forms of Catholicism, such as the milieu around the Marian apparitions in Medjugorje, have transformed the area. Population movement has altered and almost destroyed an ancient civilization of the Dinaric Mountains, which once intrigued writers such as Jovan Cvijić and Dinko Tomašić.

Violence in the late twentieth century also deepened the rift between a largely urban Muslim culture and the Christian rural population. By the twenty-first century, the population of Bosnia and Hercegovina remained divided by discursive radicalization, administrative divisions and nationalism. They have also been significantly 'unmixed' (to borrow Lord Curzon's phrase about the population transfers between Greece and Turkey in the early 1920s). The population of Bosnia and Hercegovina has been deeply affected by demographic fluctuations and political catastrophes. Since the 1870s, there have been several distinct waves of migration and new arrivals to the region. After the establishment of a Yugoslav state, Muslims chose to relocate to Islamic countries, with movements both in the 1920s and 1950s. The terrible impact of the Second World War reduced the population of the republic to just over 2.5 million in 1948 but by 1981 the population had again risen to over four million. From the 1960s onwards, Bosnians went to West Germany and Sweden to work as *Gastarbeiter*. They also moved to other neighbouring republics, working in enterprises in Serbia, Croatia and Slovenia. When they moved, they often took their traditions with them in food, music and lifestyle, which is a theme of the well-received 2003 film about Bosnians in Slovenia *Kajmac in Marmelada (Cheese and Marmalade)*. In the 1990s, hundreds of thousands of Bosnians fled the country, in particular after the outbreak of the fighting in 1992 and after the Srebrenica genocide in 1995. Most of the migrants went to Serbia, Montenegro, Croatia, Austria, Slovenia and Germany. Countries in the European Union eventually allowed Bosnians permanent residence status.[6]

Bosnia's own citizens also frequently elect to be citizens of the neighbouring former-Yugoslav republics. Although they may retain the concept of *zavičaj* or homeland, many live a long way from their place of 'origin'. Between 2002 and 2003, Ljubo Jurčić, who was born in Ružići, was Croatian economics minister. The Croatian team that won the Davis Cup in tennis in 2005 contained Marin Čilić, born in Medjugorje, and Ivan Ljubičić, born in Banja Luka. The Swiss national team that went to the World Cup in Brazil in 2014 was managed by Vladimir Petković, originally from Sarajevo, and had several players whose parents came from the former Yugoslavia, including two who had parents from Bosnia. The Bosnian census of 2013 reported an overall decline in population by 585,411 compared to the previous census of 1991 (which represents about 13 per cent). Some small towns have lost almost half their population, while the numbers in the larger cities have actually increased. Much of the change that occurred in population happened in the first half of the 1990s as well as a shift in the overall number of Serbs, Muslims and Croats living in the state. Before the 1992 war, approximately 17 per cent of the republic's population were Croats, but by 1996, according to United Nations

---

[6] Valenta, Marko and Ramet, Sabrina P. 'Bosnian Migrants: An Introduction' in Marko Valenta and Sabrina P. Ramet (eds.) *The Bosnian Diaspora: Integration in Transnational Communities* (Exeter: Ashgate, 2011), p. 3–4.

High Commissioner for Refugees, the number fell to about 14 per cent. Declared Muslims went from 43 per cent to 46 per cent of the population. The Serb minority in Krajina, Slavonija and more recently Kosovo shrank considerably in 1990s, but in Bosnia, their percentage of the overall population actually rose from 31 per cent in 1991 to just under 38 per cent in 1996. Most of the larger conurbations are in the Federation. Sarajevo and its municipal area has a population of just over 600,000 according to the last census. Only 35 per cent of the Bosnian population live in Republika Srpska, which in 2013 had only two cities with a population exceeding 100,000 (Bijeljina and Banja Luka).

The Dayton Treaty allowed for those expelled from their homes to return, but in practice it has proved very difficult to reverse the damage that the war caused. Refugee return has been very limited, with younger people now opting to live abroad or in cities. A few towns have proved exceptional including Glamoč, which although in the Federation has seen the return of some of its Serb citizens.[7] The town of Drvar has also seen returns but often people found that their former homes had been blown up or trashed. The mosque in Kostajnica was rebuilt but there were attempts to intimidate the Muslims from returning to the town by leaving a slaughtered pig in the building site to dishonour the faithful. Many Bosnians in the Federation have effectively been cut off from a rich part of their heritage as well as their former homes and religious heritage, which were largely destroyed during the war. Adil Zulfikarpašić talked rather nostalgically about his hometown, with its gardens, trees and mosques: 'My Foča does not exist ... and there are no Bosnian Muslims there anymore.'[8] An imaginary tunnel at Višegrad was an important symbolic element in the film *Lepa sela lepo gore* (lit. 'pretty villages burn more prettily') used to mark several distinct historical moments (1941, 1971, 1980 and the mid-1990s). Directed by Srdjan Dragojević and released in 1996, the film traces the end of a friendship between a Serb and Muslim. Some former citizens only venture back to Bosnia in the summer months. In

---

[7] Steele, Jonathan, 'Voters Defy Nationalists by Returning to Pre-war Home Towns', *The Guardian*, 15 September 1997, p. 12.

[8] Zulfikarpašić, *Bošnjak*, pp. 51–52.

2010, ITN reporter Penny Marshall went back to the once predominantly Muslim town of Kozarac to make the documentary *Bosnia: Unfinished Business*. Interviewing Omarska camp survivor Kemal Pervanić, they spoke to a local postman and drove past a butcher, both of whom had been camp guards. Marshall asked Pervanić how he could cope with frequent encounters with his former guards: 'It feels almost normal … this is our reality.' This does not mean that the Muslims of Kozarac accept that what happened to them was just, but it seems that they have found, as Stevan Weine put it, 'non-dichotomizing ways of making sense of the history that they have lived through'.[9]

In the Federation, Mostar has a predominantly Catholic university and different football teams, Velež and Zrinjski,[10] the latter with a decidedly Croatian history. Even language, which once united Bosnians, has been subject to change with the emergence of apparently distinct languages of Bosnian, Croatian and Serbian within the same country. Linguists have insisted that there is a fricative 'h' in *bosanski*, so that coffee becomes *kahva*, instead of *kava* or *kafa*.[11] Bosnian politicians have found the post-Dayton structures unwieldy and often refused to cooperate at the most basic level. If Bosnians believed they were voting for independence in the referendum of 1992, they found themselves subject of the most basic level of control three years later including oversight by a 'high representative' appointed by the European Community after 1995. The mission of the high representative was to ensure that the Dayton Peace Accords were being carried out. Bosnia was thus cast as a dysfunctional state rather than a new democracy, which had been undermined and attacked by an insurgency.

Nationalism divides the communities at a most basic level and the past has been kept alive by successive administrations. The internet provides space for hate speech and the raging debates between nationalists on YouTube and other social media sites often descend

---

[9] Weine, 'Redefining *Merhamet*', p. 408.

[10] Zrinjski is named after the Croatian nobleman Nikola Šubić Zrinski, who died at the Battle of Szigetvár fighting against the Ottomans in 1566. Velež is named after a nearby mountain.

[11] Isaković, Alija *Rječnik karakteristične leksike u Bosanskome jeziku* (Sarajevo: Svjetlost, 1993), p. 6.

into vulgar swearing and libellous attacks on dissonant individuals. In Višegrad in 2014, the town council contentiously removed the word 'genocide' from a memorial commemorating the mass slaughter of its citizens more than 20 years earlier. While a workman sanded down the stone, he was surrounded by survivors, some very elderly, who prayed with their hands turned up. The mayor Slaviša Mišković announced that, although he would allow the monument to remain, the remaining townspeople could not accept the term genocide on it.[12] Culture, politics and education in the two entities have mostly served to reify the separation. Within the Muslim-Croat Federation, the division between these two confessions, which emerged during the war in 1992–1993, has led to virtual separation in some spheres. The old high school in Mostar, designed by the Czech architect František Blažek at the turn of the twentieth century in the distinctive Habsburg 'Oriental' style, is known as *Stara Gimnazija* by local people. Muslims and Catholics, who previously attended classes together, are now taught in different sessions, although they do mix at break time. Scholars have also done their part to reify separation. In cases where there was no money to purchase textbooks with new versions of history, paragraphs were simply blocked out with dark ink to suit local purposes.[13]

In some nationalist circles, indicted war criminals remain figures that command respect and have joined a pantheon of earlier heroic figures. In 2005, a poster commemorating the tenth anniversary of the genocide at Srebrenica was defaced by Serb extremists who simply wrote 'it will happen again'.[14] Marko Perković Thompson's song *Evo zore, evo dana* tell his Ustaša brothers to cross the deep Drina and burn Serbia. In his 2013 song *Bosna*, Perković again evoked historical themes that suggest that the country rests predominantly on a Catholic heritage. In one of the verses he summarizes the old Croatian aspirations and themes in 'wounded' Bosnian. 'When you look Bosnia in the face, you see the Drina martyrs.

[12] 'Bosnie: le mot "génocide" effacé sur un monument, colère des victimes', *L'Express*, 23 January 2014.
[13] Low-Beer, Ann 'Politics, school textbooks and cultural identity: the struggle in Bosnia and Hercegovina', *Paradigm* 2(3), 2001, pp. 1–8.
[14] Miller, Paul B. 'Contested memories: the Bosnian Genocide in Serb and Muslim minds' *Journal of Genocide Research* 8(3), 2006, p. 313.

Bosnian was guarded by lone wolves, celebrated by the people and called *hajduks*. Silver Bosnia[15] preserves the faith, soul and body through the Franciscan brothers'.[16] On the other hand, some trends since 1995 do not conform particularly closely with prevailing nationalism. The gold statue of Bruce Lee in Mostar recalls the importance of the martial arts in 1970s and 1980s Yugoslavia. In Tomislavgrad, there is a large white statue of a guest worker returning to the embrace of his family. Tuzla has a bust of Martin Luther King, which was donated by the US Embassy and this has become a symbol of the town's continued tolerance. Director Emir Kusturica built an entire village called Drvengrad for his 2004 film *Život je Čudo*. Although the film is putatively about the Bosnian war in the Drina region, its main thread is a romantic tale between a Serb man and a Muslim woman. Kusturica actually built the village on the Serbian side of the Drina. In 2014, he opened another new project that is effectively a suburb of Višegrad named Andrićgrad after the Nobel Prize-winning Bosnian writer. As well as a statue of the eponymous Ivo Andrić, the development also has a mosaic of the young assassin Gavrilo Princip. In 2006, the mayor of Bijeljina announced plans to build a cabbage monument (*kupus-spomenik*) in the town to acknowledge the importance of the vegetable in the local economy. It has not been erected, but the notion of a new civic monument drew poignant attention once again to the destruction of the town's Ottoman heritage during the war. In the Muslim Croat Federation, the towns such as Glamoč and Drvar retained their Serb populations who preferred to stay in their native region than live in Republika Srpska. A new generation of more pragmatic politicians in Republika Srpska helped to improve the image of the entity. In early 1998, Milorad Dodik moved the capital from Pale to Banja Luka, which had been Karadžić's power base.

Sarajevo in the twenty-first century represents a distinctive Islamic modernity but with apartment blocks from the Communist era and different styles and moral codes. The enormous King Fahd Mosque

---

[15] A reference to the Franciscan province of Bosna Srebrena, i.e., Catholic Bosnia.
[16] 'Kada Bosni pogledaš u lice, u suzi joj vidiš Drinske mučenice. Čuvali te Bosno usamljeni vuci. Slavio ih narod, zvali se hajduci. A Srebrnu Bosnu sačuvaše vjerom, franjevačka braća i dušom i tijelom.'

Fig. 19 Dress codes in post-Dayton Bosnia (by Richard Mills)

built after the end of the war was financed by the Saudis. In 2001, the Istiqlal Mosque was completed, financed through a gift from the Indonesian government. Some of the foreign volunteers in the El Mudžahid brigade stayed in the city, some now selling carpets in the bazaar known as the *baščaršija*. In a stroll around Sarajevo or what the locals call the *korso*, women in white hijabs walk out with men in casual sports gear. In the 1991 census, about 50 per cent of the city's population were nominally Christian. The present tends to dictate how past is remembered. Gavrilo Princip's memorial 'footsteps', which were once imprinted into the street in Sarajevo have been removed, just as the Habsburg memorial to Franz Ferdinand and Sophie was removed by the Karadjordjević state. As the war continued, Muslim paramilitaries arrived and the graveyards were dominated by cults of the *šehidi* (Islamic military martyrs). The attacks on the United States in September 2001 gave a further boost to anti-Islamic discourses in the Balkans, with newspaper editorials in Serbia reminding their readers about links between Osama bin Laden and the Bosnian Muslim militants.[17]

[17] Dikić, Božidar 'Bin Laden na Baščaršiji', *Politika*, 4 October 2001.

Fig. 20 Waterfall at Kravice (by Jessica Sharkey)

Sarajevan tolerance has not disappeared despite the growth in obvious Muslim piety. Two of the most well-known Bosnians outside their country are composer and musician Goran Bregović and film director Emir Kusturica, who both grew up in the heady mix of élan and opportunity that was Sarajevo in the 1960s. Like many others of their generation, including Haris Dzinović and Zdravko Čolić, they chose to move to Belgrade, the great Balkan cosmos. Leaving Sarajevo was often about simple physical survival, but also meant moving away from a past that could never be fully recreated in that town. Kusturica even changed his first name to the Serbian 'Nemanje', explaining that his family had been Orthodox hundreds of years before. Many former Sarajevans return to rapturous applause. A Serb from the suburb of Grbavica, Čolić, received a moving spontaneous standing ovation when he sang in the Ferhatović stadium with Kemal Monteno in 2012. Although many towns removed the 'Tito' from their names quickly, small clusters of Yugonostalgics still exist across Bosnia. Impersonators are hired to celebrate Tito's official birthday and there is a Tito café in Sarajevo, which specializes in socialist-era kitsch.

In the summer months in recent years, a number of volunteers arrive in the small Bosnian town of Visoko for an archaeological adventure and a chance to buy pyramid-inspired gifts. They claim to want to establish that the eponymous high peak or Visočica that dominates the local landscape is actually an ancient man-made structure that dates back to unrecorded civilizations millennia ago. An American of Bosnian origin, Semir Osmanagić, has called it 'the pyramid of the sun'. Symmetrical pyramids are an infrequent, but not completely unknown geological phenomenon known as a flatiron. To believe therefore that Visočica is man-made is something of an act of faith inspired by romance rather that obvious (at this stage) evidence.[18] This was not the first time that Bosnia had been the subject of eccentric historical speculation. In 1985, Mexican writer Roberto Salinas Price caused a minor media flurry when he published *Homer's Blind Audience*, in which he claimed that Gabela in Hercegovina was in fact ancient Troy. Local people quickly saw opportunity in the structure, and during the long summer vacation that year, dozens of school children were drafted in to clear the stony fields in anticipation of spending tourists.

Despite difficulties within an unwieldy political system, the people of Bosnia and Hercegovina get on remarkably well in their daily lives considering the enormity of the war crimes committed just a few years ago. Popular culture indicates that this will continue to be the case as long as political crises can be avoided. Pjer Žalica's 2003 film *Gori Vatra* (*A Fire is Burning*) is a portrait of the citizens of Tesanj returning to the wreckage of their former homes in the Muslim-Croat Federation. Corruption is widespread and many in the town are living on the proceeds of illegal trades. This is a bleak comedy and deals with issues such as landmines, unknown causes of death during the war, the black market, human trafficking, generational conflicts, post-traumatic illness, illegal arms, Serb–Muslim relations and international intervention. The film emphasizes both the differences and similarities between the entities, so near but in some sense quite far apart. There is an everyday awkwardness about the partition of Bosnia, which is acknowledged here often

---

[18] Irna* 'Les "pyramides" de Bosnie-Herzégovine: une affaire de pseudo-archéologie dans le contexte bosnien' *Balkanologie* 13(1–2), 2011.

through humour. Žalica has described his ambition to develop a 'mikrohirurgija ljudske duše' ('microsurgery on the soul').[19]

More than 20 years after the demise of a common Yugoslav state, Bosnians can still watch and enjoy the same films and programmes and listen to the same music as their neighbours. Actors and singers can work in all of the industries. The soap opera *Lud, zbunjen, normalan* (*Mad, Confused, Normal*) has been watched avidly across the entire region since 2007. Bosnian Croat singer Davor Badrov's 2010 hit song *Ja baraba, sve joj džaba* (*I am a Vagabond, Everything is Free for Her*) is peppered with Turkish words used in dialect and was played in Croatia, Bosnia and Serbia with great popularity. Since 1995, leading actors such as Mirjana Karanović, Emir Hadžihafizbegović and Mustafa Nadarević have variously played Croat, Bosniak or Serb characters with no apparent existential dilemma. *Ničija zemlja* (*No Man's Land*) is one of the best known films about the Bosnian War. Directed by Danis Tanović in 2001, it won an Oscar in the category of Best Foreign Film. Set in and around a trench, it involves long dialogues between two Bosnians, Čiki (Branko Djurić) and Nino (Rene Bitorajac). Much of the dialogue is deliberately absurd and has the effect of making the two main characters look irrational. Especially well-known are the exchanges between Čiki and Nino about 'who started the war'. For most of the film, one of the other characters, Cero (Filip Šovagović), is lying across a mine injured and the drama revolves around how to rescue him. The Bosnian men are from the same town who find themselves on different sides in the war. Like other many films about the Yugoslavian Wars, it intersperses genuine news footage with fictional scenes.

Since the Dayton Treaty, an entire generation has grown up without the experience of shared living and overlapping culture that made Bosnia unique. The idea of a core ancient civilization in the region, one that transcends religious and ethnic conflicts, border changes and uncertainty is perhaps even more chimerical than ever. That does not mean, however, that it does not exist. Throughout this book, I have argued that a distinct Bosnian civilization still exists despite war, the erection of internal boundaries and supranational

---

[19] Burić, Ahmet 'Nije lako odlučiti da budeš sretan', *Dani* 376, 2004, p. 46.

loyalties that test local resolve. Furthermore this distinct civilization is continuously revealed through language, culture and mentalities. In the years before the creation of the South Slav states, peoples of the region – especially those who spoke the same language – genuinely admired the culture of their neighbours. Bosnia will prosper, either as separate entities or even separate states, if neighbours can rediscover the things that they like about each other. As the poet Mak Dizdar put it (in words known to most Bosnians and meditated upon by those who have suffered) '*Valja nama preko rijeke*' ('we need to cross the river').[20]

---

[20] We could interpret this as meaning that sometimes we need to do things that are difficult, but will lead us to the right place. Dizdar, Mak *Modra rijeka i Druge pjesme* (Sarajevo: Veselin Masleša, 1982), p. 18.

BIBLIOGRAPHY

Aleksov, Bojan 'Adamant and Treacherous: Serbian Historians on Religious Conversions' in Pål Kolstø (ed.) *Myths and Boundaries in South-Eastern Europe* (London: Hurst, 2005), pp. 158–190

Allcock, John B. *Explaining Yugoslavia* (London: Hurst, 2000)

Andjelić, Neven *Bosnia-Herzegovina: The End of a Legacy* (London: Routledge, 2003)

Andrić, Ivo *Die Entwicklung des geistigen Lebens in Bosnien unter der Einwirkung der türkischen Herrschaft* (Klagenfurt: Wieser, 2011)

Armakolas, Ioannis 'The "Paradox" of Tuzla City: Explaining Non-nationalist Local Politics during the Bosnian War', *Europe-Asia Studies* 63(2), 2011, pp. 229–261

Arslanagić, Naima, Bokonjić, M. and Macanović, K. 'Eradication of Endemic Syphilis in Bosnia', *Genitourin Med*, 65(1), 1989, pp. 4–7

Banac, Ivo *The National Question in Yugoslavia: Origins, History, Politics* (Ithaca: Cornell University Press, 1984)

Bandžović, Safet 'Koncepcije Srpskog kulturnog kluba o preuredjenju Jugoslavije 1937–1941', *Prilozi*, 30, 2001, pp. 163–193

Bandžović, Safet 'Ratovi i demografska deosmanizacija Balkana (1912–1941)', *Prilozi*, 32, 2003, pp. 179–229

Bartulin, Nevenko *The Racial Idea in the Independent State of Croatia: Origins and Theory* (Leiden: Brill, 2014)

Baskar, Bojan *Dvoumni Mediteran: Študije o regionalnem prekrivanju na vzhodnojadranskem območju* (Koper: Knjižnica Annales, 2002)

Baskar, Bojan 'Komišluk and Taking Care of the Neighbor's Shrine in Bosnia-Herzegovina' in Dionigi Albera and Maria Couroucl (eds.) *Sharing Sacred Spaces in the Mediterranean: Christians, Muslims, and*

Jews at Shrines and Sanctuaries (Bloomington, IN: Indiana University Press, 2012), pp. 51–59

Bayarri, Francesc *Cita en Sarajevo* (Valencia: Montesinos, 2009)

Bax, Mart 'The Madonna of Medjugorje: Religious Rivalry and the Formation of a Devotional Movement in Yugoslavia', *Anthropological Quarterly* 63(2), 1990, pp. 63–76

Beci, Bahri 'Les minorités ethniques en Albanie' in Denise Eeckaute-Bardery (ed.) *Les oubliés des Balkans* (Paris: Publications Langues'O, 1998), pp. 19–26

Bećirević, Edina 'Hotel Vilina Vlas, Višegrad – nekad i sad, sjećanje na žrtve silovanja', *Duh Bosne* 7(1), 2012

Bećirević, Edina *Na Drini genocid: istraživanje organiziranog zločina u istočnoj Bosni* (Sarajevo: Buybook, 2009)

Belamarić, Joško 'Cloth and Geography: Townplanning and Architectural Aspects of the First Industry in Dubrovnik in the Fifteenth Century' in Alina Payne (ed.) *Dalmatia and the Mediterranean: Portable Archaeology and the Poetics of Influence* (Leiden: Brill, 2013) pp. 247–268

Bieber, Florian 'Muslim National Identity in the Balkans before the Establishment of Nation States', *Nationalities Papers* 28(1), 2000, pp. 13–28

Post-War Bosnia: Ethnic Structure, Inequality and Governance of the Public Sector (New York: Palgrave Macmillan, 2006)

Biondich, Marc *Stjepan Radić, the Croat Peasant Party and the Politics of Mass Mobilization, 1904–1928* (Toronto: University of Toronto Press, 2000)

Bjelić, Dušan I. *Normalizing the Balkans: Geopolitics of Psychoanalysis and Psychiatry* (Exeter: Ashgate, 2011)

Bose, Sumantra *Bosnia after Dayton: Nationalist Partition and International Intervention* (London: Hurst, 2002)

Bougarel, Xavier 'La "revanche des campagnes", entre réalité sociologique et mythe nationaliste', *Balkanologie* 2(1), 1998, pp. 17–36

Bracewell, Wendy 'Rape in Kosovo: Masculinity and Serbian Nationalism', *Nations and Nationalism* 6(4), 2000, pp. 563–590

Bringa, Tone *Being Muslim the Bosnian Way* (Princeton, NJ: Princeton University Press, 1995)

Brogan, Patrick 'Goals Set Out For Peace in Bosnia', *The Herald*, 2 November 1995

Burić, Ahmet 'Nije lako odlučiti da budeš sretan', *Dani* 376, 2004, p. 46

Burns, John 'A Killer's Tale – A Special Report', *New York Times*, 27 November 1992

Čajkanović, Veselin *O magiji i religiji* (Belgrade: Prosveta, 1985)

Campbell, David *National Deconstruction: Violence, Identity, and Justice in Bosnia* (Minneapolis: University of Minnesota Press, 1998)

Carmichael, Cathie *Ethnic Cleansing in the Balkans: Nationalism and the Destruction of Tradition* (London: Routledge, 2002)

Carmichael, Cathie, '"A People Exists and that People has its Language": Language and Nationalism in the Balkans' in Stephen Barbour and Cathie Carmichael (eds.) *Language and Nationalism in Europe* (Oxford: Oxford University Press, 2000), pp. 221–239

Carmichael, Cathie 'Violence and Ethnic Boundary Maintenance in Bosnia since 1992', *Journal of Genocide Research* 8(3), 2006, pp. 283–293

Cigar, Norman *Genocide in Bosnia: The Policy of 'Ethnic Cleansing'* (College Station, TX: A&M University Press, 1995)

'The Serbo-Croatian War, 1991' in Stjepan Meštrović (ed.) *Genocide after Emotion: The Postemotional Balkan War* (London: Routledge, 1996), pp. 51–90

Čolović, Ivan *Bordel ratnika. Folklor, politika i rat* (Belgrade: Biblioteka XX vek, 1993)

Čolović, Ivan *Politics of Symbol in Serbia: Essays in Political Anthropology*, translated by Celia Hawkesworth (London: Hurst, 2002)

Čolović, Ivan 'Sarajevski atentat i kosovski mit', http://fenomeni.me/sarajevski-atentat-kosovski-mit/ (accessed 30 June 2014)

Curta, Florin *The Making of the Slavs, History and Archaeology of the Lower Danube Region, c. 500–700* (Cambridge: Cambridge University Press, 2001)

Cvijić, Jovan *La péninsule balkanique: Geographie humaine* (Paris: A. Colin, 1918)

Dedijer, Jevto 'La transhumance dans les pays dinariques', *Annales de geographie* 25, 1916, pp. 347–365

Dedijer, Vladimir *The Road to Sarajevo* (London: MacGibbon and Kee, 1967)

Dedijer, Vladimir *The Yugoslav Auschwitz and the Vatican: The Croatian Massacre of Serbs during World War II* (Buffalo, NY: Prometheus Books, 1992)

Dedijer, Vladimir *Genocid nad muslimanima 1941–45, Zbornik documenta i svjedočenja* (Sarajevo: Svjetlost, 1990)

de Laveleye, Émile *The Balkan Peninsula* (New York: G. P. Putnams, 1887)

Denich, Bette 'Dismembering Yugoslavia: Nationalist Ideologies and the Symbolic Revival of Genocide', *American Ethnologist* 21(1), 1991, pp. 367–390

Dikić, Božidar 'Bin Laden na Baščaršiji', *Politika*, 4 October 2001

Dizdar, Zdravko and Sobolevski, Mihael *Prešućivani četnički zločini u Hrvatskoj i u Bosni i Hercegovini: 1941–1945* (Zagreb: Hrvatski institut za povijest: Dom i svijet, 1999)

Djilas, Aleksa *The Contested Country: Yugoslav Unity and Communist Revolution 1919–1953* (Cambridge, MA: Harvard University Press, 1991)

Diu, Nisha Lilia 'What the UN Doesn't Want You to Know', *Telegraph*, 6 February 2006

Djokić, Dejan *Elusive Compromise: A History of Interwar Yugoslavia* (New York: Columbia University Press, 2007)

Donia, Robert *Islam Under the Double Eagle: The Muslims of Bosnia and Hercegovina, 1878–1914* (Boulder, CO: East European Monographs, 1981)

  Sarajevo: A Biography (Ann Arbor: University of Michigan Press, 2006)

Donia, Robert and Fine, John *Bosnia and Hercegovina: A Tradition Betrayed* (London: Hurst, 1994)

Dragović Soso, Jasna *Saviours of the Nation? Serbia's Intellectual Opposition and the Revival of Nationalism* (London: Hurst, 2002)

Duda, Igor 'Workers into Tourists: Entitlements, Desires, and Realities of Social Tourism in Yugoslav Socialism' in Hannes Grandits and Karin Taylor (eds.) *Yugoslavia's Sunny Side: A History of Tourism in Socialism (1950s–1980s)* (Budapest: Cental European University Press, 2010)

Dulić, Tomislav 'Mass Killing in the Independent State of Croatia, 1941–1945: A Case for Comparative Research', *Journal of Genocide Research* 8(3), 2006, pp. 255–281

Dulić, Tomislav *Utopias of Nation: Local Mass Killing in Bosnia and Herzegovina, 1941–42* (Uppsala: Acta Universitatis Upsaliensis, 2005)

Durham, Mary Edith *Some Tribal Origins, Laws and Customs of the Balkans* (London: George Allen and Unwin, 1928)

Dunford, Mark and Holland, Jack *The Rough Guide to Yugoslavia* (London: Routledge and Kegan Paul, 1985)

Dvorniković, Vladimir *Karakterologija Jugoslovena* (Belgrade: Kosmos, 1939)

Džaja, Srećko *Bosnien-Herzegowina in der österreichisch-ungarischen Epoche (1878–1918): die Intelligentsia zwischen Tradition und Ideologie* (Munich: Oldenbourg, 1994)

Džaja, Srećko 'Bosnian Historical Reality and its reflection in myth' in Pål Kolstø (ed.) *Myths and Boundaries in South-Eastern Europe* (London: Hurst, 2005), pp. 106–129

Džaja, Srećko *Die politische Realität des Jugoslawismus 1918–1991: Mit besonderer Berücksichtigung Bosnien-Herzegowina* (Munich: Oldenbourg, 2002)

Džaja, Srećko *Konfessionalität und Nationalität Bosniens und der Herzegowina* (Munich: Oldenbourg, 1984)

Ekmečić, Milorad 'Nacionalna politika Srbije prema Bosni i Hercegovini i agrarno pitanje (1844–1875)', *Godišnjak Istorijskog društva Bosne i Hercegovine* 10, 1959, pp. 197–219

Faroqhi, Suraiya *The Ottoman Empire* (Princeton, NJ: Princeton University Press, 2010)

Travel and Artisans in the Ottoman Empire: Employment and Mobility in the Early Modern Era (London: I.B. Tauris, 2014)

Fine, John V.A. *The Late Medieval Balkans, A Critical Survey from the Late Twelfth Century to the Ottoman Conquest* (Ann Arbor: University of Michigan Press, 1994)

'The Medieval and Ottoman Roots of Modern Bosnian Society' in Mark Pinson (ed.) *The Muslims of Bosnia-Herzegovina: Their Historic Development from the Middle Ages to the Dissolution of Yugoslavia* (Cambridge, MA: Harvard University Press, 1996)

Friedman, Francine *Bosnia and Herzegovina: A Polity on the Brink* (New York: Routledge, 2004)

The Bosnian Muslims: Denial of a Nation (Boulder, CO: Westview, 1996)

Glaurdić, Josip *The Hour of Europe: Western Powers and the Breakup of Yugoslavia* (New Haven: Yale University Press, 2011)

Godelier, Maurice 'Infrastructures, Societies and History', *Current Anthropology* 19(4), 1978, pp. 763–771

Goldstein, Ivo 'The Boundary on the Drina: The Meaning and Development of the Mythologem' in Pål Kolstø (ed.) *Myths and Boundaries in South Eastern Europe* (London: Hurst, 2005), pp. 77–105

Goldstein, Ivo *Croatia: A History* (London: Hurst, 1999)

Goldstein, Ivo 'Zemljica 'Bosna – to horion Bosona u "De administrando imperio" Konstantina VII Porfirogeneta' in Marko Karamatić (ed.) *Zbornik o Pavlu Andjeliću* (Sarajevo: Franjevačka Teologija, 2008), pp. 97–110

Grandits, Hannes *Herrschaft und Loyalität in der spätosmanischen Gesellschaft. Das Beispiel der multikonfessionellen Herzegowina* (Vienna: Böhlau, 2008)

Greble, Emily *Sarajevo, 1941–1945: Muslims, Christians, and Jews in Hitler's Europe* (Ithaca: Cornell University Press, 2011)

Greenberg, Robert *Language and Identity in the Balkans* (Oxford: Oxford University Press, 2004)

Gow, James *The Serbian Project and its Adversaries: A Strategy of War Crimes* (London: Hurst, 2003)

Triumph of the Lack of Will: International Diplomacy and the Yugoslav War (London: Hurst, 1997)

Hadžihuseinović, Salih Sidki Muvekkit *Povijest Bosne* (Sarajevo: El-Kalem, 1999)

Halilovich, Hariz *Places of Pain: Forced Displacement, Popular Memory and Trans-local Identities in Bosnian War-torn Communities* (Oxford: Berghahn, 2013)

Halpern, Joel M. and Kideckel, David A. (eds.) *Neighbors at War: Anthropological Perspectives on Yugoslav Ethnicity, Culture and History* (Pennsylvania: Penn State University Press, 2000)

Hartmann, Florence *Milošević. La Diagonale du Fou* (Paris: Denoël, 1999)

Herak, Marijan and Herak, Davorka 'Analiza seizmičnosti kao preduslov za procenu zemljotresnog hazarda u Bosni i Hercegovini', *Izgradnja* 64(5–6), 2010, pp. 263–281

Higginbotham, Adam 'Beauty and the Beast', *The Observer*, 4 January 2004

Hladnik-Milharčič, Ervin and Standeker, Ivo 'Tako v nebesih kot na zemlji', *Mladina*, 7 June 1989

Hoare, Marko Attila *The Bosnian Muslims in the Second World War* (Oxford: Oxford University Press, 2006)

Genocide and Resistance in Hitler's Bosnia: The Partisans and the Četniks, 1941–1943 (Oxford: Oxford University Press, 2006)

How Bosnia Armed (London: Saqi, 2004)

Hockenos, Paul *Homeland Calling: Exile Patriotism and the Balkan Wars* (Ithaca: Cornell University Press, 2003)

Honig, Jan Willem and Both, Norbert *Srebrenica: Record of a War Crime* (Harmondsworth: Penguin, 1996)

Hosking, Geoffrey *A History of the Soviet Union* (London: Fontana, 1985)

Ibrahimagić, Omer *Srpsko osporavanje Bosne i Bošnjaka* (Sarajevo: Magistrat, 2001)

Isaković, Alija (ed.) *Biserje: izbor iz muslimanske književnosti* (Zagreb: Globus, 1972)

İsen, Mustafa *Osmanisches Erbe am Balkan: Eine Spurensuche* (Klagenfurt: Wieser Verlag, 2008)

Jahn, George 'Bosnian Children Born of War Rape Start Asking Questions', *Seattle Times*, 31 May 2005

Jančar, Barbara 'Ecology and Self-Management: A Balance Sheet for the 1980s' in John B. Allcock, John J. Horton and Marko Milivojević (eds.) *Yugoslavia in Transition* (Oxford: Berg, 1992) pp. 337–370

Jansen, Stef *Anti-nationalism: Post-Yugoslav Resistance and Narratives of Self and Society*, doctoral dissertation, University of Hull, 2000

Jelavich, Barbara *History of the Balkans*, 2 vols (Cambridge: Cambridge University Press, 1983)

Jezernik, Božidar *Wild Europe: The Balkans in the Gaze of Western Travellers* (London: Saqi, 2004)

Jireček, Konstantin *Die Handelsstrassen und Bergwerke von Serbien und Bosnien während des Mittelalters: Historisch-geographische Studien* (Verlag der kön böhmischen Gesellschaft der Wissenschaften, 1879)

Kalčić, Špela *Nisem jaz Barbika: oblačilne prakse, Islam in identitetni procesi med Bošnjakinjami v Sloveniji* (Ljubljana: Filozofska fakulteta, 2007)

Karpat, Kemal H. 'The Migration of the Bosnian Muslims to the Ottoman State 1878–1914: An Account based on Turkish Sources' in Markus Koller and Kemal H. Karpat (eds.) *Ottoman Bosnia: A History in Peril* (Madison, WI: University of Wisconsin Press, 2004), pp. 121–140

Kaser, Karl *Hirten, Kämpfer, Stammeshelden: Ursprünge und Gegenwart des balkanischen Patriarchats* (Vienna: Böhlau, 1992)

Kennedy-Pipe Caroline and Stanley, Penny 'Rape in War: Lesssons of the Balkan Conflicts in the 1990s' in Ken Booth (ed.) *The Kosovo Tragedy: The Human Rights Dimension* (London: Frank Cass, 2001), pp. 67–84

Kesić, Obrad 'Women and Gender Imagery in Bosnia: Amazons, Sluts, Victims, Witches and Wombs' in Sabrina P. Ramet (ed.) *Gender Politics in the Western Balkans: Women and Society in Yugoslavia and the Yugoslav Successor States* (Pennsylvania: Penn State University Press, 1999)

Kolar-Panov, Dona *Video, War and the Diasporic Imagination* (London: Routledge, 1997)

Koljević, Svetozar, *The Epic in the Making* (Oxford: Clarendon Press, 1980), pp. 311–13

Koller, Markus 'Introduction: An Approach to Bosnian History' in Markus Koller and Kemal H. Karpat (eds.) *Ottoman Bosnia: A History in Peril*, (Madison, WI: University of Wisconsin Press, 2004)

Korb, Alexander 'Understanding Ustaša Violence', *Journal of Genocide Research* 12, 2010, pp. 1–18

Krestić, Vasilije *La grande Croatie: le génocide comme projet politique* (Paris: L'Age d'Homme Editions, 2000)

Krizman, Bogdan *Pavelić u Bjekstvu* (Zagreb: Globus, 1986)

Kržisnik-Bukić, Vera *Cazinska buna 1950* (Sarajevo: Svjetlost, 1991)

Lampe, John R. *Yugoslavia as History: Twice there was a Country* (Cambridge: Cambridge University Press, 2000)

Lemkin, Raphaël *Axis Rule in Occupied Europe. Laws of Occupation, Analysis of Government. Proposals for Redress* (Clark, NJ: The Lawbook Exchange, 2005)

Lieberman, Benjamin 'Nationalist Narratives, Violence Between Neighbours and Ethnic Cleansing in Bosnia-Hercegovina: A Case of Cognitive Dissonance?' *Journal of Genocide Research* 8(3), 2006, pp. 295–310

Terrible Fate: Ethnic Cleansing in the Making of Modern Europe (Chicago: Ivan R. Dee, 2006)

Lockwood, William G. *European Moslems: Economy and Ethnicity in Western Bosnia* (New York: Academic Press, 1975)

Lord, Albert Bates *The Singer of Tales* (Cambridge, MA: Harvard University Press, 1960)

Lovrenović, Ivan *Bosnia: A Cultural History* (London: Saqi, 2001)

Low-Beer, Ann 'Politics, School Textbooks and Cultural Identity: The Struggle in Bosnia and Hercegovina', *Paradigm* 2(3), 2001, pp. 1–8

MacDowall, Andrew 'Sarajevo: City Commemorates End to 'a Century of Conflict', but Divisions Still Run Deep', *Observer*, 28 June 2014

Maček, Ivana 'Predicament of War: Sarajevo Experience and the Ethics of War' in Bettina E. Schmidt and Ingo W. Schröder (eds.) *Anthopology of Violence and Conflict* (London: Routledge, 2001)

Maček, Ivana *Sarajevo under Siege: Anthropology in Wartime* (Philadelphia: Penn State Press, 2009)

Mahmutćehajić, Rusmir *Maintaining the Sacred Center: The Bosnian City of Stolac* (Bloomington, IN: Worldwisdom, 2011)

Malcolm, Noel *Bosnia: A Short History* (London: Macmillan, 1994)

Marjanović Damir, Fornarino, S., Montagna, S., Primorac, D., Hadžiselimovič, R., Vidovič, S., Pojskič, N., Battaglia, V., Achilli, A., Drobnic, K., Andjelinovic, S., Torroni, A., Santachiara-Benerecetti, A.S. and Semino, O. 'The Peopling of Modern Bosnia-Herzegovina : Y-chromosome Haplogroups in the Three Main Ethnic Groups', *Annals of Human Genetics* 69, 2005, pp. 757–763

Marjanović, Damir, Kapur, L., Drobnič, K., Budowle, B. and Hadžiselimovič, R. 'Comparative Study of Genetic Variation at 15 STR Loci in Three Isolated Populations of the Bosnian Mountain Area', *Human Biology* 76(1), 2004, pp. 15–31

Markowitz, Fran 'Census and Sensibilities in Sarajevo', *Comparative Studies in Society and History* 49(1), 2007, pp. 40–73

Markowitz, Fran *Sarajevo: A Bosnian Kaleidoscope* (Urbana, IL: University of Illinois Press, 2010)

Marriott, John A.R. *The Eastern Question: An Historical Study in European Diplomacy* (Oxford: Clarendon Press, 1940)

McCarthy, Justin 'Archival Sources Concerning Serb Rebellions in Bosnia 1875–76' in Markus Koller and Kemal H. Karpat (eds.) *Ottoman Bosnia: A History in Peril* (Madison, WI: University of Wisconsin Press, 2004), pp. 141–145

McCarthy Justin *Death and Exile: The Ethnic Cleansing of Ottoman Muslims 1821–1922* (Princeton: Darwin Press, 1996)

Meštrović, Stjepan, Letica, Slaven and Goreta, Miroslav *Habits of the Balkan Heart: Social Character and the Fall of Communism* (College Station, TX: A&M University Press, 1993)

Milazzo, Matteo *The Četnik Movement and Yugoslav Resistance* (Baltimore and London: John Hopkins University Press, 1975)

Miller, Paul B. 'Contested Memories: The Bosnian Genocide in Serb and Muslim Minds', *Journal of Genocide Research* 8(3), 2006, pp. 311–324

Mills, Richard 'Fighters, Footballers and Nation Builders: Wartime Football in the Serb-held Territories in the Former Yugoslavia', *Sport in Society* 16(8), 2013, pp. 945–972

'Velež Mostar Football Club and the Demise of "Brotherhood and Unity" in Yugoslavia, 1922–2009', *Europe-Asia Studies* 62(7), 2010, pp. 1107–1133

Mitrović, Andrej *Serbia's Great War 1914–1918* (London: Hurst, 2007)

Morrison, Kenneth *Wahhabism in the Balkans* (London: Conflict Studies Research Centre, 2008)

Mujanović, Jasmin 'Princip, Valter, Pejić and the Raja: Elite Domination and Betrayal in Bosnia-Herzegovina', *South-East European Journal of Political Science* 1(3), 2013, pp. 106–120

Nettlefield, Lara *Courting Democracy in Bosnia and Herzegovina: The Hague Tribunal's Impact in a Postwar State* (Cambridge: Cambridge University Press, 2010)

Neuffer, Elizabeth *The Key to My Neighbor's House: Seeking Justice in Bosnia and Rwanda* (London: Picador, 2002)

Newman, John Paul 'Les héritages de la Première Guerre mondiale en Croatie' in François Bouloc, Rémy Cazals and André Loez (eds.) *Identités Troublées 1914–1918: Les appartenances sociales et nationales à l'épreuve de la guerre* (Toulouse: Privat, 2011), pp. 141–152

Niškanović, Miroslav 'Ilindanski dernek kod turbeta Djerzelez Alije u Gerzovu', *Novopazarski zbornik* 2, 1978, pp. 163–186

Novak, Viktor *Magnum crimen: pola vijeka klerikalizma u Hrvatskoj* (Zagreb: Nakladni zavod Hrvatske, 1948)

Okey, Robin *Taming Balkan Nationalism: The Habsburg 'Civilizing Mission' in Bosnia, 1878–1914* (Oxford: Oxford University Press, 2007)

Olivier, Louis Pierre Frédéric *La Bosnie et l'Herzégovine* (Paris: A. Colin, 1890)

Ondřej, Daniel 'Gastarbajteri: Rethinking Yugoslav: Economic Migrations towards the European North-West through Transnationalism and Popular Culture' in Stephen G. Ellis and Lud'a Klusáková (eds.) *Imagining Frontiers, Contesting Identities* (Pisa: Pisa University Press, 2007), pp. 277–302

Palairet, Michael R. *The Balkan Economies c. 1800–1914: Evolution without Development* (Cambridge: Cambridge University Press, 2003)

Palmer, Bryan D. *E.P. Thompson: Objections and Oppositions* (London: Verso, 1994)

Paris, Erna *Long Shadows: Truth, Lies and History* (London: Bloomsbury, 2003)

Pavlovitch, Stevan K. 'Serbia and Yugoslavia: The Relationship', *Southeast European and Black Sea Studies* 4(1), 2004, pp. 96–106

Peco, Asim *Turcizmi u Vukovim Rječnicima* (Belgrade: Vuk Karadžić, 1987)

Perica, Vjekoslav *Balkan Idols: Religion and Nationalism in Yugoslav States* (Oxford: Oxford University Press, 2002)

Pineau, Jean-Claude, Delamarche, Paul and Bozinovic, Stipe 'Les Alpes Dinariques: un peuple de sujets de grande taille', *Comptes Rendus Biologies*, 328, 2005, pp. 841–846

Pinson, Mark 'The Muslims of Bosnia-Herzegovina under Austrian Rule 1878–1918' in Mark Pinson (ed.) *The Muslims of Bosnia-Herzegovina: Their Historic Development from the Middle Ages to the Dissolution of Yugoslavia* (Cambridge, MA: Harvard University Press, 1996)

Ramet, Sabrina P. *Nationalism and Federalism in Yugoslavia 1962–1991* (Bloomington: Indiana University Press, 1994)

Redžić, Enver *Bosnia and Herzegovina in the Second World War* (London: Routledge, 2004)

Rendić-Miočević, Ivo *Zlo velike jetre: povijest i nepovijest Crnogoraca, Hrvata, Muslimana i Srba* (Split: Književni krug, 1996)

Rihtman-Auguštin, Dunja 'O susjedima' in Božidar Jakšić (ed.) *Tolerancija*, (Zemun: Biblioteka XX vek, 1999), pp. 151–164

Rusinow, Dennison *The Yugoslav Experiment, 1948–1974* (London: Hurst, 1977)

Šašel Kos, Marjeta 'Bistue Nova', *Enzyklopädie der Antike*, 2, 1997

Savelli, Mat 'Diseased, Depraved or just Drunk? The Psychiatric Panic Over Alcoholism in Communist Yugoslavia', *Social History of Medicine* 25(2), 2012, pp. 462–480

Schindler, John R. 'Defeating Balkan Insurgency: The Austro-Hungarian Army in Bosnia-Hercegovina, 1878–82', *Journal of Strategic Studies* 27(3), 2004, pp. 528–552

Isonzo: The Forgotten Sacrifice of the Great War (Westport, CO: Greenwood, 2001)

(2003) 'Yugoslavia's First Ethnic Cleansing: The Expulsion of the Danubian Germans 1944–46' in Steven Béla Várdy and T. Hunt Tooley (eds.) *Ethnic Cleansing in 20th-Century Europe* (Boulder, CO: Social Science Monographs/Columbia University Press, 2003), pp. 359–372

Schlick, Irvin Çemıl 'Christian Maidens, Turkish Ravishers: The Sexualization of National Conflict in the Late Ottoman Period' in Amila Buturović and I. Ç. Schlick (eds.) *Women in the Ottoman Balkans: Gender, Culture, and History* (London: I. B. Tauris, 2007)

Šehić, Nusret *Četništvo u Bosni i Hercegovini (1918–1941). Politička uloga i oblici djelatnosti Četničkih udruženja* (Sarajevo: Akademija nauka i umjetnosti Bosne i Hercegovine, 1971)

Sekulić, Milisav *Knin je pao u Beogradu* (Bad Vilbel: Nidda Verlag, 2000)

Sells, Michael *The Bridge Betrayed: Religion and Genocide in Bosnia*, 2nd edn (Berkeley, CA: University of California Press, 1998)

Shepherd, Ben *Terror in the Balkans: German Armies and Partisan Warfare* (Cambridge, MA: Harvard University Press, 2012)

Simić, Andrei 'Machismo and Cryptomatriarchy: Power, Authority in the Traditional Yugoslav Family' in Sabrina P. Ramet (ed.) *Gender Politics in the Western Balkans: Women and Society in Yugoslavia and the Yugoslav Successor States* (Pennsylvania: Penn State Press, 1999), pp. 11–29

Simić, Andrei 'Nationalism as Folk Ideology: The Case of the Former Yugoslavia', in Joel M. Halpern and David A. Kideckel (eds.) *Neighbors at War: Anthropological Perspectives on Yugoslav Ethnicity, Culture and History* (Pennsylvania: Penn State Press, 2000)

Simms, Brendan *Unfinest Hour: How Britain Helped to Destroy Bosnia* (Harmondsworth: Penguin, 2001)

Skendi, Stavro 'Crypto-Christianity in the Balkan Area under the Ottomans', *Slavic Review* 26(2), 1967, pp. 227–246

Skrbiš, Zlatko 'The Apparitions of the Virgin Mary of Medjugorje: The Convergence of Croatian Nationalism and her Apparitions', *Nations and Nationalism* 11(3), 2005, pp. 443–461

Slapšak, Svetlana, Milošević, Milan, Cvetićanin, Radivoj, Mihailović, Srećko, Curgus Kazimir, Velimir and Gredelj, Stjepan *The War Started at Maksimir: Hate Speech in the Media: Content Analyses of Politika and Borba Newspapers, 1987–1991* (Belgrade: Media Centre, 1997)

Slijepčević, Djoko M. *Pitanje Bosne i Hercegovine u XIX veku* (Keln: Iskra, 1981)

Sokolović, Džemal and Bieber, Florian (eds.) *Reconstructing Multiethnic Societies: The Case of Bosnia-Herzegovina* (Exeter: Ashgate, 2001)

Šolić, Mirna 'Women in Ottoman Bosnia as Seen Through the Eyes of Luka Botić, a Christian poet' in A. Buturović and I. Ç. Schlick (eds.) *Women in the Ottoman Balkans: Gender, Culture, and History* (London: I.B. Tauris, 2007)

Sorabji, Cornelia 'Islam and Bosnia's Muslim Nation' in F.W. Carter and H.T. Norris (eds.) *The Changing Shape of the Balkans* (London: University College Press, 1996)

Sorabji, Cornelia 'Islamic Revival and Marriage in Bosnia', *Journal of the Institute of Muslim Minority Affairs* 9(2), 1988, pp. 331–337

Sorabji, Cornelia 'Muslim Identity and Islamic Faith in Sarajevo', Cambridge University PhD thesis, 1989

Sorabji, Cornelia 'A Very Modern War: Terror and Territory in Bosnia-Hercegovina' in Robert A. Hinde and Helen E. Watson (ed.) *War: A Cruel Necessity? The Bases of Institutionalized Violence* (London: I.B. Tauris, 1995)

Spalatin, Mario S. 'The Croatian Nationalism of Ante Starcevic, 1845–1871', *Journal of Croatian Studies* 16, 1975, pp. 94–100

Spence, Richard B. 'General Stephan Freiherr Sarkotić von Lovćen and Croatian Nationalism', *Croatian Review of Studies in Nationalism* 17(1–2), 1990, pp. 147–155

Steele, Jonathan, 'Voters Defy Nationalists by Returning to Pre-war Home Towns', *The Guardian*, 15 September 1997, p. 12

Stein Erlich, Vera *Family in Transition: A Study of 300 Yugoslav Villages* (Princeton, NJ: Princeton University Press, 1966)

Sućić, Daria Sito 'The Fragmentation of Serbo-Croatian into Three New Languages', *Transition* 2(24), 1996

Sugar, Peter F. *Industrialization of Bosnia-Hercegovina, 1878–1918* (Seattle: University of Washington Press, 1963)

Swales, Peter 'Freud, Death and Sexual Pleasures: On the Psychical Mechanism of Dr. Sigm. Freud', *Arc de Cercle* 1, 2003, pp. 4–74

Tanović, Nenad *Stećci ili Oblici Bosanskih Duša* (Sarajevo: Bosanska riječ, 1994)

Terzić, Smail F. *Musa Ćazim Ćatić* (Sarajevo: Bosanska riječ, 1996)

Thompson, Mark *Forging War: The Media in Serbia, Croatia, Bosnia and Hercegovina* (Luton: Article 19, 1999)

The White War: Life and Death on the Italian Front, 1915–1919 (London: Faber, 2008)

Todorova, Maria *Imagining the Balkans* (Oxford: Oxford University Press, 1997)

Tomasević, Jozo *Četnici u drugom svjetskom ratu 1941–1945*, translated Nikica Petrak (Zagreb: Sveučilisna Nakalda Liber, 1979)

Tomasevich, Jozo *War and Revolution in Yugoslavia* (Stanford: Stanford University Press, 1975)

Tomašić, Dinko *Personality and Culture in East European Politics* (New York: G.W. Stewart, 1948)

Truhelka, Ćiro 'Testament gosta Radina – Prinos pataranskom pitanju', *Glasnik Zemaljskog muzeja*, 24, 1911, pp. 355–376

Valenta, Anto *Podjela Bosne i Borba za Cjelovitost* (Vitez: HKD Napredak, 1991)

Valenta, Marko and Ramet, Sabrina P. 'Bosnian Migrants: An Introduction' in Marko Valenta and Sabrina P. Ramet (eds.) *The Bosnian Diaspora: Integration in Transnational Communities* (Exeter: Ashgate, 2011)

Velikonja, Mitja *Religious Separation and Political Intolerance in Bosnia and Herzegovina* (College Station, TX: A&M University Press, 2003)

Vidan, Aida *Embroidered with Gold, Strung with Pearls: The Traditional Ballads of Bosnian Women* (Cambridge, MA: Harvard University Press, 2003)

Vodopivec, Nina 'On the Road to Modernity: Textile Workers and Post-Socialist Transformations in Slovenia', *History* 97(328), 2012, pp. 609–629

Voigt, Vilmos 'Primus Inter Pares: Why Was Vuk Karadžić the Most Influential Folk Lore Scholar in South Eastern Europe in the Nineteenth Century?' in Michael Branch and Celia Hawkesworth (eds.) *The Uses of Tradition: A Comparative Enquiry into the Nature, Uses and Functions of Oral Poetry in the Balkans, the Baltic and Africa* (London: School of Slavonic and East European Studies, 1994), pp. 179–193

Vojvoda, Gabriela *Raum und Identitätskonstruktion im Erzählen Dževad Karahasans* (Münster: Lit Verlag, 2013)

Volčič, Zoran 'Yugo-nostalgia: Cultural Memory and Media in the Former Yugoslavia', *Critical Studies in Media Communication* 24(1), 2007, pp. 21–38

Wachtel, Andrew B. 'How to Use a Classic: Petar Petrović Njegoš in the Twentieth Century', in John R. Lampe and Mark Mazower (eds.) *Ideologies and National Identities: The Case of Twentieth-Century* (Budapest: Central European University Press, 2004), pp. 131–153

Wagner, Sarah E. *To Know Where He Lies: DNA Technology and the Search for Srebrenica's Missing* (Berkeley, CA: University of California Press, 2008)

Walasek, Helen 'Marian Wenzel 18 December 1932–6 January 2002', *Bosnia Report*, 27–18, 2002

Weine, Stevan 'Redefining *Merhamet* after a Historical Nightmare' in Joel M. Halpern and David A. Kideckel (eds.) *Neighbors at War: Anthropological Perspectives on Yugoslav Ethnicity, Culture and History* (Pennsylvania: Penn State Press, 2000), pp. 401–412

Weine, Stevan *When History is a Nightmare: Lives and Memories of Ethnic Cleansing in Bosnia-Herzegovina* (New Brunswick, NJ: Rutgers University Press, 1999)

Wenzel, Marian *Ukrasni motivi na stećcima* (Sarajevo: Masleša, 1965)

West, Richard *Tito and the Rise and Fall of Yugoslavia* (New York: Carroll and Graf, 1995)

Woodward, Susan *Balkan Tragedy: Chaos and Dissolution after the Cold War* (Washington: Brookings Institute, 1995)

Yeomans, Rory *Visions of Annihilation: The Ustasha Regime and the Cultural Politics of Fascism, 1941–1945* (Pittsburgh: University of Pittsburgh Press, 2013)

Žanić, Ivo *Prevarena povijest. Guslarska estrada, kult Hajduka i rat u Hrvatskoj i Bosni i Hercegovini 1990–1995. Godine* (Zagreb: Durieux, 1998)

Živković, Marko *Serbian Dreambook: National Imaginary in the Time of Milošević* (Bloomington, IN: Indiana University Press, 2011)

LITERATURE, MEMOIRS, AUTOBIOGRAPHIES AND POLITICAL ESSAYS

Adamič, Louis 'Sarajevo – Mustafa's Home Town', *The Rotarian*, 1936, pp. 34–36, 69–73

Andrić, Ivo *The Damned Yard and Other Stories* (Dufour: Forest Books, 1993)

Andrić, Ivo *Na Drini ćuprija* (Belgrade: Prosveta, 1945)
Andrić, Ivo *Nobel Prize Library: S. Y. Agnon, Ivo Andric* (New York: Alexis Gregory/Helvetica Press, 1971)
Andrić, Ivo *Travnička hronika* (Belgrade: Državni izdavački zavod Jugoslavije, 1945)
Aralica, Ivan *Asmodejev šal* (Zagreb: Naprijed, 1988)
Aralica, Ivan *Duše robova* (Zagreb: Naprijed, 1984)
Aralica, Ivan *Graditelj svratišta* (Zagreb: Naprijed, 1986)1
Aralica, Ivan *Konjanik* (Zagreb: Naprijed, 1971)
Aralica, Ivan *Psi u trgovištu* (Zagreb: Naprijed, 1979)
Arbuthnot, George *Herzegovina: or Omer Pacha and the Christian Rebels* (London: Green, Longman, Roberts and Green, 1862)
Bašeskija, Mula Mustafa Ševki *Ljetopis (1746–1804)*, translated from the Turkish by Mehmet Mujezinović (Sarajevo: Veselin Maleša, 1987)
Bartók, Béla and Lord, Albert Bates (eds.) *Serbo-Croatian Folk Songs; Texts and Transcriptions of Seventy-five Folk Songs from the Milman Parry Collection and a Morphology of Serbo-Croatian Folk Melodies* (New York: Columbia University Press, 1951)
Bell, Martin *In Harm's Way: Reflections of a War-Zone Thug* (Harmondsworth: Penguin, 1996)
Benić, Bono *Ljetopis sutješkoga samostana* (Sarajevo: Synopsis, 2003)
Berić, Gojko *Letters to the Celestial Serbs* (London: Saqi, 2002)
Bićanić, Rudolf *Kako živi narod: Život u pasivnim krajevima* (Zagreb: Tisak Tipografija, 1936)
Blau, Otto and Kiepert, Heinrich *Reisen in Bosnien und der Hertzegowina* (Berlin: D. Reimer, 1877)
Brenan, Gerald *A Life of One's Own: Childhood and Youth* (Cambridge: Cambridge University Press, 1979)
Broz, Svetlana and Hart, Laurie Kain (eds.) *Good People in an Evil Time: Portraits of Complicity and Resistance in the Bosnian War* (New York: Other Press, 2004)
Capus, Guillaume *A travers la Bosnie et l'Herzégovine. Études et impressions de voyage* (Paris: Librairie Hachette, 1896)
Catić, Musa Ćazim *Pjesme: (izbor)*, edited by Medhija Mušović (Sarajevo: Veselin Masleša, 1991)
Chopin, Jean-Marie *Provinces Danubiènnes et Roumaines: Bosnie, Servie, Herzegovine, Bulgarie, Slavonie, Illyrie, Croatie, Montenegro, Albanie, Valachie, Moldavie et Bucovine*, 2 vols (Paris: Firmin Didot Frères Editeurs, 1856)
Ciliga, Ante *Sam kroz Europu u ratu* (Rome: Na pragu sutranšnjice, 1978)

Čolaković, Rodoljub *Zapisi iz oslobodilačkog rata*, 3 vols (Zagreb: Naprijed, 1961)

Ćorović, Vladimir (ed.) *Memoari prote Matije Nenadovića* (Belgrade: G. Kon, 1926)

Corwin, Phillip *Dubious Mandate: A Memoir of the UN in Bosnia, Summer 1995* (Durham, NC: Duke University Press, 1999)

Čubrilović, Vaso 'Iseljavanje Arnauta' in Miroslav Brandt, Bože Čović, Radovan Pavić, Zdravko Tomac, Mirko Valentić and Stanko Zuljić (eds.) *Izvori velikosrpske agresije: Rasprave, dokumenti, kartografski prikazi* (Zagreb: August Cesarec, Školska knjiga, 1991), pp. 106–124

Dankoff, Robert and Kim, Sooyong (eds.) *An Ottoman Traveller: Selections from the Book of Travels of Evliya Çelebi*, 2nd edn (London: Eland Publishing, 2011)

Davidson, Basil *Partisan Picture* (Bedford: Bedford Books, 1946)

Deakin, William *The Embattled Mountain* (Oxford: Oxford University Press, 1971)

de Asbóth, János *An Official Tour Through Bosnia and Herzegovina: With an Account of the History, Antiquities, Agrarian Conditions, Religion, Ethnology, Folk Lore, and Social Life of the People* (London: S. Sonnenschein, 1890)

Dedijer, Vladimir *The Beloved Land* (London: MacGibbon and Kee, 1961)

Dedijer, Vladimir *The War Diaries of Vladimir Dedijer*, Vol. I (Ann Arbor: University of Michigan Press, 1990)

Die Türkische Nachbarländer an der Südostgrenze Österreichs: Serbien, Bosnien, Türkisch-Kroatien, Herzegovina und Montenegro (Pest, Wien and Leipzig: Hartleben's Verlag-Expedition, 1854)

Dizdar, Mak *Kameni spavač* (Sarajevo: Veselin Masleša, 1970)

Dizdar, Mak *Modra rijeka i Druge pjesme* (Sarajevo: Veselin Masleša, 1982)

Djikić, Ivica *Cirkus Columbia* (Sarajevo: Civitas, 2005)

Djilas, Milovan *Land Without Justice* (New York: Harcourt Brace Jovanovich, 1958)

Djilas, Milovan *Wartime* (New York: Harcourt Brace Jovanovich 1977)

Drašković, Vuk *Nož* (Belgrade: Nova Knjiga, 1985)

Du Preez Bezrob, Anne Marie *Sarajevo Roses: War Memoir of a Peacekeeper* (Cape Town: Struik Publishers, 2006)

Durham, Mary Edith *Diary from 1900*, Royal Anthropological Institute (RAI MS)

Evans, Arthur J. *Through Bosnia and the Herzegóvina on Foot During the Insurrection, August and September 1875* (London: Longmans, Green, 1876)

Filipović, Zlata *Zlata's Diary: A Child's Life in Sarajevo* (Harmondsworth: Penguin, 1994)

Fortis, Alberto *Viaggio in Dalmazia* (Venice: Alvise Milocco, 1774)

Freud, Sigmund *Die Traumdeutung* (Leipzig/Wien: Franz Deuticke, 1914)

Freud, Sigmund *Das Unbehagen in der Kultur* (Wien: Internationaler Psychoanalytischer Verlag, 1930)

Freud, Sigmund *Zur Psychopathologie des Alltagslebens (Über Vergessen, Versprechen, Vergreifen, Aberglaube und Irrtum)* (Berlin: Verlag von S. Karger, 1904)

Gajić-Sikirić, Nadžija *Sjećanja iz Bosne* (Raleigh, NC: Lulu, 2012)

Gorkić, Milan *Revolucija pod okriljem Kominterne*, edited by Božidar Jakšić (Filip Višnjić: Belgrade, 1987)

Gutman, Roy *A Witness to Genocide: The First Inside Account of the Horrors of Ethnic Cleansing in Bosnia* (Shaftesbury: Element, 1993)

Hadžišehović, Munevera *A Muslim Woman in Tito's Yugoslavia*, translated by Thomas J. Butler and Saba Risaluddin (College Station, TX: A&M University Press, 2003)

Halilović, Sefer *Lukava Strategija* (Sarajevo: Matica, 1998)

Hangi, Antun *Die Moslim's in Bosnien-Hercegovina* (Sarajevo: D.A. Kajon, 1907)

Hoernes, Moritz *Dinarische Wanderungen: Cultur- und Landschaftsbilder aus Bosnien und der Hercegovina* (Vienna: C. Graeser, 1894)

Holbach, Maude *Bosnia and Herzegovina, Some Wayside Wanderings* (New York: J. Lane, 1910)

Holbach, Maude *Dalmatia: The Land where East meets West* (London: J. Lane, 1910)

Holbrooke, Richard *To End a War* (London: Random House, 2011)

Hukanović, Rezak *The Tenth Circle of Hell: A Memoir of Life in the Death Camps of Bosnia* (London: Abacus, 1998)

Irna 'Les "pyramides" de Bosnie-Herzégovine: une affaire de pseudo-archéologie dans le contexte bosnien' *Balkanologie* 13(1–2), 2011

Ibrahimović, Zlaten *I am Zlaten Ibrahimović* (Harmondsworth: Penguin, 2013)

Isaković, Alija *Rječnik karakteristične leksike u Bosanskome jeziku* (Sarajevo: Svjetlost, 1993)

Izetbegović, Alija *Islam between East and West* (Selangor: Islamic Book Trust, 1993)

Izetbegović, Alija 'The Islamic Declaration: A Programme for the Islamicisation of Muslims and the Muslim Peoples', *South Slav Journal*, 6, 1983, pp. 56–89

Izetbegović, Alija *Sjećanja: autobiografski zapis* (Sarajevo: OKO, 2005)

Jackson, Thomas Graham *Memories of Travel* (Cambridge: Cambridge University Press, 1923)

Jergović, Miljenko *Sarajevski Marlboro* (Sarajevo: TKD Šahinpašić, 2008)

Kadare, Ismail *Elegy for Kosovo: A Novel* (London: Vintage Classics, 2010)

Karadžić, Vuk 'Srbi svi i svuda' in Mirko Grmek, Marc Gjidara and Neven Simac (eds.) *Etničko Čišćenje. Povijesni dokumenti o jednoj srpskoj ideologiji* (Zagreb: Nakladni zavod Globus, 1993)

Kinsley Hutchinson, Frances *Motoring in the Balkans: Along the Highways of Dalmatia, Montenegro, the Herzegovina and Bosnia …* (Chicago: McClugh, 1909)

Krauss, Alfred *Das 'Wunder von Karfreit': im besonderen der Durchbruch bei Flitsch und die Bezwingung des Tagliamento* (Munich: J.F. Lehmann, 1926)

Krauss, Friedrich Salomon *Sitte und Brauch der Südslaven* (Vienna: A. Hölder, 1885)

Kurspahić, Kemal *Pisma iz rata* (Sarajevo: Bosanski mostovi, 1994)

Kočić, Petar *Jazavac pred sudom* (Zagreb: Savez kulturno-prosvjetnih društava Hrvatske, 1950)

Maass, Peter *Love thy Neighbor: A Story of War* (New York: Vintage, 1996)

Maček, Vladko *In the Struggle for Freedom* (Philadelphia: Penn State University Press, 1968)

Maclean, Fitzroy *Eastern Approaches* (London: Jonathan Cape 1951)

Mažuranić, Matija *A Glance into Ottoman Bosnia* (London: Saqi, 2007)

Mažuranić, Matija *Pogled u Bosnu ili kratak put u onu krajinu, učinjen 1839–40* (Zagreb: Ljudevita Gaja, 1842)

Mehmedinović, Semezdin *Sarajevo Blues* (San Francisco: City Light Books, 1998)

Mertus, Julie Jasmina, Tesanović, Habiba Metikos and Borić, Rada (eds.) *The Suitcase: Refugee Voices from Bosnia and Croatia* (Berkeley: University of California Press, 1997)

Muir Sebright Mackenzie, Georgina Mary and Irby, Adelina Paulina *The Turks, Greeks and Slavons: Travels in the Slavonic Provinces of Turkey-in Europe* (London: Bell and Daldy, 1877)

Pejanović, Mirko *Through Bosnian Eyes: The Political Memoir of a Bosnian Serb West* (Lafayette, IN: Purdue University Press, 2004)

Philips Price, Morgan *Through the Iron Curtain: A Record of a Journey through the Balkans in 1946* (London: Sampson Low, 1949)

Plavšić, Biljana. *Svedočim* (Banjaluka: Trioprint, 2005)

Preindlsberger, Milena Theresia *Bosnisches Skizzenbuch; Landschafts- und Kultur-Bilder aus Bosnien und der Hercegovina* (Dresden: E. Pierson, 1900)

Rašković, Jovan *Luda zemlja* (Belgrade: Akvarijus, 1990)

Renner, Heinrich *Durch Bosnien und die Hercegovina kreuz und quer* (Berlin: D. Reimer, 1896)

Rieff, David *Slaughterhouse: Bosnia and the Failure of the West* (New York: Simon and Schuster, 1995)

Sarajlić, Izet *Sarajevska ratna zbirka* (Sarajevo: OKO, 1995)

Selimović, Meša *Derviš i smrt* (Sarajevo: Svjetlost, 1967)

Šešelj, Vojislav *Pravo na istinu* (Belgrade: Multiprint, 1988)

Softić, Elma *Sarajevski dani, sarajevske noći* (Zagreb: VBZ, 1994)

Šop, Nikola *Božanski pastir* (Zagreb: Mozaik knjiga, 1997)

Thompson, Mark *Paper House: The Ending of Yugoslavia* (London: Hutchinson Radius, 1992)

Tomašević, Bato *Life and Death in the Balkans: A Family Saga in a Century of Conflict* (London: Hurst, 2008)

Ugrešić, Dubravka *The Culture of Lies* (Pennsylvania: Penn State Press, 1998)

Vucetić, Srdjan 'Identity is a Joking Matter: Intergroup Humor in Bosnia', *Spaces of Identity* 4(1), 2004

Vulliamy, Ed *Seasons in Hell: Understanding Bosnia's War* (London: Simon and Schuster, 1994)

West, Rebecca *Black Lamb and Grey Falcon: A Journey through Yugoslavia* (Edinburgh: Cannongate, 1993)

Yriarte, Charles *Bosnie et Herzégovine: souvenirs de voyage pendant l'insurrection* (Paris: E. Plon, 1876)

Zulfikarpašić, Adil *Bošnjak* (with Milovan Djilas and Nadežda Gaće) (Zurich: Bošnjački institut, 1994)

NEWPAPERS AND ONLINE SOURCES

The United Nations International Criminal Court for the former Yugoslavia (www.icty.org) is an incredibly detailed ledger for historians of the 1990s. Careful records were kept, trial transcripts were translated and all the trials were published on the internet. Newspapers and newsletters, many of them now online, are also an invaluable source. Many journalists have taken considerable personal risks to keep the rest of the world informed about events in Bosnia. Among them are *Bosnia Report* (London); *B2* (Belgrade); *Dani* (Sarajevo); *Guardian* (London);

Independent (London); *L'Express* (Paris); *Mladina* (Ljubljana); *New York Times* (New York); *Observer* (London); *Politika* (Belgrade); *Oslobodjenje* (Sarajevo); *Telegraph* (London).

FILMS AND DOCUMENTARIES ABOUT BOSNIA AND ITS NEIGHBOURS DISCUSSED IN THE TEXT

Otac Domovine (*Father of the Nation*) (Hrvatski slikopis, 1942)
Straža na Drini (*Watch on the Drina*) (dir. Branko Marjanović 1942)
Marš na Drinu (*The Drina March*) (dir. Žika Mitrović 1964)
Valter brani Sarajevo (*Valter Defends Sarajevo*) (dir. Hajrudin Krvavac 1972)
Sutjeska (*The Fifth Offensive*) (dir. Stipe Delić 1973)
Drviš i Smrt (*The Dervish and Death*) (dir. Zdravko Velimirović 1974)
Sjećaš li se Doli Bel? (*Do You Remember Dolly Bell?*) (dir. Emir Kustarica 1981)
Miris Dunja (*The Scent of Quinces*) (dir. Mirza Idrizović 1982)
Otac na službenom putu (*Father is on a Business Trip*) (dir. Emir Kustarica 1985)
Serbian Epics (dir. Paweł Pawlikowski 1992)
Gospa (dir. Jakov Sedlar 1995)
Lepa sela, lepo gore (*Beautiful Villages Burn in a Beautiful Way*) (dir. Srdjan Dragojević 1996)
Trying Tadić (dir. Belinda Giles 1996)
Savršeni krug (*A Perfect Circle*) (dir. Ademir Kenović 1997)
The Reckoning (dir. Kevin Sim 1998)
A Cry from the Grave (dir. Leslie Woodhead 1999)
Ničija Zemlja (*No Man's Land*) (dir. Danis Tanović 2001)
Kajmac i Marmelada (*Cheese and Marmelade*) (dir. Branko Djurić 2003)
Gori vatra (*A Fire is Burning*) (dir. Pjer Žalica 2003)
Ljeto u zlatnoj dolini (*Summer in the Golden Valley*) (dir. Srdjan Vuletić 2003)
Život je Čudo (*Life is a Miracle*) (dir. Emir Kustarica 2004)
Grbavica (dir. Jasmila Žbanić 2006)
Turneja (*The Tour*) (dir. Goran Marković 2008)
Kenjac (*Donkey/Ass*) (dir. Antonio Nuić 2009)
Winterslaap in Lukomir (dir. Niels van Koevorden 2010)
Bosnia – Unfinished Business (ITN, broadcast 2010)
Halimin put (*Halima's Path*) (dir. Arsen Ostojić 2012)
The Love of Books: A Sarajevo Story (BBC Storyville, broadcast 19 September 2012)

INDEX

tuberculosis, xviii, 53, 55, 64
Tudjman, Franjo, ix, xx, xxi, 82,
　126, 127, 128, 132, 136, 168,
　178, 179
Turkey, 10, 31, 38, 63, 83, 96, 118, 178,
　180
Turkish, 65, 99, 106, 123
Turks, xvii, 3, 7, 9, 10, 13, 18–23,
　26–31, 33, 35, 36, 44–8, 61, 62,
　65, 66, 110, 118, 121, 127, 133,
　143, 144, 153, 162, 165, 189
Tuzla, xx, xxii, 1, 12, 55, 58, 78, 86, 94,
　99, 109, 110, 116, 127, 153, 155,
　165, 175, 185

UDBA, 101, 104, 144
Ugljen, Zlatko, 111
Ugrešić, Dubravka, 163
United Nations, xx, xxi, 130, 136, 148,
　151, 152, 153, 154, 156, 164,
　165, 166, 167, 172, 174, 175,
　176, 181
United States, iv, xx, 54, 59, 64, 124,
　156, 167, 168, 170, 186
Ustaša, xiv, xviii, xix, 52, 59, 68, 69, 71,
　72, 74, 77–90, 122, 124, 129,
　143, 146, 152, 157, 161, 171,
　184
Užice, 87, 90

Valencia, 104
Valenta, Anto, 131, 181
Valter brani Sarajevo, film, 116
Valtorta, Maria, 120
van Renssen, Raviv, 153
Vance, Cyrus, xx, 165, 166, 171
Varešanin, Marijan, 51
Vasiljević, Dušan, 59
Velika Kladuša, 151
Veliki Školj, 10
Venice, 10, 11, 20, 26, 30, 39, 102
Via Reggio, 120
Vidoši, 5
Vidovdan, xvi, xvii, 51, 52, 56, 61,
　146, 164
Vidovdan, 28 June, 52, 61, 68
Vienna, 2, 18, 23, 28, 34, 39, 40, 41,
　45, 46, 47, 48, 49, 50, 58, 60,
　62, 161

Vijećnica, viii, 35, 44, 45, 53, 80, 146
Vilajetović, Salih, 40
Vionica, 120
Višegrad, viii, xvii, 23, 24, 73, 84, 163,
　173, 182, 184, 185
Višević, Mihajlo, 11
Višnjić, Filip, 28, 30, 161, 207
Visočica, 188
Visoko, 1, 13, 113, 188
Vistula, river, 11
Vitez, 11
Vitezović, Pavao Ritter, 50
Vlach, xiv, 3, 17, 18, 19, 78
Vlachs, 17, 65, 79
Vladimir, Bishop of the Bosnian
　Diocese, 16
Vojvodina, 40, 59, 74, 153
von Krempler, Karl, 96
Voorhoeve, Joris, 154
Vrančić, Faust, 20
Vranduk, 11
Vratac, 1
Vratar, 1
Vratnik, 178
Vrbanje, bridge, 139
Vrbaska, *banovina* of, xviii, 70
Vrelo Bune, 1
Vucetić, Srdjan, 18
Vuk Karadžić, 61
Vukovar, xx, 86, 136, 141
Vulliamy, Ed, 143, 146, 159

Wacht an der Drina, film, 74
Wagner, Richard, 76, 140
Washington Peace Agreement, xxi
Weine, Stevan, 147, 183
Wenzel, Marian, 14, 146
West, Rebecca, 35, 49, 55, 81
Wildeshausen, Bishop Johannes von, 16
Windhorst, 102
Winterslaap in Lukomir, film, 9
Withopf, Ekkehard, 167
Wittek, Alexander, 45
Wrench, Evelyn, 32

Yad Vashem, 80
Yeomans, Rory, 71, 74
Young Pioneers, 100
Yugoslav Air Force, 89